# Jack Hanna's Ultimate Guide to Pets

**Other books by Jack Hanna**

*Monkeys on the Interstate*

*Let's Go to the Petting Zoo*

*Jungle Jack Hanna's Safari Adventure*

*Jungle Jack Hanna's Pocketful of Bugs*

*The Lion's Share*

# Jack Hanna's Ultimate Guide to Pets

## Jack Hanna

### with Hester Mundis

G. P. PUTNAM'S SONS
*New York*

G. P. Putnam's Sons
*Publishers Since 1838*
200 Madison Avenue
New York, NY 10016

Photographs by Rick A. Prebeg © 1996 World Class Images

Library of Congress Cataloging-in-Publication Data

Hanna, Jack, date.
    [Ultimate guide to pets]
    Jack Hanna's ultimate guide to pets / by Jack Hanna with Hester Mundis.
        p.      cm.
    Includes bibliographical references and index.
    ISBN 0-399-14193-6 (alk. paper)
    1. Pets.    I. Mundis, Hester.    II. Title.
SF411.5.H37    1996                    96-28560 CIP
636.088'7—dc20

*Printed in the United States of America*
10   9   8   7   6   5   4   3   2   1

This book is printed on acid-free paper. ∞

BOOK DESIGN BY LAURA HAMMOND HOUGH

*To my daughter Julie,*

*whose love for animals*

*helped her overcome serious illness;*

*to Stephen Kritsick, D.V.M. (1951–1994),*

*"The Gentle Doctor" and veterinary correspondent*

*for Good Morning America,*

*who dedicated his life to caring*

*for all of God's creatures;*

*and to three men who are responsible*

*for fostering my animal enthusiasm,*

*Dr. Warren Roberts, Dr. Bill Montgomery,*

*and Guy Smith*

# Contents

# A Note to the Reader

This book is based on what I've learned over the years from my personal experience with animals, zoologists, veterinarians, animal behaviorists, writers in the field, and just plain pet owners. It is intended only as a guide to aid in your selection of an animal companion by providing numerous options and important considerations. Although extensive research has gone into its preparation, it is not all-inclusive, and no endorsement of any breeder or practitioner contacted through information obtained from this book (or such breeder or practitioner's diagnosis, treatments, or credentials) is implied or should be inferred.

ONE MORE REMINDER: *The diet, health, and medical suggestions throughout this book are recommendations, not prescriptions, and are not intended as veterinary advice.*

# Acknowledgments

I wish to gratefully express sincere appreciation to all my friends and colleagues whose help, advice, encouragement, support, and patience were invaluable in the preparation of this book, especially Hester Mundis; Nancy Rose; Rick A. Prebeg; Julie Estadt; Sally South; Ginger Earley; Doug Warmolts; Susan Phillips Cohen, M.S.W., A.C.S.W; Ron VanWarmer; and, of course, my wife, Suzi Hanna.

For their assistance with cover and interior photos (and much more) I want to thank Andy Lightfoot; Suzi Rapp; Sean Greene; Bob Macklin; Susie Schmidt, Jack's Aquarium & Pets; Jim Waters, Noah's Ark Pets; Jim Cunningham, Canine Companions for Independence; Allan and Neda Shaub; and, particularly, the Columbus Zoo and Video Tours.

I would also like to thank, for their invaluable contributions to this guide, the American Veterinary Medical Association; the American Kennel Club; the Animal Medical Center; the Delta Society; Canine Companions for Independence; Cornell Feline Health Center; the Wildlife Conservation Society; American Society for the Prevention of Cruelty to Animals; Dick Schroeder; Jane Bicks, D.V.M.; The House Rabbit Society; Arlen M. Wilbers, D.V.M.; K. L. Laytin, Ph.D.; Paul V. Loiselle; Dean Hougen; Elaine Thompson; Sharon and Richard Rothe, Pet Fare; Lynn Schiowitz-Fox; Jane Doughterty; and Richard Curtis, without whom a work of this scope could never have been completed.

# Preface

I've lived with animals all my life. I've loved animals all my life. In fact, animals *are* my life (a given that my wife, Suzi, accepted when we married and my daughters have never questioned), which is why I care so much for their well-being—as well as the beings who care for them—and why I wrote this book.

Having witnessed too often that people learn animal parenting truths the hard way (over twenty million pets end up in shelters every year), I realized that a user-friendly reference guide to picking the right pet was long overdue. So, never one to shy away from the challenge of entertaining while enlightening the public about animals (as my continuing appearances on *Good Morning America*, the *Late Show with David Letterman*, and *Larry King Live* attest), I decided to do it. And with the invaluable help of some of the world's best veterinarians, animal behaviorists, trainers, zoologists, pet experts, breeders, humane societies, wildlife organizations—along with knowledgeable owners and friends—I did.

This guide (written with love, sweat, and lots of unforgettable memories) is intended as an owner's manual for anyone who wants a pet, has one and wants another, needs more information about the one he or she already has—or is merely curious about the range of fauna options available. My feeling has always been that knowing what to expect from an animal, before it becomes *your* animal, gives you the chance to weigh the positives against the negatives; in other words, how much pleasure/comfort/company a pet will give you versus how much work/space/time it will take for you to enjoy it. Also, because all species are not created equal—or naturally friendly to each other—it's important (to say nothing of *safer* and *cheaper*) to be aware of potential "petfalls" before they happen to you or your pet. For this reason, I've included not only pros and cons to consider for all the animals—but cautions, general health care, diet and housing tips, socialization needs, compatible roommates, solutions to common (and uncommon) pet problems, as well as easy-to-locate sections for fingertip reference, and some of the most fascinating and outrageous animal facts I could find.

Most important, though, I've tried to stress that exotic animals are *not* pets, should not be considered as pets, and should absolutely not be kept as pets. It's a scenario for disaster. People buy exotic animals as babies and then discover that, as they mature, they can no longer house, feed, or handle them, so they decide to give them to a zoo. Unfortunately, most zoos can't or won't accept them for a variety of reasons—and the consequences are almost always tragic.

It's very easy to fall in love with an animal. Believe me, I know. If I had a nickel for every one that captured my heart over the years I'd never run out of change. But loving an animal is one thing, raising that animal in your home as part of your family is a whole different story—a story that deserves a happy ending every time. My hope is that this guide will make living happily-ever-after a joyful reality for you and all the pets of your dreams for a long time to come.

*—Jack Hanna*

# Part One

# A Pet Primer

# 1

# Pets as Part of Our Lives

## What Is a Pet?

A pet is a living creature that you bring into your home, your life, and your family. It is totally dependent on you, its owner—its *parent*—for just about everything. In many cases ample food is not enough, shelter is not enough, sometimes even love is not enough. Having a pet means assuming responsibility, a responsibility for another living creature's quality of life. Because of this—and I can't stress this strongly enough—it's extremely important to understand the basic nature and essential needs of any animal desired as a human companion—*before* the animal enters your life.

This is not to say that if you already have a pet it's too late to learn about it; it's never too late for that. It's just that I've discovered, having lived with an ark-ful of animals in my time, that a little pre-pet understanding can prevent a lot of pet-owning heartache.

## How Animals Became Pets

Nope, it wasn't love at first sight. In fact, there's little doubt that primitive man (and woman and child) was more interested in animals as dinner than as pets. In those days, "fast food" was what got away. Hunting was, by far, the most popular occupation of the time, which made sense since hunger was, by far, the most widespread preoccupation of the time. Although archaeological finds have indicated that certain animals during that long ago period around 12,000 BC were tamed, it is debatable whether those creatures were kept for the pleasure of their company—or as backup for a bad hunting season.

## World's First Pet

The quest for food, not companionship, was what forged the first people-pet bond. It was a give-and-take relationship that began over 14,000 years ago and continues—in somewhat different form—to this day: the relationship between *Homo sapiens* and *Canis familiaris*, human and dog, teaming up to bring down the evening meal. Today *Homo sapiens* brings in the meals and *Canis familiaris* wolfs them down. ("Wolfing" things down is an inherited canine tradition.)

By following primitive hunters on their raids, increasing their success in bagging prey, and always hoping for leftovers (some things never change), the wild dog—with its greater sense of smell and weapon-sharp teeth—soon became a welcome addition to prehistoric caves and the undisputed, paws-down title holder as the world's first pet!

**JACK'S FACTS:**
## We Are Family
As opposite as most people think they are, dogs and cats actually share an ancestor—a tree-climbing meat-eater called *Miacis* that lived 40 million years ago and who evolved into a four-legged forebear of both species! It just goes to show what you'll find if you climb far enough back into a family tree.

## The Early Days of Pets

When people first began keeping animals as friends instead of food, the animals were rarely just companions. Almost all pets in those days served double duty. For instance, dogs were expected to be herders, hunters or protectors; goofy, tail-wagging, Frisbee-chasers were not in demand. Birds were kept as pets for home entertainment and—in the case of canaries—to warn miners of toxic fumes; today those purposes are more easily served by CDs and smoke alarms. Goldfish were originally prized by the Chinese as symbols of wealth; today Rolexes are preferred. And cats, well, cats were revered as oracles, treated as deities and extolled as exterminators; for cat fanciers, of course, nothing's changed.

---

**JACK'S FACTS: Domestication Birthdays**

| | | |
|---|---|---|
| Dogs: 12,000 BC | Donkeys: 4,000 BC | Guinea Pigs: 1800 |
| Horses: 5,000 BC | Cats: 3,000 BC | Parakeets: 1840 |
| Goats: 5,000 BC | Rabbits: 449 BC | Gerbils: 1935 |
| Pigs: 4,000 BC | Canaries: 1600 | Hamsters: 1939 |
| | Goldfish: 1700 | |

---

## Pets as Wonder Workers for People

Anyone who has ever loved an animal knows the joy that human-animal bonding can bring. But what many people don't know is that pets can do much more than ever imagined. Dogs, cats, rabbits, horses, gerbils, birds, fish, and even reptiles can provide remarkable physical and psychological health benefits to humans, as recent research at hospitals, institutions, schools, and nursing homes has shown. Personally, I have never doubted the benefits of having an animal companion.

### Wonders Pets Can Work
- Pets can increase medical patients' survival chances.
- Pets can decrease stress.
- People with pets get fewer colds than people without pets.
- Pets can help adults lower their blood pressure.
- People with pets live longer.
- Pets can relax children during medical exams and aid in their recovery from serious illness.
- Pets can motivate children to improve motor skills.
- Pets can help children overcome behavior problems.

### JACK'S FACTS: **When Animals Work Wonders**

At the age of two, our daughter Julie suddenly became ill, running a temperature of 105° F. We rushed her to Children's Hospital in Knoxville, where she was diagnosed with leukemia. Due to her lack of immunity, she had developed pneumonia and a staph infection, and the prognosis was terrifyingly grim. In fact, our doctor told us that she needed immediate treatment. We had to get her to St. Jude's Hospital in Memphis, some 450 miles away, as fast as possible, or it might be too late. Driving was out of the question, so I phoned Harold "Bubba" Beal, a local Knoxville realtor who I knew was a pilot; a few hours later we were in Memphis.

Upon her arrival, Julie was placed in a sterile intensive-care unit where she spent the next two months in isolation to protect her from infectious diseases. It was a long, slow ordeal for everyone—especially Julie—who had to endure years of chemotherapy, radiation, bone-marrow transplants, and spinal taps to beat the odds. But she did. And as important as all those medical procedures were, it was Julie's connection with animals, especially her favorite bunny, Flopsy, that through it all provided her with the indomitable will to get well. Since then I have never stopped being grateful to modern medicine—or ever questioned the healing wonders of animals.

- Pets can provide emotional support for seriously ill children and the elderly.
- Pets can listen without judging and love unequivocally.

## Animal Helpers Among Us

Every minute of every day there is an animal somewhere helping a human. Cats, rabbits, horses, even tropical fish, perform therapeutic miracles, but dogs—well, dogs have made professional careers out of working for us.

### JACK'S FACTS: **Nothing but the Best**

If it's good enough for humans, it's out there for pets. There are fast-food restaurants for dogs (and if they eat too much, there's liposuction). There are also luxury day-care centers, hotels, grooming parlors, dating services, personal trainers, therapists, and designer fashions for dogs and cats; voice coaches, manicurists, and avian counselors for birds; aquascapers for tropical fish; weight counselors for potbellied pigs; posh playpens for reptiles and amphibians; plus antique furniture, electronic toys, and gourmet treats for every animal companion under the sun. From heated nurseries and surrogate-parenting aids to CAT scans and pacemakers to elaborate caskets, monuments, and funerals, Americans tend to feel that their personal fauna deserve nothing but the best.

Search-and-rescue dogs are used to locate disaster victims, missing children, people buried under snow, rubble, or lost in the wilderness.

Drug dogs are used specifically to sniff out illegal substances.

Bomb dogs have saved millions just by using their noses.

Guard dogs are put in charge of security at everything from small businesses to important military installations.

Personal protection dogs work as full-time bodyguards.

Service dogs are specially trained pets to help physically and emotionally disabled individuals live fuller, more independent lives. They include: guide dogs for the blind; signal dogs for the hearing impaired; seizure-alert dogs for epileptics; emotional support dogs for agoraphobics fearful of leaving the house; and companion dogs that—among many other things—can open doors, pull wheelchairs, turn light switches on and off, and retrieve objects from pockets, shelves and drawers for their physically disabled owners.

JACK'S FACTS:
## Guide Dog Eye-Opener

It's easier for a totally blind person to work with a guide dog than for someone with a small amount of vision.

## Vets as Part of Our Pets' Lives

If you have a pet, you need a vet. Fortunately, your chances of locating a good veterinarian today are better than they have ever been. According to the American Veterinary Association, there are more board-certified specialists in all fields than ever before, as well as more accredited alternative practitioners.

I've had years of experience with veterinarians. In fact, one of the most influential people in my life was Dr. Warren Roberts. He was the local vet when I was growing up on our farm in Knoxville, Tennessee. I was fascinated by every aspect of his work and loved watching him, whether he was treating our horses at the farm or working at his clinic in town.

One day, during the summer when I was eleven, my Dad told Dr. Roberts that I really wanted to work for him. As a favor to my father, Dr. Roberts gave me a job. It was for no pay, but that didn't bother me a bit. It didn't even bother me when Dr. Roberts started me right off cleaning cages. I'm talking dog-doo *big time*—scrubbing, scraping, and hosing the cages of over forty dogs! Maybe I'm crazy, but I still wouldn't mind doing it today, because it's a way to get to know if you really like animals. If you can somehow enjoy cleaning out their cages, then you know you genuinely love animals.

To me, aside from being well-trained technically, truly good veterinarians are those with a special compassion that shows in their faces, is heard in their voices, and is seen in the touch of a hand on an animal's head.

Knowing how to handle animals is important for a veterinarian, but being a good people communicator is equally important. Animals are people's kids, they want to take the best care of them. All the veterinary knowledge in the world is worth nothing if it can't be communicated. What I've learned over the years working with vets and animals is that wisdom is more important than knowledge.

## How to Find the Right Vet for You and Your Pet

- Ask pet owners you know for recommendations.
- Find out whom area breeders use.
- Enquire at local animal shelters.
- Call your local or state veterinary association.
- Contact the closest college of veterinary medicine. (Your local library can help.)
- Write to the American Animal Hospital Association (AAHA), Member Services, PO Box 150899, Denver, CO 80215, for a list of member practitioners in your area.
- For a board-certified specialist anywhere in the United States, phone the American Veterinary Medical Association at (708) 925–8070.
- For an alternative veterinary practitioner in your area you can phone the American Holistic Veterinary Medical Association at (410) 569–0795, or write to them at 2214 Old Emmorton Road, Bel Air, MD 21015. Enclose a stamped self-addressed envelope.
- For information about homeopathic veterinarians in your locality contact the National Center for Homeopathy, 801 North Fairfax St., Suite 306, Alexandria, VA 22314, or phone (708) 548–7790. (An information packet and directory of practitioners costs $6.00.)

**Note:** *It should be understood that no endorsement of any practitioner contacted through these services—or such practitioner's diagnoses, treatments, or credentials—is implied or should be inferred.*

## Did You Know . . .

- More than half of all pet owners would rather be with their pet on a desert island than with another person.
- Patients in the waiting rooms of doctors and dentists have been found to be more relaxed in the presence of fish tanks.
- According to the Ego Strength Scale of Minnesota Multiphasic Personality Inventory (MMPI), dog ownership can contribute to a strong self-image.
- Researchers have found that if you own a snake, you are a seeker of novelty and a challenger of the rules of convention.
- If you own a bird you tend to be socially outgoing and expressive.

- A New Jersey specialty company, run by Patricia Henderson, made a mink coat for a parrot who recited Chaucer!
- King Henry III of France kept two thousand lap dogs in lavishly cushioned apartments in his palace.
- In ancient times the priests of Lake Shedit kept crocodiles as divine pets and adorned them with gold bracelets. Because they were well-fed and stayed pretty much on the shore sunning themselves the jewelry was rarely lost; and because they were crocodiles it was never stolen.
- It was not uncommon for cats in ancient Egypt to wear gold earrings and dogs to wear silver necklaces. (*Sure beats flea collars!*)
- In medieval times gentlemen used dogs to keep their feet warm. (*The original hot dogs!*)
- Americans spend more than $20 billion a year on their pets. That's more than they spend on movies and home videos combined!
- People with animals are assumed to be nicer, which is why politicians like to be seen with them.
- More than half of all U.S. households have pets.

---

**JACK'S FACTS: Talk About a Pampered Pet!**

I've heard about a lot of pampered pets, but there's one that I still talk about. In fact, if I hadn't seen her with my own eyes, I wouldn't have believed it. She is a miniature horse named Penelope, who belongs to a woman in Webster, New York, and she lives the life of a queen. She has the run of the house—literally! Whenever she wants a carrot, she goes right to the fridge, whinnies, and gets it. (When she doesn't want something she just says, "Neigh!") She sleeps on a plush pillow dog bed and has her own monogrammed blanket. She even has her own pet—a kitten that cuddles with her. Penelope also has special sneakers so she can have better traction indoors, wears pink dresses (with bunny slippers on Easter), and she watches my show on television! As far as I'm concerned, she may be pampered, but she obviously has good taste.

---

## Questions and Answers About Pets as Part of Our Lives

### When "No Pets" Are Allowed

My mother has epilepsy. She takes medication, but would really like to have one of those dogs that sense oncoming seizures—only her building doesn't allow pets. Would a dog like that be considered a pet?

It shouldn't be, not if it's a service animal trained to help someone with a seizure disorder. I'd suggest, though, that you contact the Service Dog Center (SDC) of the Delta Society. They will explain all the rules and state-by-state regulations of the Americans with Disabilities Act and can provide you with all the information you'll need concerning the laws affecting public access and housing—as well as how to go about obtaining the right dog for your mother. The center can be reached by telephone at 1–800–869–6898, or contacted by mail: Delta Society Service Dog Center, PO Box 1080, Renton, WA 98057–9906.

### Seeing Eye to Eye
Is there a difference between a "guide dog" and a "Seeing Eye dog"?

In name only. A guide dog is the generic term for any dog formally trained to help the blind get around—cross streets, move through crowds, avoid obstacles, board vehicles, climb stairs; essentially, attain as much independence as possible. A "Seeing Eye dog" is a specific trademark of the organization Seeing Eye, Inc.

### No Petting Allowed
Can any animal be a pet?

Any animal *can* be a pet, but that doesn't mean it *should* be. Wild and exotic creatures belong in their natural habitat or zoos. Pets are domesticated animals. These animals have been raised and bred to live with humans; captive wild animals have not. Many types of captive wild animals may be trained by professionals, but there is a big difference between trained and *domesticated*. Bringing a wild animal into your home and family as a pet is setting yourself up for the inevitable heartbreak—as my wife, Suzi, and I learned the hard way. Daisy was the first lion cub we owned and she became like a member of our family. Of course, when she grew to her full size—a hefty three hundred pounds—we had to keep her outdoors. I'd go to her large enclosure every day, talk to her softly and she'd respond—we were close. It was hard to think of her as a wild animal—and that was a mistake. I treated her as a pet, never even imagining that in one moment she could casually swing a powerful paw and maim a child forever. But she did. The child survived, Daisy was taken to a zoo, but it was a nightmare for everyone involved, and haunts me still.

# Getting into Petting

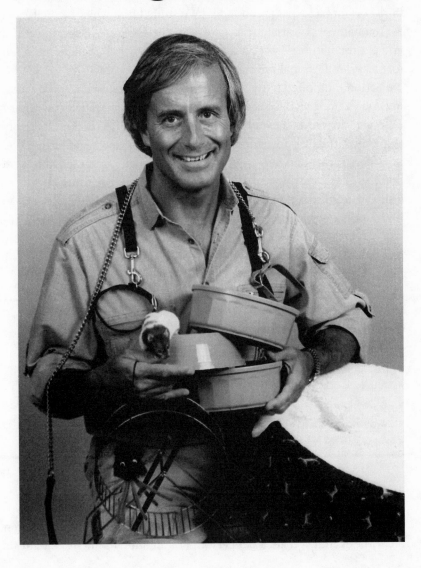

# 2

## How I Did (or Confessions of an Animal Addict)

It started when I was five years old growing up in Knoxville, on our farm, which my dad named Bu-Ja-Su, after my brother, Bush, my sister, Sue, and me. It wasn't a working farm, but it sure was an animal farm. Especially after I got going!

My first two pets were a couple of collies, Lance and Vandy. Pretty normal, right? Well, from there, with the encouragement of my brother and sister, it was just about anything we could handle that moved—pigs, goats, horses, rabbits, birds. I even had a pet groundhog. (We stuffed him when he died.)

You name it, I wanted it as part of my menagerie. I'd catch fish from the creek and put them in little ponds, using our toilet bowl as a temporary holding tank before transfer. (Animal raising was always a risky business for me.) When my rabbit collection multiplied to over one hundred, and I refused to part with a single one, my dad decided to have someone "dispose" of them. Well, the night before "The Disposer" arrived I let every one of those cotton-tailed suckers loose on the farm. (I think my father was ready to send "The Disposer" for me after that!)

When I was fourteen, I got the Christmas gift of my dreams—two miniature donkeys, Doc and Flower. (Doc later helped me get the girl of my dreams, my future wife, Suzi.) After that there were three ducks (Aquaduck, Viaduck, and Ovaduck), a pygmy goat—and the animals just kept coming, llamas, lions, chimpanzees, a baby elephant. (Move over, Noah!) My life had become a zoo in progress. And I'm happy to say that it still is.

## JACK'S FACTS: The Five Best and Worst Reasons for Getting into Petting

| BEST | WORST |
|---|---|
| • Desire for companionship | • Wanting a toy for your kids |
| • A reason to exercise | • An impulse decision |
| • A way to raise your spirits | • An excuse not to visit family |
| • Wanting an unequivocal love object | • A way to use up leftovers |
| • A longing for a specific pet | • Desire for food |

## "Pet-People Compatibility Quiz"

If you've never had a pet, there might be a reason. Some folks just aren't "pet people." But even if you are a pet person, not all animals might be right for you. (One species does not fit all!) Picking the right pet is sort of like picking the right spouse; when you do, you both live happily ever after, when you don't, your life becomes a double nightmare.

Ask yourself the following questions and discover what pets might—or might not—be right for you:

1. Do you enjoy spending time outdoors?     YES     NO

IF YOU ANSWERED YES

You have the basic pet-compatibility requirement for all-size dog ownership.

IF YOU ANSWERED NO

Forget Fido and focus on a more indoor-oriented companion. A cat, bird, or ferret would be a more compatible pet for year-round enjoyment.

2. Are you a night person?     YES     NO

IF YOU ANSWERED YES

The one pet I'd suggest you avoid is a bird. With the exception of owls and bats (which are illegal), a feathered friend is generally an early riser and lets you know it.

IF YOU ANSWERED NO

Pets with few exceptions are not naturally nocturnal and will adjust happily to your lifestyle.

3. Are you afraid of mice?     YES     NO

IF YOU ANSWERED YES

You should think twice about getting either a cat or a snake. There are few pleasures more enjoyable for a cat than bringing her owner a present that she's caught—which in most cases is a mouse. (And unfortunately for you it's not always dead.) And if you get a snake as a pet, their cuisine of choice is mouse, not mousse—preferably alive and squeaking. (You can buy flash-frozen mice, but some snakes are picky eaters and still want a little excitement with their meals.)

IF YOU ANSWERED NO

Cats, snakes—heck, you can even go for the rodent itself as a pet. White mice make great pets for small apartments (provided a pair doesn't escape and inadvertently repopulate your building). Other rodentlike potential companions are hamsters. Or, if you prefer a larger pet, a guinea pig.

4. Are you allergic to dust?                  YES        NO

IF YOU ANSWERED YES

Think twice before making a bird your pet of choice. Even when they're not molting, their wing flapping can send dust flying faster than a pickup on an Arizona highway. Also, if you have allergies to dust, you might also be allergic to certain cat dander. And if you're prone to allergies in general, it's wise to spend time with any pet you're thinking of making a part of your family before you make it part of your family. It's easier to prevent heartache than go through it.

IF YOU ANSWERED NO

You're ahead of the game when it comes to people-pet compatibility. Even the cleanest cats and best-groomed dogs are dust catchers. (If you want them to stay off the furniture and on the floor, what do you expect?) As for other pets, if they have fur, feathers, or require litter trays, you might as well resign yourself to more dusting around the house on a regular basis.

5. Do you have noise-tolerant neighbors?     YES        NO

IF YOU ANSWERED YES

You're lucky. You have your pick of the vocal pets—and, in case you didn't realize it, birds rank right up there with the loudest. (I've known lovebirds whose "cooing" could out-decibel two barking Dobermans!)

IF YOU ANSWERED NO

Think fish, gerbils, guinea pigs, hamsters, and reptiles. Though cats are fairly quiet—provided, that is, they're not in heat, going whisker on whisker with another Tom, or bringing you a rodent present. (A Siamese cat can yowl as loud as a baby—and just as often!) As for a dog, unless it's a Basenji, or you're planning to move soon (or frequently) forget it.

6. Are there small children in your household?  YES       NO

IF YOU ANSWERED YES

Small children and animals of any size need supervision. A child may accidentally hurt a kitten and a cat may deliberately hurt a small child. Birds of any feather should be kept safely away from small children, and vice versa. (Parrots have frequently bitten the hands that feed them—and are particularly fond of tempting little fingers.) Look but don't touch should be the rule until a child is old enough to be left alone with a pet.

IF YOU ANSWERED NO

Well, the moment you get a pet you'll feel as if you do.

7. Are you a vegetarian?        YES      NO

IF YOU ANSWERED YES

There's nothing wrong with your being a vegetarian as long as you don't expect a carnivorous pet to share your dietary habits. *And cats are carnivores!* Whether shy domestic pets or ferocious feline predators, cats need meat to get the nutrients they need. (See Chapter 5.) Though some people have put their dogs (who are omnivores and can survive on animal and plant food) as well as cats on vegan diets, my experience is the animals' natural nutritional health is poorer for it. I'm not saying you should give them raw meat (in fact, you shouldn't), but they do need to eat a complete and balanced diet rich in animal proteins. Your best assurance that your pet is getting all the nutrients it needs is to read labels. (All foods should be tested according to American Association of Feed Control Officials—AAFCO.) They now have vegetarian pet foods that contain *synthetic* meat proteins and amino acids made from petroleum-based products, but I'd advise checking with your veterinarian before relying on them for your pet's optimal health. On the other hand, if your pet enjoys a side salad of greens or veggies, by all means indulge it.

8. Do you travel frequently?        YES      NO

IF YOU ANSWERED YES

Lucky you, but not so lucky for your pet—unless you are prepared to provide it with a responsible caretaker when you're away. There's more to keeping a pet healthy than just quality food, fresh water, and exercise. I've known birds to die from lack of attention due to an owner's absence. Leaving your cat for an occasional weekend with an ample supply of dry food and water is all right, but realize that the less attention the animal gets from you, the less social it's going to be. Sometimes two cats are easier to keep happy than one because they can keep each other company when you're away. Then again, just because two animals are of the same species doesn't mean they're going to get along—as attested to by politics, divorce, and wars.

9. Do you work at home?        YES      NO

IF YOU ANSWERED YES

You're definitely going to want a compatible, pattable pet. And, depending on what it is you do at home, you're going to want a pet that can adapt to your work schedule and not intrude on it. If, for instance, you need quiet to concentrate, a squawking conure might not be the best pet to share your workspace. Keeping in mind that pets like routine, and routine is helpful to anyone who works at home, you should feel free to have your pick of animal companions and it can be a win-win situation all around.

IF YOU ANSWERED NO

Depending on where you *do* work, and the hours that you do your work, should influence your choice of pet. If, for instance, your hours are erratic, training a puppy or raising a dog can be a problem—for both you and the animal. Cats, fish, rodents, reptiles—even birds—are much more forgiving (and self-reliant) when you're unexpectedly detained at the office.

10. Do you have a cat?  YES  NO

IF YOU ANSWERED YES

The best way to expand your home pet world would be to introduce another cat. Wanting to add a bird to your household would be a bad idea, as would adding a gerbil, mouse, hamster, or fish tank. Most cats (depending on personality, age, and previous experiences) can usually handle themselves around dogs, provided the dog is introduced as a puppy or is an older animal that's used to living with felines. Some cats may get along with ferrets, but it depends on the individual cat. In any case, it's usually best to own the ferret before the cat and introduce the cat as a kitten.

11. Does your home have expensive carpets?  YES  NO

IF YOU ANSWERED YES

If you're planning to share your home with a pet, be prepared to compromise your carpets. Even the best-trained animals have accidents on occasion. So, if the mere thought of Fifi barfing on the broadloom sends chills through your checkbook, it's time to think "tank," as in fish for pets.

IF YOU ANSWERED NO

You'll be happy to know that neither does mine.

12. Do you plan to keep your pet outdoors?  YES  NO

IF YOU ANSWERED YES

That's okay, as long as you're prepared to provide your animal with adequate shelter, food, and attention. Just because a pet is housed outside your home doesn't mean it requires less TLC. Dogs and cats are social creatures; they thrive on human praise and love. Simply keeping an animal in a pen or on a chain makes it more of a prisoner than a pet. Then again, if you think that letting your dog or cat roam the neighborhood is better, you're wrong. Your pet is your responsibility, not your neighbor's; if you don't care to care for it, you don't care. And people who don't care shouldn't have pets.

## Pets by the Pound: Shelters and Rescue Services as Super Sources

Whether you're thinking about a kitten, a puppy, or a rabbit—or even a pig, a ferret, or a goat—humane societies, local pounds and breed rescue services are fine and affordable ways to get into pet owning.

If you're looking for a particular breed of dog or cat or rabbit, your best bet is to go through the breed's rescue league. Rescue leagues generally know more than shelters do about their animals' breed characteristics and background, which is a definite plus when adopting a pet. Required veterinary care—including, in most cases, spaying or neutering—is provided by these rescue organizations before adoption. (An adoption fee is charged to help cover their costs.) Prospective owners are interviewed so that animals can be matched with compatible human companions. (They don't want the animals to have to be re-rescued!) And, though rescued purebreds do not as a rule come with papers, you can still enter a dog in AKC (American Kennel Club) sanctioned events by obtaining an ILP (Indefinite Listing Privilege) from the club, and unpapered felines may enter cat shows in the HHP (Household Pet) category.

### Ways to Locate a Breed Rescue Organization
- Call your local animal-control officer.
- Call your local animal shelter.
- Ask veterinarians in your area.
- Contact reputable breeders.
- Get in touch with breed clubs.
- Attend breed shows.
- Search on-line services or the Internet for breed rescue organizations.
- Ask your local library for the *Project Breed* directory.

If you're not set on a particular breed, humane society shelters are great sources of home-hungry pets. Most of these shelters also have counselors who can guide you in making the right mixed-breed choice for your family and lifestyle.

Before you do adopt, though, it's wise to find out all you can about your potential pet. The information is not always available, but it is always wise to ask.

### What You Want to Know

- How long the animal has been at the shelter.
- Where it came from.
- Why it was given up.
- Whether it was an indoor or outdoor pet.
- Whether it was raised with children.
- How it gets along with other animals.
- Whether it has been adopted before (and if so, why it was returned).
- Any health problems.
- Any unusual habits.

I'd also suggest giving it what I call a basic LAB test (that's L for looks, A for attitude, and B for behavior) before you decide to make it part of your family.

### Jack's LAB Test

#### LOOKS

Is its coat in good condition? Are its eyes clear, bright and alert? Are its ears clean? Is its nose healthy-looking? Is its skin free of sores?

#### ATTITUDE

Does it move with confidence? Does it enjoy being petted? Is it inquisitive? Is it friendly?

#### BEHAVIOR

Can you encourage it to come to you? Will it play with a toy? Does it respond non-aggressively to other animals? To children? Will it accept a treat from you?

Of course, just because an animal passes this LAB test with flying colors doesn't mean it's the perfect pet, but at least you'll have a better chance of making it one.

### Making an Outside Animal a Pet Project

Every once in a while people get into petting by accident, and sometimes it's because the pet-to-be was involved in an accident. Wild animals and birds that have been either injured or orphaned are frequently rescued by well-meaning humans and cared for as pets. As rewarding as this can be, for both human and animal, there are risks involved for both.

## Cautions to Consider

- Bringing an injured bird into your home can endanger your own pet bird's health.
- In the United States it is illegal to keep a wild bird in captivity—even if you've saved its life. The one exception is the starling. Introduced in the nineteenth century from Europe, starlings are now the most numerous and unwanted birds in the wild, primarily because they've taken over the feeding and breeding grounds of many of our native American birds. So, if you want a pet starling— it's all yours.

  NOTE: You may be allowed to keep a native bird in captivity if you obtain a license from your local or state Department of Wildlife, Department of Environmental Conservation, or Department of Natural Resources. (Your local Audubon Society can supply you with the proper requirements and phone numbers.) As a rule, though, children under eighteen years of age are ineligible for licenses to keep wild birds.
- The legality of making any wild animal a pet varies from state to state; check with your department of conservation or wildlife before becoming too attached.
- Wild animals, such as raccoons, squirrels, and skunks can, without proper inoculations and environmental supervision, endanger the health and well-being of other pets and family members.
- Treating a wild animal as a pet can cause it to become dangerously dependent on you, which could seriously compromise its natural survival instincts.
- If you offer deer a benevolent food handout in the winter, they'll come back for your flowers in the spring. (CAUTION: Regular food handouts may undermine natural foraging instincts and actually endanger the animals.)

## Hanna's Hints:

- Leaving out bread crumbs to feed wild birds and squirrels is fine, but leaving out meat scraps, poultry carcasses, or bones is not advisable. Aside from attracting bears, skunks, and raccoons (which have a high rabies potential in many areas), the scraps can also attract neighborhood dogs and cats—and they're not the most polite communal diners.
- If you're going to feed outside birds, think of it as a year-round hobby. Aside from winter, when their food supplies are virtually gone, they need food in the spring when supplies are low and calcium needs are high for egg laying; in summer when they have fledglings to care for; and in fall, when they need fuel for migrating flights. (For year-round feeding in most areas, sunflower seed is best.)

- The National Audubon Society recommends that bird feeders, especially hummingbird feeders, be cleaned regularly, and rinsed thoroughly with hot water.
- Check bird feeders weekly to make sure that seed is dry; damp seed can become moldy and cause illness in birds.
- In heavy-snow areas, when natural substitutes for grain are not available to birds, the scattering of grain and corn can cause ground-feeding types to become so dependent on you that if you stop feeding them—even for a few days—they may starve to death.
- Soak dried fruits before feeding them to wild birds.
- Peanut butter is a great high-energy treat for wild birds, but it's best to mix it with fat or cornmeal—or spread it thinly on pinecones—to prevent birds from possibly choking on too big a beakful of the sticky treat.

## JACK'S FACTS: Now That's a Pet Project!

Several years ago I got a request from the Columbus, Ohio, water department to investigate a report from a meter reader who claimed he had nearly stepped on a large alligator sleeping in the backyard of a house. I said I'd check it out (secretly believing that the meter reader had mistaken a garden hose for a gator) and got one of the biggest surprises of my life—a twelve-foot-long, three-hundred-pound alligator! The owner had gotten him in Florida when he was just twelve *inches* long, and had kept him as a pet for fourteen years! The guy didn't know it was against the law to keep an exotic animal within city limits—he just loved "Allie." He raised rabbits to feed it, kept it company in the shower (and vice versa) and though *I* knew the law, and am very much against people keeping wild animals as pets, this was one time I knew it was best for all involved to let sleeping alligators—and zookeepers—*lie*. I told the water department that all I saw was a garden hose.

## Adoption Program Alternatives

If you'd like to get into petting without worrying about fur on the furniture, feathers in the blender, fleas, leashes, litterboxes, walks, water dishes, bites, or allergies—and you really have your heart set on a pet a bit more exotic than a dog, cat, or canary—you do have an option. Adoption! And I highly recommend it.

Most zoos, aquariums, and humane societies operate "animal adoption" programs. Virtually all animals are "up" for adoption—however, there may be some favorites that have already been adopted. ("Sorry, Billy, you can't have the platypus; how about a cobra?")

Zoo programs vary, but—aside from the satisfaction you get from directly contributing to a specific animal's food and care—you will usually get a photo of your particular "pet," a fact sheet profiling the animal, a bumper sticker ("I ♥ my hippo"), or a bookmark, and sometimes even your name on a plaque at the zoo.

Costs vary with zoos, adoption programs, and, of course, the animal being adopted. Obviously, an elephant eats more than a frog (even if the frog is very, very hungry). Most reptiles, amphibians, fish, arthropods (bugs), some birds, and small mammals will cost under $100 to adopt—and perhaps as little as $15. Larger mammals are more expensive. And though you might think that an elephant would be the most expensive adoptee, costing over $4,000 a year to feed, the koala—because of its specialized, difficult-to-obtain diet of eucalyptus leaves—costs $15,000 annually.

The Wildlife Conservation Society has a "Sponsor-A-Species" program designed to give the gift of life to animals in danger of becoming extinct. This society participates in forty international Species Survival Programs (SSPs).

SSPs are cooperative breeding efforts; sort of a computer-mating service for zoo animals around the world designed to increase the population of rare, threatened, or endangered species that are vanishing from our earth.

## *Species That Need Sponsoring in Order to Survive*

| | | |
|---|---|---|
| Arabian Oryx | Golden Lion Tamarin | Red-Fronted Macaw |
| Asian Elephant | Grevy's Zebra | Red Panda |
| Bali Mynah | Hawksbill Turtle | Rhinoceros Hornbill |
| Beluga Whale | King Cobra | Ring-Tailed Lemur |
| Black Rhino | Malayan Tapir | Rodrigues Fruit Bat |
| Bog Turtle | Mongolian Wild Horse | Siberian Tiger |
| California Sea Otter | Pacific Walrus | Slender-Horned Gazelle |
| Cheetah | Poison-Arrow Frog | Snow Leopard |
| Chilean Flamingo | Polar Bear | Western Lowland Gorilla |
| Chinese Alligator | Proboscis Monkey | White-Cheeked Gibbon |
| Chinstrap Penguin | Pudu | White-Naped Crane |
| Gelada Baboon | Red Bird of Paradise | |

You can obtain all the information you need on adopting an animal by contacting almost any zoological park or humane society.

## Questions and Answers About Getting into Petting

### *Unpapered Pets*

How can I be sure that the animal I get from a breed rescue group is a purebred if it has no papers?

You can't. In fact, some breed rescue operations will even find homes for animals that aren't purebred as long as they have most of the purebred's physical and behavioral characteristics. But since these animals are spayed and neutered and can't be bred, the only real handicap is being unable to enter your pet in a Best of Breed show that requires a pedigree. And, as any animal lover will tell you, a pedigree has very little to do with making a wonderful pet.

### *Rabies Resistance*

We live in the country. Our dogs and cats have all their shots, but I still worry about rabid animals. Is there any way to keep them away?

When an animal has rabies, it often does not behave normally. Raccoons and skunks, for instance, normally nocturnal and cautious, will appear friendly and approach humans in the daytime. My suggestion is to keep your garage and shed doors—as well as your chimney flue—closed when not in use; these seem to be appealing nesting places for animals. In addition, I'd advise checking your attic for outside openings that could let in bats.

# 3

# Pet Myths and Myth-stakes

## Misconceptions About Pets

There are probably as many misconceptions about animal companions as there are animals. I know, because I've been the victim of quite a few myself. As a kid I thought worms had brains, which stopped me from fishing because I figured all they could think about was drowning. As an adult, I learned the hard way that when an elephant waves his ears, it's not always a friendly greeting. So, before you decide on a pet you think you know, find out if what you think you know about it is true.

### *True or False?*

1. Large dogs always need more exercise than small dogs. T □  F □

    FALSE. Some large dogs, such as the mastiff, for instance, are gentle giants that prefer lounging around an apartment to jogging around the park. All dogs, of course, need exercise, but some less than others. (See Chapter 6.)

    HANNA'S HINT: Research the breeds! Be sure you know how much exercise a dog needs *before* you bring it home. You want it to be your pet, not your pet peeve.

2. Food that's good for dogs is good for cats. T □  F □

    FALSE: Dog food is nutritionally deficient for cats because adult cats need almost five times more protein than do adult dogs. Additionally cats—unlike dogs—must have the amino acid taurine in their daily diet.

3. You can't teach an old dog new tricks. T □  F □

    FALSE: Older animals, provided they're not ill, injured or geriatric, can learn new tricks. Not jumping through hoops, perhaps, but sitting on command, barking when the doorbell rings and fetching a toy are options. Depending on the age of the dog, though, teaching it to play dead might be inadvisable.

4. A wagging tail means a friendly dog. T □  F □

    FALSE: Not necessarily. And there are many dog bites on record to prove it. While it is true that dogs do wag their tails when they feel friendly, they also wag them when they're excited, ready to fight, tense, anxious, and annoyed. (Sometimes just because they have a fly on their flanks.)

    HANNA'S HINT: Unless you know the dog the wagging tail belongs to, handle your hands with care.

T      F

5. Pigs are dirty animals. ☐    ☐

FALSE: Pigs, by nature, are clean animals. They just happen to like mud. If there's a puddle around, they'll wallow in it.

T      F

6. Cats are smarter than dogs. ☐    ☐

FALSE: Dogs are smarter than cats—except when it comes to catching mice, climbing trees, and visually surveying their surroundings. But to keep pet perspectives in place, pigs are smarter than dogs.

T      F

7. You should offer an outstretched palm to an unknown ☐    ☐
dog before petting it.

FALSE: Fingers are canine temptations. A closed fist is the recommended, safer approach.

T      F

8. Before spaying cats and dogs it's better for their ☐    ☐
personalities to let them have a litter.

FALSE: How loud can I say "NO!" Millions of unwanted pets are put to death every year because of this myth. As far as affecting personalities, spaying and neutering only help pets become more focused on their owners. The advantages of spaying and neutering are many—including increasing longevity, by reducing the incidence of certain tumors (breast cancer in females and testicular and prostate cancer in males). Some animals can be sterilized as early as eight weeks. Ask your vet what's best for your pet.

T      F

9. Only male birds will sing or talk. ☐    ☐

FALSE: Male birds are better singers and talkers than female birds, but that doesn't mean the females are unable to complete a sentence or carry a tune. (See Chapter 4.) In fact, birds are often so hard to sex you can't tell if it's a male or female vocalist—until it lays an egg.

T      F

10. Fish are easy pets because they don't demand much ☐    ☐
attention.

FALSE: An aquarium requires a good deal of time-consuming maintenance. (See Chapter 10.) Just because fish are naturally good swimmers doesn't mean they don't need supervision.

|  | T | F |
|---|---|---|
| 11. Rabbits make cuddly pets. | ☐ | ☐ |

FALSE: Most rabbits do *not* like to be held; they prefer to sit beside you.

|  | T | F |
|---|---|---|
| 12. Feeding a dog red meat will make it vicious. | ☐ | ☐ |

FALSE: Food does not make a dog vicious; not even bad food. But bad conditioning, treatment, and training can.

HANNA'S HINT: Some breeds are more prone to aggressive behavior than others—particularly working dogs bred for protection. (See Chapter 6.)

|  | T | F |
|---|---|---|
| 13. Cats can't catch a disease from humans. | ☐ | ☐ |

FALSE: Cats can catch tuberculosis from humans. Unfortunately, the disease can be passed on to other humans as well as cats; fortunately, the occurrences are rare.

|  | T | F |
|---|---|---|
| 14. Cat fur causes allergies. | ☐ | ☐ |

FALSE: It's not the cat's fur that's the culprit; it's the dander in the cat's fur or the cat's saliva. When the cat washes itself, the proteins in its saliva adhere to the fur, then dry and fall off, much like dander (tiny scales in the cat's fur) causing uncomfortable reactions in allergic people. Some breeds are better than others for people with allergies. (See Chapter 5.)

HANNA'S HINT: Wash your hands after petting or playing with your feline. This should not only help you alleviate allergic reactions and prevent disease, but also make a better impression when greeting guests.

|  | T | F |
|---|---|---|
| 15. A cat purrs because it's happy. | ☐ | ☐ |

TRUE AND FALSE: A cat does purr when it's content, but it will also purr when it's in pain.

|  | T | F |
|---|---|---|
| 16. Cats can transmit AIDS. | ☐ | ☐ |

FALSE: Feline AIDS is caused by a totally different virus and cannot be transmitted to humans—even through a bite or a scratch.

|  | T | F |
|---|---|---|
| 17. One cat year is the equivalent of seven human years. | ☐ | ☐ |

FALSE: After the first two years a cat's life goes more slowly, the subsequent years are equal to about four human years. (See Chapter 5.)

|  | T | F |
|---|---|---|
| 18. Cats can see in the dark. | ☐ | ☐ |

FALSE: They can smell in the dark, feel in the dark, hear in the dark, but without a flashlight, their night vision is pretty much the same as ours. And although cats' long-distance vision is superb (they can spot a mouse forty yards away!), if you put something up really close to their eyes, they're virtually blind as bats.

|  | T | F |
|---|---|---|
| 19. A baby rabbit is a great pet for a child. | ☐ | ☐ |

FALSE: Baby rabbits are not good pets for children. They are delicate—easily injured if improperly picked up—and destructive if not supervised by an adult. They have been known to chew through anything they can get their budding buckteeth into, from rugs to rain boots. (See Chapter 8.)

|  | T | F |
|---|---|---|
| 20. You can't keep poinsettia plants in your house if you have cats or birds. | ☐ | ☐ |

FALSE: These holiday plants have gotten a bum rap for years, but the word is out: they are not poisonous. It is possible that excessive consumption of poinsettia leaves and flowers could give an animal an upset stomach, but it's unlikely that a cat or bird will find the plant tasty enough to do more than taste. (See pp. 74 and 99 for plants that are poisonous for pets.)

|  | T | F |
|---|---|---|
| 21. Hitting a puppy with a newspaper is a good method of discipline. | ☐ | ☐ |

FALSE: Hitting a puppy with anything is not a good disciplinary method. Rolling up a newspaper and smacking it against your hand as you utter a loud "no" serves an equally effective disciplinary purpose.

|  | T | F |
|---|---|---|
| 22. Most dogs' barks are worse than their bites. | ☐ | ☐ |

FALSE: Don't bet on it!

**Letting the Cat out of the Bag**

This expression, which sounds as if it has something to do with rescuing an imprisoned cat (or giving a reprieve to one on the way to the vet), means suddenly revealing a secret. It comes from the days in old England when suckling pigs were brought to market and sold in a sack. Frequently, though, unscrupulous vendors would trick buyers by putting a cat instead of a piglet inside the bag. Smart shoppers who wanted to see their bacon-to-be before they shelled out the shillings, opened the bag on the spot, thereby *letting the cat out of the bag*.

## Myth-stakes and Superstitions

From earliest times, animals have been the source of myths and superstitions, influencing everything from the most mundane human decisions to the fate of nations. Here are some that might strike you as laughable, but they're still around:

- In the South it is believed that if a cat sniffs at a dead body, disaster will befall the entire family.
- If a girl is undecided about accepting a proposal of marriage, she is supposed to take three hairs from a cat's tail, wrap them in white paper, and leave it overnight. The next morning, after carefully unfolding the paper, if the hairs are arranged in the shape of the letter Y, her answer should be yes; if it's in the shape of an N, she's wise to stay single.
- In the fur of every black cat there is believed to be a perfect white hair. If you find it and tear it out without getting scratched, it will make you rich or reward you with true love.
- In Holland, it is believed that if you don't like cats, it will rain at your funeral.
- In Britain it is bad luck for fishermen to even mention the word "rabbit," particularly while on a fishing boat. If, for some reason, "rabbit" has to be mentioned, it is referred to as "coney."
- It is also a British superstition that if you call out the word "rabbit" three times quickly on the first day of a new month, you'll have good luck throughout that month. (*Provided, one assumes, you're not a fisherman.*)
- The Scots believe it is unlucky to mention the word "pig" while preparing for, or during, a fishing trip.
- A rabbit foot should always be kept in the makeup box of an actor for good luck; loss of it (the rabbit foot . . . or the makeup box) is bad luck.
- If a girl steps on a cat's tail, she won't find a husband that year.

- In the Ozarks, it is believed that if a bird defecates on a girl's hat, it is positive evidence that her parents are stingy.
- If a cat sneezes, it's a sign of rain.
- If a cat sneezes three times, the family will catch cold.
- If a cat sneezes near a bride, she'll have a happy marriage.
- In Lancashire, England, it is believed unlucky to let a cat die in the house. (*Particularly for the cat!*)
- To break a cat of catching birds, rub a burned match or charred wood three times over the cat's nose.
- If you can make friends with strange cats, you will be lucky.
- If your cat walks to the door and then comes back and lies down in the center of the room with all four feet in the air, company from out of town will arrive that day.
- In Ireland it's unlucky to take a cat with you when moving from one house to another.
- If a bird flies in and out of a room through an open window, there will be a death in the house.
- If a caged bird dies on the morning of a family member's wedding, the married couple will separate.
- Whatever you are doing when you first hear a cuckoo in any year, you will do most frequently all that year.
- The gypsies believe that if a dog digs a big hole in your garden, there will be a death in the family. (*Probably the dog's.*)
- If your dog barks at night, knock three times on the wall and he'll stop.
- A strange dog following you is good luck.
- If you bury under your house a few hairs from a dog's tail, the dog will never run away.
- Jumping over a dog will bring you bad luck. (*Especially if it stands up suddenly.*)
- If you put a hat over the head of a sleeping dog, that night you'll have his dreams.
- It's good luck to step in dog poop. (*Except if you're wearing really expensive shoes.*)
- The Irish believe it is unlucky to meet a barking dog early in the morning.
- If a dog passes between a couple who are about to be married, bad luck will befall them.
- To cure a cough, place a hair of the patient's head between two pieces of buttered bread and give it to the dog. The dog will catch the cold, and the patient will lose it.

JACK'S FACTS:
## Now Hare This!
The basis of the superstition that the rabbit's foot is a good-luck charm stems from the belief that young rabbits are born with their eyes open and therefore have the power of the Evil Eye, enabling them to ward off evil. The truth is, young *rabbits* are born blind; it's young *hares* that are born open-eyed.

JACK'S FACTS:
## Why It Rains
## Cats and Dogs
Norse meteorologists of
old, having no access
to satellite photos or
weather radar, believed
that witches rode the
storms in the form of
cats, which symbolized
rain, and that dogs,
which surrounded
Odin, the god of
storms, provided the
howling winds. (Mod-
ern meteorologists be-
lieve that the expression
evolved because torren-
tial storms sound like
cats fighting with dogs;
but then modern meteo-
rologists believe their
forecasts, too.)

- It's good luck if a spider falls from the ceiling onto your face.
- In Britain it is believed that if you find a spider on your clothes, you'll soon receive money. (*Especially if you've just brought the clothes home from the dry cleaner.*)
- If you wear a snakeskin around your head, you will never have a headache.
- Snakes never die until the sun goes down.
- A frog brings good luck to the house it enters.
- A greyhound with a white spot on its forehead will bring luck.
- To see a black goat on a lonely bridle path means that treasure is hidden there.
- If a dog, snake, lizard, or hare crosses the path of a bridal party on its way to the wedding, the marriage will never be happy. If a spider or toad cross their path, happiness for the couple is virtually guaranteed.
- If a mouse runs over a person, it's a sign that the person is doomed. (*If a person runs over a mouse, it's a certainty that the mouse is doomed.*)
- An old folk remedy for asthma was to collect spiders' webs, roll them into a ball in the palm of your hand—then swallow them.
- An old folk remedy to cure bed-wetting was to roast a mouse and give it to the child.

## Pet Stars' Stories

Rin Tin Tin, one of Hollywood's early great animal stars, was discovered in a trench during World War I by an American Army officer, Captain Lee Duncan. He starred in over forty films, starting in 1922, and, amazingly, continued to do so for quite a few years after his death in 1932. Even for a canine that could climb ladders, leap ravines, and rescue unconscious females, this was a truly remarkable dog trick. (Hollywood magic made possible by Rin Tin Tin, Jr.—and the quiet unleashing of a few other juniors.)

JACK'S FACTS: **FIRST FIDO OF FILM**
The first animal ever to receive star billing in a movie was a German shepherd dog, Etzel von Oeringen, whose name was immediately changed for publicity purposes to "Strongheart." Strongheart made his debut in 1921 in a film titled *The Silent Call*, and was an instant screen sensation—emphasis on the "instant." Strongheart's dreams of rolling in Milk-Bones for the rest of his dog days were short-lived. The following year—in true back-barking Tinseltown tradition—he was usurped by another German shepherd, Rin Tin Tin.

Unquestionably, one of the best animal pet tricks in screen history is the female impersonation carried off by the screen's most famous canine, Lassie. This collie, who in reality was a male named Pal, became a true Hollywood celebrity after the release of his first movie, and soon gained fame around the world. He traveled first-class, had his special meals flown to wherever he was appearing and even had a fan club. One film reviewer said, "This dog is so human he does everything but talk—and he doesn't have to do that." Evidently, Lassie didn't; he wound up getting his own weekly national *radio* show! And later, a hit television series that lasted twenty years (which would have been 101 in dog years!)

Another gender-bending canine who made it big by reversing sexes was Budweiser beer superstar Spuds MacKenzie. A macho-looking party animal, "he" was in reality a "she," a sweet bull terrier bitch named Evie. S/he made commercials, print ads, a movie, *People*'s Best Dressed List and a lot of money. Pretty good for a female that everyone thought was a dog!

Name changes have also seemed to do a lot for animal careers. (And are much easier to get away with than sex changes.) The lovable mutt who played Higgins on the TV series *Petticoat Junction* for seven years had his name changed to Benji and suddenly made the leap to the big screen in *Benji*—the first of several box-office hits.

Cats, who have the reputation of being more difficult stars to work with than dogs or horses, have nonetheless scratched their niches in the media. Rhubarb, the star of the 1951 film of the same name, was an extraordinary alley cat who at the age of sixteen (which in human years made him the George Burns of cats) became one of Hollywood's most famous feline stars. He could swim, roll over, chase a ball like a dog, feign sleep, or hiss and attack on command—and uncomplainingly repeat these actions take after take (which is more than you can say about a lot of two-footed actors).

Morris, the cat who was rescued from an animal shelter and went on to become the original TV and print spokespuss for 9-Lives catfood in the 1980s, was such a popular animal star that he ran for president of the United States. (He didn't win; the job went to another Hollywood celebrity.)

JACK'S FACTS:
**Dog-Gone It!**
During World War II, Lassie's fame spread to the army's canine division, and a pin-up photo of Lassie (strategically air brushed) hung on the kennel wall of a Dalmatian guard dog named Togo, at Fort McPherson, Georgia. No one had the heart—or nerve—to break it to Togo that there was more to his pin-up pooch than met the eye.

## Questions and Answers About Pet Lore

### Which Is Witch?

Why are black cats considered to be bad luck?

They aren't bad luck if you live in parts of Britain, Brittany, or the Midi of France, among other places (namely homes of people who own black cats). In fact, in these places, as in ancient Egypt (where all cats were revered as gods) they are considered lucky.

The bad luck part goes back to the Middle Ages in Europe, when it was believed that witches could take the form of black cats, and that all black cats were actually transformed witches. To have one cross your path was, therefore, considered unlucky. (It was particularly unlucky for the black cat, which was singled out for persecution, resulting in thousands being shamefully destroyed.)

### Sizzler Puzzler

Why are really hot summer days called "dog days"?

I used to think it was because that's when most people barbecue hot dogs, but it's not. The expression originated in Roman times when they believed that during July and the first part of August, the rising "dog star" Sirius (which means "scorching" in Greek) gave its heat to the sun. Those sweltering weeks became known to friends, Romans, and countrymen as "days of the dog," to us, just plain "dog days."

### Putting On the Dog

When anyone acts snooty or show-offy around my landlord, she usually says that they are "putting on the dog." Is this some sort of cat person versus dog person expression? (She is a cat owner, and dogs aren't allowed in our building.)

Your landlord might be a biased cat person, which could be why she favors the expression "putting on the dog," but that has nothing to do with where it originated. It goes back to after the Civil War when the nouveau riche, who made their fortunes during the conflict, wanted to flaunt their wealth. Small, expensive lap dogs became symbols of wealth for the wives of the riche, and they lavished excessive amounts on these pampered pets. Today, anyone who puts on snooty airs—even if they don't have a pup to their name—is said to be "putting on the dog."

Part Two

# Picking the Perfect Pet

# Strictly for the Birds

4

## Birds as Pets

Feathered friends make great pets. They are terrific companions. They come in all different sizes, an amazing variety of colors, have an extraordinary range of vocal talents—from whistles to words to trilling symphonies—and they exhibit personalities as diverse as those of the people who buy them. A bird can be as much of a buddy as a dog, as playful and cuddly as a kitten—and as obnoxious as a toddler with a tantrum. It all depends on you!

### *Know Your Bird*

Before you bring a bird into your home, your family and your life, be sure you know what you're letting yourself in for.

- Read up on the type of bird you're interested in, then speak to people who've actually owned one of them.
  HANNA'S HINT: Birds that in books might be deemed "vocal," may in reality be squawking screechers capable of driving you bonkers—or out of your apartment.
- Find out how much time and attention the bird you're thinking about needs.
  HANNA'S HINT: Birds are social animals, they hate being ignored. Some will pluck out their feathers, or even die, if left alone too much of the time. And *time* is an important consideration when it comes to pet birds, especially since most are long-lived. If you're thinking bird, you are talking commitment. It is not uncommon for parrots to live sixty years, and often more! Even cockatiels can easily have a life span of two decades.
- Check into how much space your bird is going to need. Cage requirements vary for different species, but keep in mind that some small birds can be very active and need room to thrive.
  HANNA'S HINT: Just because your quarters are small—or your budget won't allow a large cage—doesn't mean you have to count out an active bird pet. You can make it up to the bird by letting it fly or play outside its cage on a daily basis.
- Be sure you know what sort of diet your bird of choice requires, and if you can—or care to—deal with it.
  HANNA'S HINT: A little warning about lories and lorikeets. These birds are so colorful and adorable that many people buy them on impulse, unaware that their diet regularly contains liquid mixtures—which makes for very messy

droppings, frequently expelled with significant force. Not an indoor bird for neatniks!

- Stop, look, and definitely listen to your bird before you buy. Decibel levels vary between species—and between individual birds.

  HANNA'S HINT: If you live in an apartment, I'd suggest you check with your neighbors—and landlord—before bringing home a Moluccan cockatoo or an Aratinga conure. I'd also suggest a pair of those ear protectors they wear at shooting ranges.

- Find out if there is an avian veterinarian in your area. Hookbills shouldn't go to horse doctors—and vice versa. If your special bird needs veterinary attention, you want a vet who knows avian medicine. And it's better to know where one is *before* you bring your bird home!

  HANNA'S HINT: The breeder or pet store where you purchase your bird should be able to help you. If not, you can contact the American Veterinary Medical Association (AVMA) at 1–800–248–2862, or the Association of Avian Veterinarians, PO Box 811720, Boca Raton, FL 33481–1720.

## How to Recognize a Healthy Bird

Trust your instincts and your senses. If you're going to purchase a bird, you shouldn't smell a rat or anything else unpleasant at the place of purchase, be it a pet store or a breeder's aviary. Check out the cages. The seed and the water dishes should look good enough for any bird to want to eat and drink from. Let me put it this way: Cleanliness is not only next to godliness, it guarantees the best breeding grounds for healthy animals.

A quick rule of thumb when bird-buying is to look immediately for what I call the Four S's:

Shiny, clear eyes
Sleek, smooth feathers
Self-confident stature
Spirited movement

HANNA'S HINT: If the bird you're considering is disinterested in you—walks away, evidences no fear or curiosity—it's not a good sign of health, and wise for you to become disinterested in that bird as a pet.

- Check your potential pet from top to toes.
- The *beak* should close properly.
- The *nostrils* should be the same size and clear.
- The *feet* should be smooth.
- The *toes* should have claws. (Although a missing claw can disqualify a show bird, it need not turn you off a great pet. On the other hand, if more than one claw is missing, the bird will have difficulty perching—making for a lifelong problem.)
- The *vent* below the tail should be clean, not stained or matted with feces.
- The *breastbone* should be surrounded by plump flesh and not protrude sharply.
- *Breathing* should be even and unmarred by wheezing.
- The *skin*, when feathers are gently parted, should be clear and unspotted.

HANNA'S HINT: If you're buying a bird, you should be able to handle it before you bring it home. Breeders and pet-store owners vary in their wariness of potential buyers, but depending on the bird—and owners' insurance policies—they'll usually allow you a tactile pre-purchase encounter.

## Trouble Signs and How to Read Them

When children get sick, parents recognize the signs instantly; anything from a lack of appetite to a disinterest in TV can be a giveaway. But when animals get sick, it's not that easy for their human parents to know there's trouble brewing, which is why it's important to familiarize yourself with potential trouble signs—and know what they could mean.

### *Your Bird Might Be Sick If . . .*
- It is puffed up and sluggish.
- It sits on both feet with its eyes closed.
- Its nostrils are wet.
- The fleshy part around its nostrils (the cere) looks scaly.
- Its eyes are dull.
- Its eye rims are inflamed or look swollen.
- Its droppings increase, change in color or consistency.
- The feathers under its tail are soiled with excrement.
- Its feet are excessively scaly.
- It begins drinking much more water than usual.

- It stops talking, whistling, or warbling.
- Its breastbone is strongly visible.
- The lower part of its body is swollen.
- Its breathing is labored.
- It begins sitting in places it usually avoids.
- Its feathers look scruffy or brushlike, and the bird is not molting.

## Common Diseases

ASPERGILLOSIS: Caused by breathing in spores from certain plants or moldy bread, old seeds, musty hay, and other mold-infested items. The disease damages tissues and causes an accumulation of pus that seriously affects the bird's respiratory system.

*Best Prevention Measures:* Purchase only fresh seed; keep bird away from damp areas where there might be mold.

COCCIDIOSIS: An illness caused by parasites that are spread through droppings. When these droppings are consumed by a bird, the parasites mature in the intestines, diminishing the bird's appetite and causing diarrhea.

*Best Prevention Measures:* Keep those cages clean!

COLDS: Yes, birds catch them. No, they don't catch them from you. But they can catch them from other birds, from viruses, from drafts, from fungi, or they can be brought on by a vitamin A deficiency or stress. Colds affect the bird's respiratory system. An open beak, labored breathing, and a tail that's bobbing up and down, coupled with sneezing, coughing, nasal discharge, and puffed-out ruffled feathers are common symptoms.

*Best Prevention Measures:* Keep cages out of drafts, room temperatures regulated, and diets well-balanced with vitamins.

DIARRHEA: More a symptom than a disease, it is serious enough to warrant a bird owner's attention but, unaccompanied by other symptoms, not a reason to panic. Diarrhea can be caused by anything from indigestion and stress to food or insecticide poisoning—or even an intake of too much protein!

*Best Prevention Measures:* Don't spray or keep poisons around where you keep your birds: provide fresh food and water daily.

EGG BINDING: Occasionally a female bird will be unable to lay an egg that's ready to emerge. The bird will have a swollen abdomen, look sick, and stay pretty quiet on the cage floor. This can be caused by a vitamin deficiency, breeding too soon, old age, stress, or a common cold.

*Best Prevention Measures:* Wait until weather is warm enough and bird is mature enough to breed.

**EYE DISEASES:** Eye infections, where rims become inflamed or small wartlike bumps appear, are not uncommon in caged birds. They are most often caused by bacteria picked up from dirty perches. They can also be caused by irritants, such as aerosol sprays, a vitamin A deficiency, complications from another illness, or burrowing mites, which also cause Scaly Face disease (see below).

*Best Prevention Measures:* Keep perches clean; check your bird's eyes daily. Fast treatment usually guarantees a quick recovery.

**FEATHER PLUCKING:** This usually starts with an after-mold-itch, then a scratch, then a pluck . . . and another, and another, and another, until the plucking goes far enough to denude the bird! Under- or overheated rooms, intestinal parasites (which can cause skin itching), boredom, or vitamin and mineral deficiencies are some of the culprits suspected of causing this behavior. Bird owners should realize that plucking out a few feathers is normal, plucking out too many can be dangerous—especially when feather stumps are left, blocking new growth, or when the feathers pulled out are blood feathers.

*Best Prevention Measures:* Give your bird room to exercise, toys to play with, and regular baths or showers in hot weather.

**FRENCH MOLT OR BFD (BUDGERIGAR FLEDGLING DISEASE):** A disease, suspected of being caused by a virus, that strikes young birds while still in the nest, causing them to lose their new tail and flight feathers.

*Best Prevention Measures:* Stop breeding the parent birds for several months.

**MITES:** There are different types of mites that afflict birds. One type lives on the feathers and skin (*Syringophilus bipectioratus*), causing itching that often leads to feather plucking (see above). Another type (*Dermoglyphus elongatus*) is more insidious, it burrows into the feather shaft and follicle. Red mites (*Dermanyssus gallinae*) falls into this second category. These mites hide in cages during the day and feed on the birds' blood at night.

*Best Prevention Measures:* Keep cages clean, provide daily opportunities for baths or showers.

**PSITTACOSIS:** Also called ornithosis, chlamydiosis, and parrot fever, this is a bacterial disease that's spread through the inhalation of fecal and feather dust and can be transmitted to humans as well as to other birds. Birds evidence coldlike symptoms (see above) and people develop flulike symptoms. Fortunately, for birds and their owners, this disease can be successfully treated with antibiotics.

*Best Prevention Measures:* Avoid unexamined imported birds; quarantine sickly birds; wash hands after handling any birds.

SCALY FACE: A contagious disease (most common in budgerigars) evidenced by scaly growths that appear primarily around the eyes and beak. It is caused by mites that burrow into the skin, laying eggs there.

*Best Prevention Measures:* Keep cages and perches clean, quarantine sick birds until infection clears.

---

JACK'S FACTS: **The Molting Ritual**

Once or more a year, your bird is going to look like, well, something the cat dragged in. It's not a pretty sight, but it happens to all birds. It's essentially out with old feathers and in with the new, but birds (and their owners) don't really consider it "a good time." Molting saps a bird's energy. It tends to act listless, often stops singing and frequently becomes downright disagreeable. (Trust me, this passes. Think of it as avian PMS—Pre-Molt Syndrome.)

Molting times vary with different species. In the wild, the lengthening of daylight, which stimulates the thyroid gland and in turn the sex organs, sets the molt in motion. Canaries, for instance, usually molt between July and September, but in captivity they might molt at a completely different time of year, which then becomes their regular molting time each year.

No two birds, even of the same species, necessarily molt alike. Some will lose lots of feathers at once, others will lose them gradually. This is all within the realm of normal molting. Generally, the process—which is influenced by heat, humidity, and diet—takes about six weeks.

During molting, it is especially important to make sure that your bird is getting enough protein and calcium in its diet! (Hard-boiled egg yolks and offerings of well-washed, boiled, and crushed egg shells make fine treats at this time.)

*Shock Molting* (sudden or out-of-season feather loss) may occur in newly acquired birds or birds frightened by traumatic changes in location or the unexpected sight of a predator, such as a cat or an unfamiliar animal.

*Abnormal Molting* (losing too many feathers or losing feathers out-of-season) may occur because of shock (see above), dramatic temperature change, or illness. When in doubt, call a vet.

## Handling Emergencies

The best way to handle any emergency is to call your vet for advice and get your pet there as soon as possible. But, what is the best way of getting to the vet?

Gently gather the bird in your hands, holding its wings against its body. Leave only its feet and head free.

HANNA'S HINT: Take toys and perches out of the cage first—more room for you to maneuver and less room for a fluttering bird to hurt himself.

For a small biting bird, grasp the neck between your thumb and middle fingers. The little guy will still be able to turn his head, but not lunch on your fingers.

For a large bird, drop a light towel over it. Drape the towel so the material will cover your fingers when gently grasping the bird's neck.

## Breeding Tips

As the song says, *"Birds do it, bees do it, even educated fleas do it."* But if you want *your* particular birds to do it, speak to breeders who've done it successfully. Before you start multiplying your pets, know what you're letting yourself *and* your pets in for. It's unfair for all involved to do otherwise.

Also, keep in mind that many birds are not sexually dimorphic, meaning you can't tell the males from the females without DNA testing, which, I've learned, tends to cause breeding problems.

## Compatible—and Incompatible—Household Pets

Before you bring a bird into your home, it's important to consider how it will be received by—and react to—*all* the members of your household.

### Birds

Unless you buy two birds of the same species together, birds of a feather do not always take an immediate liking to one another. And birds of different species can present other problems.

**KEEP IN MIND**

- All birds are territorial, so before you add a new one to a cage where there is an established resident, be sure you know what you're letting the newcomer in for.
- If you want a pal to keep your male Amazon company (not a mate), pick a bird that is as different looking as possible—and then keep their cages apart!

JACK'S FACTS:
## A Bird-Brained Love Match

One of the most mismatched love matches in my career involved a pair of orangutans, Squiggy and Lenny, acquired from another zoo on "breeding loan." After the two had spent quite a long while together and no babies were in the offing, we decided to have our vet look into things. Well, after a thorough medical examination, the vet declared that we indeed had a "pair" of orangutans, but not a breeding pair. Unfortunately, both animals were males—but the good news was, they were really quite fond of each other!

## Cats

A risky situation. Cats have bird-catching instincts that just don't disappear because they live indoors. A bird in a cage is a trapped target, one that can be terrorized (if not internalized) by a house cat. If the bird is allowed outside the cage, it's a moving target. (And if its wings are clipped, it could be a dead duck!)

**KEEP IN MIND**

- It's not impossible to have cats and birds in the same household, it is just not recommended.
- When you're away, a cat will play—so make sure your bird is out of the way.
- It works both ways. A large hookbill, such as a parrot or macaw, or even a cockatoo, can do serious damage to a cat.

## Children

Depending on their ages and personalities, children can get along famously with *some* (and I emphasize *some*) birds. Temperamental large hookbills—and temperamental kids—can be a dangerous combination. When choosing a feathered pet, consider your child's age and temperament as well as the bird's. (See breed suggestions, p. 47.) Know the appropriate bird for your child!

**KEEP IN MIND**

- Children are not always aware of the consequences of their actions and therefore should be supervised when handling birds.
- Birds are very much like little children—and you don't leave little children alone with other little children.
- Parrots can be extremely hazardous to the fingers of young children.

## Dogs

Birds and dogs can get along. Dogs will show an interest in the new arrival—and should definitely be supervised when inspecting the cage—but as long as the dog's territory is not usurped, problems can usually be worked out.

**KEEP IN MIND**

- Curious dogs, of any size, can accidentally knock over cages and inadvertently frighten a bird to death.
- When a bird is unsupervised outside its cage, a dog may mistake it for a high-tech squeak toy.
- Hunting dogs and terriers are breeds that might tend to think of your bird more as prey than playmate.

- Barking will frighten birds, but they'll get used to it—provided it's not too frequently directed at them.

### Rabbits, Mice, Hamsters, and Small Rodents

These are all compatible with birds, provided they are not allowed in the bird's cages and vice versa. (Togetherness is not advisable.)

### Reptiles

If the reptile is large and your bird is small, the bird could be dinner. If your bird is large and the reptile is small, the reptile could be dinner. But if you keep both species in separate cages—and don't let them out at the same time—they'll get along just fine.

## Cautions to Keep in Mind

Birds are hardy pets, but hazards to their health and well-being abound. Knowing what these potential hazards are—and keeping yourself aware of them—is not only important, it could be a matter of your pet's life or death.

Look over the following list carefully. Surprisingly, many things that are good for you and your family could be harmful to birds.

- There are lots of things you can share with your bird, but your morning coffee or evening wine should definitely not be among them. Caffeine and alcohol can dramatically throw off a bird's metabolic rate, and even small amounts could be toxic.
- Chocolate, avocado, and rhubarb can be lethal for birds!
- Leafy greens, carrots, and low-fat yogurt are good for birds *and* you. But if you decide to share your lunch with your pet, don't let it eat from your plate or spoon. Human saliva contains *E. coli*, a natural bacteria that is potentially dangerous to birds. (Dog and cat saliva is also a bird health hazard, so don't let your feathered pet clean your other pets' plates, either.)
- Avoid giving your pet salty, sugary, or high-fat snack foods.
- Keep chewing gum and licorice away from your birds—they could choke on them.
- Be cautious about giving your bird old nuts. Peanuts, even if unsalted or raw, could be moldy and cause aspergillosis (see p. 39).

- Don't feed your pet old or damp seed that might be moldy. (You can keep seed fresher longer by putting it in an airtight container in your refrigerator.)
- Supplementing a balanced, formulated diet with extra vitamins (unless directed to do so by a veterinarian) can result in a potentially harmful overdose.
- Adding vitamins to your bird's drinking water can encourage bacterial growth and endanger your pet's health.
- Always look behind you before you sit down—and look down before you stand up.
- You may do more harm than good by trying to treat a fracture at home; get pet to vet as soon as possible!
- Ceiling fans should always be off if your bird is out.
- Keep aquariums covered and toilets closed.
- Birds often mistake foamy surfaces for firm landing places, so keep tubs and sinks empty or covered.
- Close cabinets and drawers to prevent curious birds from getting trapped.
- Birds can easily escape up a chimney, so keep fireplaces closed with screens or doors.
- Electrical wires and outlets can cause deadly shocks. Use childproof covers for empty sockets and hide wires beneath moldings or carpets.
- Kitchens can be hazardous to birds. Beware of hot stoves, open pots, steam, gas, and cooking fumes.
- Hot spices may help your chili, but they can seriously harm your bird.
- Nonstick cookware (Teflon, Silverstone, and others), if heated to over 536° Fahrenheit, gives off highly toxic polytetrafluorethylene fumes that will kill birds!
- Crocheted afghans, sweaters, and knitting yarns can entangle—and possibly strangle—unsupervised birds.
- If you chemically color or perm your hair, it is not advisable to let your bird preen you.
- No matter how great you want your bird to look for company, *never* use oils or greasy lotions on its feathers; you'll defeat their insulating properties and can seriously endanger your pet's health!
- Picture windows and glass doors can cause quick concussions for unclipped fliers; draperies and shades can help act as preventives.
- Keep your perfume to yourself; it's poison for a bird.
- Air pollutants harmful to birds include aerosol hairsprays, room deodorizers, insecticide sprays or pest strips, paint fumes, houseplant pesticides, and carbon monoxide.

- Cigar and cigarette smoke is unhealthy for your bird; nicotine is deadly.
- Keeping a bird's cage in direct sunlight can cause heatstroke.
- Avoid commercial bird grit that contains charcoal. It's indigestible and highly absorbent, allowing it to soak up important nutrients that your pet should be getting.
- Don't let your bird peck or chew on pennies, food cans, aluminum pots, lead soldered glass, lead-painted surfaces, or anything rusty. All of these can cause chronic toxicities.
- Lead in any form is dangerous to birds, so be aware of curtain-bottom weights, fishing weights, imported glazed ceramic bowls or mugs, antique toys or trains.
- Crayons are okay for kids to play with, but they are poisonous for birds.
- Other writing implements that are hazardous to a bird's health are Magic Markers, pencil leads, and ballpoint pen refills.
- Human home remedies (unless authorized by a veterinarian) can be toxic to a bird.
- When your bird alights, make sure there are no matches around—the striking heads are poisonous. (Safety—or book—matches are nontoxic.)
- Mothballs are very appealing to pet birds; unfortunately, they are also lethal.
- Cages placed too close to a color TV may adversely affect your bird's eyes. (Birds can see the tiny, rapid dot changes that people don't.)
- Any products around the house that can harm children can kill birds. (Whatever you'd keep out of a child's reach, you want to keep away from your bird!) These include: All household cleansers, detergents, drain cleaners, paint removers, waxes, polishes, pine oil, hair dyes, fabric softeners, aspirin, medicines, bleach, suntan lotions, fuels, petroleum products, shellac.
- Rusty or plastic-coated pans can be deadly for birds.
- Wall sconces make lovely light fixtures, but they also make dangerous traps for small pet birds.

### Plants to Keep Your Bird Away from, and Vice Versa

Though greens are good for birds, not all plants are. The following lists those that could be harmful to your bird. (If you are in doubt about the poison potential of all or part of any plant you own, check with an avian vet—or play it safe and find the plant a new home.)

| | | |
|---|---|---|
| American Yew | Black Locust | Buttercup |
| Baneberry | Bloodroot | Caladium |
| Bittersweet | Buckthorn | Calla Lily |

| | | |
|---|---|---|
| Cherry Tree | Iris | Nightshade |
| Christmas Candle | Jack-in-the-pulpit | Nutmeg |
| Clematis | Jimsonweed | Pokeweed |
| Cowslip | Laburnum | Rhododendron |
| Daphne | Larkspur | Rhubarb |
| Dieffenbachia | Locoweed | Rosary Peas |
| English Yew | Lords and Ladies | Snowdrop |
| Golden Chain | May Apple | Snowflake |
| Hemlock | Mescal | Sweet Pea |
| Henbane | Mistletoe (just the berries) | Tobacco |
| Honey Locust | Monkshood | Water Hemlock |
| Horse Chestnut | Morning Glory | Western Yew |
| Indian Turnip | Mountain Laurel | |

---

JACK'S FACTS: **A Cautionary Tale**

I learned the importance of paying attention to cautions the old-fashioned way: painfully! I was with a veterinarian who had to perform a routine medical procedure on an emu, a tall, flightless bird with long, strong legs and sharp claws. "Now, don't get too close," the vet warned. "The emu is a tricky bird." I nodded, and cautiously followed him as he came up behind the emu and, with swift precision, corralled it with a tight grasp. Seeing that he had a firm grip on the bird, I decided I wanted a closer look. So, I ignored the warning. Before I knew what hit me (though I certainly knew *where* it hit me) the emu had struck out with a lightening fast kung-fu kick in the last place I ever (never) want to be kicked again!

---

## Birds by Breed

KEY: 🐾🐾🐾🐾 means easy-care family bird

🐾🐾🐾 means weigh pros and cons carefully

🐾🐾 means think twice about this bird

🐾 means this bird needs special consideration

### 🐾🐾🐾🐾 *Canaries*

PRO: Lots to recommend them. They are small (four to six inches), don't demand constant attention, are not destructive, not noisy (and if they're songsters, they're a delight to listen to), quite happy living singly, good pets for beginners and relatively inexpensive.

## JACK'S FACTS: **Did You Know . . .**

- Birds extract oxygen from the air about seven times more effectively than humans; unfortunately, they also extract pollutants from the air at the same accelerated rate. (Miners used to carry a caged canary with them into mines, using the poor bird as an expendable, early-warning toxic-fume detector.)

- The single feature that makes a bird a bird is that it has one thing no other animal has—feathers! (For those of you who thought "beak," be aware that there is actually a species of whale that has a beak!)

- Birds that live with people tend to think of them as their flock members—and can be influenced by their daily moods.

- A talking bird can learn hundreds of words (an African grey named Prudle made *The Guinness Book of Pet Records* for having a vocabulary of over 800 words), but it cannot *unlearn* one!

- A bird can take off faster, in less distance, and fly further on less fuel than any aircraft ever invented.

- Birds are the only living creatures that close their eyes in death.

- A bird can starve to death in twenty-four to forty-eight hours.

- Birds exert the most physical effort when they exhale, which is just the opposite of us; it takes more effort to inhale.

- Birds often bite the one they loves the most—especially when a stranger or new pet comes around.

CON: They're not cuddly, prefer not to be handled. They spend most of their lives caged, so they need enough space in the cage for flying exercise. The recommended cage for keeping a canary healthy should be at least thirty inches long, with perches placed at either end for landing.

CREATURE COMFORTS: Your canary will appreciate a swing, a toy bell—or play equivalent—and a daily bath in its own shallow tub. (Place room-temperature water in tub for your pet to splash in.) Most canaries like the security of a cage covering in the evening, preferably away from the TV.

DIET NEEDS AND TREATS: Though natural seed-eaters, canaries can now thrive hassle-free on a nutritionally complete pelleted diet that's been formulated especially for them. Healthy supplements to offer are fresh greens (kale, spinach, dandelion leaves, etc.), mashed hard-boiled eggs, peeled orange and apple slices, or

JACK'S FACTS: **Buyer Beware**

If you are thinking of buying a bird as a pet, buy one that's been bred domestically. Hand-raised or captive-bred birds not only make for better and healthier pets, they save the lives and protect the future of dozens of endangered species that are smuggled illegally (and inhumanely) into the country each year. Keep in mind that people who don't care about the lives of endangered species aren't going to worry about falsifying a leg band on an exotic bird, so learn as much as you can about the seller of your bird-to-be as about the bird itself before you buy.

other fresh fruits. They also need a cuttlebone in their cage, a mineral mixture and some grit. Some Red-Factor canaries need color food, which is high in beta-carotene or contains artificial coloring, to remain red.

**MORE INFO**

There are different types of canaries—some bred for shape, some for coloring, some for song. They vary in price and personal appeal, so take time to shop, look and listen before you buy.

## 🐦🐦🐦🐦 *Finches*

PRO: Like canaries (who are a species of finch), finches are small, lively, undemanding, not destructive, not noisy, generally affordable and great pets for kids or beginners.

CON: They are not fond of being cuddled, kissed, or petted. They're not natural loners. They thrive on pairing off with birds of finch feather—especially those of the opposite sex. (It's not always easy to tell a boy finch from a girl finch, but, as a rule, singing is a guy thing.)

CREATURE COMFORTS: Same as for canaries. Also, many finches enjoy roosting nests to sleep in. (These can be purchased inexpensively at pet stores.) They need flying room, so cages should be at least thirty inches long.

DIET NEEDS AND TREATS: Seed-eating finches also have a complete pelleted food that's been specially formulated to simplify your life and supply all their necessary nutrients. Finches enjoy the same healthy supplements as canaries (see above) with the occasional addition of live food—mealworms, aphids, and fruit flies. (Not all finches take to these treats—but neither do all owners!)

**MORE INFO**

There are many different types of finches to choose from. African finches have special diet requirements, are fairly high-maintenance birds and not recommended for beginners. Zebra finches are the easiest to keep. They're well-domesticated, affordable, and sexually distinguishable—which always makes breeding a lot easier!

### ✹✹✹✹ *Budgerigars (Budgies—also known as Parakeets)*

**PRO:** They're delightful little parrot companions for older or physically-challenged persons, as well as responsible youngsters. Small (six to eight inches), with a life span of ten to fifteen years, these talkative, affordable, easy-to-tame-and-train pets make great first birds. Vocal enough for amusement, not too loud for apartment dwellers.

**CON:** Out-of-cage playtime with human companion an hour or two each day—or a full-time budgie playmate—is essential for budgie happiness.

**CREATURE COMFORTS:** Toys and swings. They'll turn anything into a toy, so make sure they don't get into trouble when they're out and about. (See "Cautions" section, p. 44.)

**DIET NEEDS AND TREATS:** Complete pelleted budgie diets are available. But you'll want to serve a treat to these high-energy pets of occasional leafy greens, as well as raw grated carrots, broccoli, cooked corn, fresh fruit, whole-grain toast, and even cooked pasta!

**MORE INFO**

You can usually tell a male from a female by the color of its cere, which is the soft strip right above the beak. If it's blue (or purple) it's a boy; if pink (or tan), a girl. Though the guys have the gift of gab, gals will speak, too.

### ✹✹✹ *Cockatiels*

**PRO:** Great personalities, good whistlers, and mimics of short phrases, like to be cuddled, easy-to-tame, average life span ten to twenty years, nice for handling (ten to twelve inches), fine choice for a beginner bird.

**CON:** They are messy seed-scatterers, and they're dusty. (Their outer feathers are covered with a thin powder that prevents water from reaching their skin and interfering with their body's insulation system.) They can screech on occasion. Single birds become very dependent on their owners and demand playtime and attention. They are very fast flyers and need room to exercise.

**CREATURE COMFORTS:** Cockatiels need their space—and prefer when it's outside of a cage! If your pet is going to spend much time confined, the cage should be at least thirty-six inches long, eighteen inches wide, and twenty-four inches high, with bars no more than ¾-inch apart. They enjoy taking a daily bath—or getting a fine-spray shower with a plant mister. Perches of varied thicknesses, toys, swings, and particularly ladders to climb on make for happy cockatiels.

**DIET NEEDS AND TREATS:** Cockatiels are finicky eaters (and stubborn), so starting them on a nutritionally complete pelleted diet is best for them—and you. Offering a variety of healthy treats—hard-boiled egg, broccoli, corn, peas, whole-wheat bread—is always a good idea. A cuttlebone or mineral block in the cage is a necessity. Avoid the temptation to spoil your new pal with sugary snacks—cockatiels have a high risk of diabetes.

#### MORE INFO

The best time to buy a cockatiel is in the early fall, when there should be the largest selection to choose from. When very young, both males and females look like their mother. Cockatiels are normally gray, with white patches on their wings and bright-orange patches on their cheeks, and generally cost between $50 and $150. The color mutations (pied, lutino, albino, cinnamon, etc.) are more expensive.

### 🐦🐦🐦 *Lovebirds*

**PRO:** They are intelligent, affectionate, affordable, come in thousands of colors (literally!), can be happily kept as a single bird, will bond with owner, and can be trained to talk and perform tricks. They are small by hookbill standards (about six inches) and have an average life span of about ten years. They are fine for beginners and best for people seeking a feathered pet that's more than a budgie but less than an Amazon parrot.

**CON:** They have high-pitched voices and, though not overly loud, they do vocalize often. They are not dimorphic, which means you can't visually tell the males from the females in most cases, which causes problems if you plan to breed. They are natural paper shredders and can turn important documents into confetti in no time!

CREATURE COMFORTS: A cage large enough for energetic birds to play in, a minimum of eighteen inches long, wide and high. Toys, ladders, swings—perhaps a nest to sleep in.

DIET NEEDS AND TREATS: A nutritionally complete pelleted food will save your sanity and keep your pet healthy. The cage should always contain a cuttlebone and a mineral block. For treats that your pet will enjoy, try apples, pears, rehydrated raisins, cornbread, sunflower seeds, and beans.

### MORE INFO

Of the three most available species of lovebirds (there are nine)—the peachface, the masked, and the Fischer's—the peachface is the most popular. If you are buying a pair of lovebirds, make sure they are of the same species; a peachface and a masked are more likely to fight than cuddle. Also, lovebird pairs—even those that bill and coo—tend to become aggressive with humans when they have each other. Keep in mind that hand-fed birds will make better pets, so be sure to shop around!

## 🐚 Lories and Lorikeets

PRO: They're playful, they're colorful, great mimics, and they come in sizes from small to medium.

CON: They're expensive, they need special cages (which need to be on washable surfaces) because of the liquidity of their droppings. They're noisy, territorial, jealous of other birds, require special foods, they bite when annoyed. They are not dimorphic, so you can't tell the males from the females by looks. They are high-maintenance birds; not for beginners.

CREATURE COMFORTS: A large cage designed for easy cleaning—which, as a rule, is not available at most pet stores and has to be ordered specially. A sleeping nest. Daily baths or showers. Swings. Toys—especially those that make noise!

DIET NEEDS AND TREATS: Though there are nutritionally complete dry foods formulated for lories and lorikeets, these birds are essentially nectar, pollen, and fruit-eaters. Commercially prepared nectar diets are available, but the birds still require supplements of fresh fruits (which they love squeezing the juice out of) and vegetables for their health and happiness, which seems to increase proportionately with the mess they make of meals.

**MORE INFO**

The larger lories (black caps, yellow backs) are the best talkers—but they're also the loudest. They are called "brush-tongued" parrots because the raised papillae at the end of their tongues (used for gathering nectar from flowers) is much like a brush. Lories sometimes sleep on their backs with their feet in the air (so don't rush out looking for a shoebox right away). Never try to discipline a lory with a slap; it may carry a grudge against you for months. Throw out any soft food that's been left uneaten for too long, especially in warm weather!

## 🐾🐾 *Conures*

PRO: They are intelligent, affectionate and love being around—and riding on—their owners. There are several different species of conures, ranging in size from a small six inches to a substantial twenty inches. They're outgoing and long-lived, with life spans of fifteen to fifty years.

CON: They have a high-pitched screech and can be very, *very* noisy. Many have a tendency to be jealous and can become nippy. They need attention and know how to demand it.

CREATURE COMFORTS: For small conures, a cage that's sturdy, approximately thirty-six inches long by eighteen inches wide and twenty-four inches high, with ½-to-¾-inch spacing between the bars. Cuttlefish, mineral block, toys, swings, and substantial perches.

DIET NEEDS AND TREATS: Early training with a nutritionally complete pelleted formula is best for basic health. Supplements of fresh (or defrosted) veggies, chopped fruits, cheese, mashed hard-boiled eggs, and toasted whole-grain breads fit all sizes of conures.

**MORE INFO**

It is possible to reprogram—or at least vary—a conure's screech by exposing it to a variety of other sounds as a baby. Sun conures are reputed to have the highest-pitched screech, but they can be trained (without yelling) to go to their cage for quality "quiet time."

## 🐾 *Toucans*

PRO: Intelligent, curious, colorful, neat eaters, not very noisy, won't damage furniture.

CON: Expensive, large (twelve to fifteen inches), require fresh fruit daily, and are prone to messy loose stools. Hard to train unless hand-reared. Non-talkers. Not for beginners.

CREATURE COMFORTS: A large cage, warm and humid environment. Branches to fly to.

DIET NEEDS AND TREATS: These softbills are fruit-eaters and will *not* thrive on a dry pelleted diet alone. Pet stores have fruit mixes available, but chopped fresh apples, bananas, grapes, and even cooked carrots should be daily treats. (CAUTION: Tomatoes, pineapple, oranges, and other citrus fruits should be avoided because their high-acid content can adversely affect the bird's metabolism.)

### MORE INFO

A toucan is a "softbill" not because it has a soft bill (it doesn't), but because it eats soft foods. Toucans don't have enough strength in their beak to chew things. They often have to pound small pieces of fruit against a hard surface in order to eat them. (But don't be fooled. Toucans can actually kill birds with whom they share a cage . . . including another toucan!)

## 🐦🐦 *African Grey Parrots*

PRO: The best talkers in the pet kingdom. Beyond mimicry, they've been found to understand and use human speech. (Probably the most amazing African grey I've met has been Alex, trained by psychologist Dr. Irene Pepperberg at the University of Arizona. Alex can identify objects and distinguish similarities and differences between them, as well as name their colors and shapes. I can't vouch for what he really "knows," but it's quite a bit—and a lot more than just rote training.) They are beautiful, intelligent, and empathetic. They're a nice size for a pet, twelve to fifteen inches and have an estimated life span of thirty-five to fifty years.

CON: They are expensive, can be temperamental, tend to bond to one person, can be nippy, not good with young children.

CREATURE COMFORTS: A large, roomy cage with a large roomy door, and latches that will stay latched. (Parrots are notorious escape artists.) Locking feeders with outside access, because African greys don't generally like strangers' hands in their cages. An assortment of perches, different widths. Toys to chew, swings, a cage-top—or free-standing—gym.

DIET NEEDS AND TREATS: Nutritionally complete pelleted foods are available, but African greys like their fruits and vegetables, and just about anything that you eat and they can get their beaks on. Because they are susceptible to calcium deficiency, emphasis on natural calcium-rich treats such as broccoli, bok choy, collard and turnip greens, almonds, soybeans, and tofu are good choices.

## MORE INFO

There are two types of African greys—the large Congo (black beak, bright-red tail) and the smaller Timneh (reddish beak, dull red tail). Intellectually, African greys are reputed to be the equal of three- to five-year-old children, emotionally, they're like toddlers in the terrible twos. The Jardine, Sengal, and Meyers are *Poicerphalus* parrots. They're expensive and beautiful and not great talkers—and not for beginner pets.

## 🐦 *Amazon Parrots*

PRO: Playful, colorful, entertaining, talkative. A large variety of species to choose from (twenty-seven without counting subspecies). Extremely intelligent. Fine singers. Enjoy human companions. Great powers of retention. The most popular types range in size from fourteen to sixteen inches and are long-lived, with estimated average life spans of thirty to seventy years.

CON: Can be stubborn. Can screech loudly and/or talk incessantly. May bite when excited, angry, hungry, annoyed, or jealous. Can't be trusted unsupervised around young children. Expensive.

CREATURE COMFORTS: A large rectangular cage (large enough for bird to spread his wings up and out without touching the bars), with ¾-inch to one-inch spacing between the bars. Outside-access feeding doors, with locked-on feeding dishes. Secure door latches (or locks for them). Sturdy perches, a swing, toys to chew, horizontal bars, or sturdy gym ladders for climbing exercise. Give regular misting showers or have bathing facilities available.

DIET NEEDS AND TREATS: Amazon owners have to watch their pets' weight, because these birds sure won't. They're natural noshers and tend to become unhealthily obese as they get older. A nutritionally complete pelleted diet should be augmented with fresh fruits and vegetables, chopped raw carrots, corn, sweet potatoes, cantaloupe, dark leafy greens, and especially other vitamin A-rich foods. (If adding seeds, go easy on high-fat ones like safflower and sunflower seeds. Older Amazons are reported to be susceptible to clogged and hardened arteries.)

### MORE INFO

The three most popular types of Amazons are the Double yellowhead, the Blue front and the Yellow nape. (Yellow napes are reported to be the best talkers. These reports, of course, come from Yellow nape owners.) Amazons tend to learn most of their speech during the first two years of life. If you buy an older bird, he may be difficult to train—or, depending on what he has learned already, even more difficult to *untrain!* Amazons tend to develop a musty bird odor when they're excited or agitated. Regular mistings with a fine spray of room temperature water (or a shower or a bath) helps. Amazons are expensive birds, ranging in price from $400 to $1,500 and more. If you are offered a bargain bird, be wary. It could be ill or illegal, or possibly have the personality of a feathered serial killer, and it's not worth taking the chance. Amazons have a very long life span, so it is neither foolish nor morbid to make arrangements in writing for your pet's well-being if you happen to die first.

### 🦜🦜 *Cockatoos*

**PRO:** The most affectionate of all parrots. Social, lovable, acrobatic. There are several different types of cockatoos, with different personalities—some more suited for families than others (see "More Info" below). They range in size from fourteen to twenty inches and have estimated life spans of thirty to fifty years.

**CON:** Can be very demanding. Need lots of activity and/or attention. Can be destructive. Need room for a large cage. Expensive.

**CREATURE COMFORTS:** A strong large cage, with bar spacing from ¾ inch to 1½ inches, depending on type of cockatoo. Locking, outside-access feeder doors—with bolt-on feeding dishes. Secure latches or locks for cage. (Some cockatoos can pull off Houdinilike escapes from cages that their owners thought were locked!) Toys galore (not all in the cage at once), especially those they can chew. Extra perches, ladders, horizontal bars. Daily showers with a mist sprayer.

**DIET NEEDS AND TREATS:** Cuttlebone, mineral block. A nutritionally pelleted diet formulated for cockatoos, supplemented with a variety of fresh fruits (especially oranges, grapes, kiwis, and pineapple chunks) and vegetables (raw, cooked, fresh, or defrosted).

**MORE INFO**

Not all cockatoos are family-friendly. Even in a particular species, like the umbrella cockatoo, there could be a bird that's a "bad seed." Most umbrellas, though, are happy in households with children, provided they get enough attention and toys. (That goes for the children, too.) All cockatoos are noisy at times. Some can be very noisy, and some, like the Moluccan cockatoo, can be really noisy. Because all cockatoos are not like Baretta's Fred, speak to people who've lived with the type you're thinking about—*before* you bring it home!

## 🐦 *Macaws*

PRO: Loving, intelligent talkers, laughers, and whistlers. Fast-learners and born acrobats. Large in size (thirty to thirty-six inches), these parrots can qualify as roommates as well as pets. They have an estimated life span of more than sixty years. They also come in mini-macaw sizes (eleven to fifteen inches), with big-bird personalities.

CON: They are very expensive, some of the large birds running from $8,000 to $10,000. (The mini-macaws are less expensive—around $300 and up—but still not cheap.) They are big, very loud, have extremely powerful beaks, and are chewers. They require large, *strong* cages. Not good for households with young children.

CREATURE COMFORTS: A large cage with ¾-inch to 1½-inch bar spacing, depending on the macaw's size. (Check with breeder or seller for measurements right for your type of macaw.) Lots of challenging puzzle-type toys that keep their beaks and minds engaged for long periods of time. (These toys usually have nuts trapped inside treated wood that the birds have to chew open.)

DIET NEEDS AND TREATS: Cuttlebone or mineral block. A nutritionally complete pelleted food, supplemented (preferably daily) with fresh fruit (apples, pears, kiwis, grapes, oranges, cantaloupe, strawberries), vegetables (carrots, brussels sprouts, cucumbers, peppers, broccoli, corn), cooked beans, pasta, pumpkin seeds, large unsalted raw nuts.

**MORE INFO**

Macaws can learn all sorts of tricks—including how to eat from a spoon. (Or maybe how to eat a spoon.) The most common types of large pet macaws are the blue and gold macaw, the scarlet macaw, the hyacinth macaw, and the green wing macaw. The macaw type that's reported least likely to get along with other pets and children is the scarlet macaw. Mini-macaws will also learn to perform tricks—and children can safely be around to enjoy them.

## Other Bird Choices

**PARROTLETS:** Small, sociable, not too noisy. Happy enough with a species playmate or quality time with owners who'll give them out-of-cage time at least once a day. Will thrive on complete pelleted food, subsidized by daily fresh fruits and veggies.

**INDIAN RINGNECKS:** Colorful, talkative, attention-demanding birds in the parakeet family. Cockatiel-sized and expensive, ringnecks have average life spans of twenty to thirty years and exceptionally clear speaking voices. Foods and treats are similar to those of cockatiels. Not for beginners.

**PIONUS PARROTS:** Pricey ($200 to $1,200), depending on which of the five available species you choose, these mid-sized parrots—relatively new in the domestic pet market—provide a lot of bird bang for the buck. They're quiet, they talk, they play, they'll eat a pelleted diet and whatever fruits and vegetables you let them get their beaks on. Once you speak to people who've owned them, you'll probably want one.

**ECLECTUS PARROTS:** Beautiful, personable, good talkers, playful. Companion-sized at about fourteen inches, eclectus parrots enjoy socializing with their owners and need large cages with plenty of room for toys and swings. They'll eat a pelleted diet, but—like all parrots—they thrive on regular supplements of fresh fruits, vegetables, and nuts.

**QUAKER (MONK) PARAKEETS:** A medium-sized bird (about eleven inches) that's great with families. Quakers love to talk, mimic, whistle—and can be noisy. (Apartment dwellers, beware.) They're hardy birds, eat pelleted diets supplemented with fresh fruits, vegetables and healthy people snacks. But they are costly (anywhere from $160 to $1,000) and, at this writing, they are illegal in many states—including California, Connecticut, Georgia, New Jersey, and Wyoming. (This is because they've been found able to survive in the wild and have taken over habitats of native birds.)

**TOURACOS:** Softbilled, quiet, smaller, less showy than their toucan relatives. Their diet requirements are the same, but touracos seem to enjoy flying much more than performing stunts. Not a small-cage apartment bird.

🐦 **MYNAH BIRDS:** Glossy-black with a purple sheen, these relatives of starlings are among the best feathered talkers and sound mimics there are. I can vouch for that, having lived with one when I was director of the Central Florida Zoo in Sanford, Florida. Mynahs are softbilled birds (see lories and lorikeets for dietary tastes), but they are not easily bred in captivity, and are frequently brought into the country illegally.

---

JACK'S FACTS: **My Major Mynah**

One of the most talkative animals I've known personally was a mynah bird named Joe. I got him from a bar that was going out of business, so he had a pretty colorful vocabulary—every thing from "Aw . . . [you-know-what]" to "I wanna take your order." I kept him with me at the Central Florida Zoo, where one day someone broke into my office and stole him. Because Joe was a sort of mynah zoo celebrity, and visitors loved him, the police were determined to help me find him. The local papers ran a story headlined: "He's mine a bird, not yours." This led to a tip and an address. Without a search warrant, there wasn't much the police could do. They told the woman who unknowingly bought the bird that they thought it was mine. She wanted proof. I told her that, without even seeing the bird, once he heard my voice, he was going to curse and then say, "I wanna take your order." Sure enough, I said, "Hey, Joe," and he said, "Aw, shit!" Before he even finished saying, "I wanna take your order," the policeman said: "That's your bird!"

Many owners of talking birds are now advised to teach their expensive pet to learn to say their names and phone numbers as a positive means of identification in case of theft.

---

## Big Names and Their Birds' Names
Some famous names and names of their feathered friends to help you find a name for yours.

*Calvin Coolidge:* Nip and Tuck (Canaries)
*Bo Derek:* Angus (Parrot)
*Shannen Doherty:* Julio, Paloma, Pissaro (Doves)
*Louise DuArt:* Wazzo (Cockatiel)
*Shelley Duvall:* Mowgli and Scarley-Wharley (Macaws); Gorby, Humpty, Sunny (Parrots)
*Greta Garbo:* Polly (Parrot)
*Earl Holliman:* Walter (Pigeon)

*Andrew Jackson:* Poor Poll (Parrot)
*Thomas Jefferson:* Dick (Mockingbird)
*John F. Kennedy:* Robin (Canary); Bluebell and Maybell (Parakeets)
*Vincent Price:* Pocahontas (Parakeet)
*Elizabeth Taylor:* Alvin (Parrot)
*Betty White:* Woodstock (Parakeet)
*Robin Williams:* Big Sal (Parrot)

And in my travels I've also met a parrot named Wannacracker, a cockatoo named Cageybee, and a canary called Sing Sing.

## Questions and Answers About Strictly for the Birds

### Feathers Apart
What's the difference between an English budgie and an American parakeet?

Though they are members of the same species, the English budgie is larger and (in British fashion) more reserved than its American relative. Not that they're stuffy, "stiff-upper-beak" types—just generally more reserved.

### Polly Want to Potty?
I love Mombockis, my African grey, but I'd love him even more if I didn't have to clean up after him when he's not in his cage. Is it possible to potty-train a parrot?

If you have the patience, yes, it can be done! They can be taught to relieve themselves from a perch onto newspaper, a special tray, a garbage can—even into the toilet. By putting the bird in the same place each time, repeating the same trigger word (say, "Potty"), then rewarding him with praise and play when he does what he's supposed to do where he's supposed to do it, you can develop a fairly well-trained pet. Just keep in mind, that accidents do happen.

### Training No-Nos to Know
Whenever my cockatiel, Bowie, nips my finger, I yell at him. He does it again and when I yell at him again his behavior just gets worse. I may be imagining it, but he seems to enjoy getting me angry. Do birds do this?

You're not imagining it. Birds are a lot like kids: if they can get a reaction out of you—even a negative one—they'll take it over being ignored. Bowie sounds as if he needs some mellow, full-attention quality time with you. Try whistling together—but pick a tune you like. I knew someone who taught her bird "It's a Small World After All"—and has regretted it for years!

## Bird Talk You Should Know

ALBINO: a mutation in which melanin or all—or virtually all—of the dark coloring is absent, leaving only white. Eyes are red.

AVIARY: a large cage or room where birds fly free

BLOOD FEATHER: a feather that still has a blood supply to it

CERE: the fleshy, unfeathered piece across the top of the bill

CLOACA: the outlet at the end of the large intestine or rectum that excretes waste from the digestive tract as well as from the kidneys. Reproductive organs of both males and females open at the cloaca.

CLOSED-BAND: a completely closed metal ring providing hatch date and place of birth; used as proof of age and domesticity (An "open-band," one that isn't *completely* closed, indicates an imported bird.)

CLUTCH: a hatch of eggs; the chicks that hatch from them

COCK: a male bird

DIMORPHIC: when there are distinct visual characteristics between the sexes

DOMESTIC: a bird bred in the United States

FLEDGLING: a baby bird that is out of the nest, but cannot yet feed itself

GRANULOMAS: masses of dry, hard pus

HAND-RAISED: when young fledglings are taken from their parents and fed by people to promote bonding to humans, making the birds friendlier and easier to train

HEN: a female bird

IMPORTED: a bird brought in from another country

MOLTING: the shedding and replacing of feathers

MONOMORPHIC: both sexes of the bird seem identical

**OMNIVOROUS:** birds that eat all kinds of food—plant and animal

**OPEN-BAND:** an incompletely closed leg-band that indicates an imported bird

**ORNITHOLOGY:** the branch of zoology that deals with birds

**PBFD:** Psittacine Beak and Feather Disease

**PSITTACINE:** parrot or parrotlike birds, hookbills

**PSITTACOSIS:** a curable bacterial illness, spread through inhalation of feather and fecal dust, that affects humans *and* birds

**SOFTBILLS:** birds that feed on insects, nectar, and plants

**ZOONOSIS:** any animal disease that can be contracted by a human

---

JACK'S FACTS: **Five Top Books for Bird Owners**

*You and Your Pet Bird* by David Alderton (Knopf)

*Simon & Schuster Guide to Pet Birds* by Matthew M. Vriends

*Birds for Pets and Pleasure* by Nealy Haley (Delacorte)

*Encyclopedia of Cage and Aviary Birds* by Cyril H. Rogers (Macmillan)

*Birds as Pets* by Paul Villiard (Doubleday)

Plus: *Bird Talk Magazine*, P.O. Box 57347, Boulder, CO 80322–7347. (303) 666–8504. A monthly publication with the latest information on the care and keeping of birds.

# 5

# The Cats' Meows

**Cats as Pets**

Cats rule! Anyone who has ever owned a cat, been around a cat and a dog—or a cat and any other animal—knows this. Cats do not perceive owners as "masters," they think of them more in the way teenagers think of parents. They'll snuggle up to them when they're feeling cuddly or want something, usually attention (or in the case of kids, car keys), ignore them when preoccupied with bird watching or sleep, and generally tolerate them as roommates in what they unquestionably believe is their domain.

There are about forty recognized cat breeds—and about a million unrecognized ones. In fact, it is estimated that only 1 percent to 3 percent of all cats are purebred. They come in all sorts of colors—and snazzy combinations thereof—as well as a variety of shapes and sizes (from a hairless Sphynx and tail-less Manx to a dog-eared Scottish fold and macho-sized Maine Coon) and, additionally, in more long and shorthaired variations than Dolly Parton's wigs!

Cats have become the most popular housepet in America, for many good reasons.

• They can be kept in small apartments.
• They don't have to be walked outside on cold and rainy days.
• They can amuse themselves when you are not around.
• They're quiet, loving, and—with a few exceptions—very good self-groomers.
• They enjoy what we offer without being emotionally dependent.
• Local animal shelters afford a large selection of fine affordable feline friends.
• They generally play and work well with other animals.

Before you decide to bring a cat into your life, there are things to think about.

## *What You Should Know*
• Cats have an average lifespan of about fifteen years, which means a long-term commitment.
• Cats are independent creatures, but they do require veterinary care—particularly annual inoculations and boosters to protect them *and you* from diseases. HANNA'S HINT: Even if you plan to keep your kitten or cat indoors, vaccinations are advisable. In many states, certain inoculations are required by law. Kittens are especially vulnerable to illnesses and should receive their shots starting at seven to nine weeks. Check with your vet.

- Kittens are an easy impulse pet to bring home—mostly because there are, regrettably, so many given away for free. But owning a pet is a financial as well as an emotional responsibility, so if you can't handle the expenses involved in keeping it—primarily veterinary care, food, housing, and litter facilities—resist that impulse!

  HANNA'S HINT: Unless you are a breeder, have your cat neutered! Aside from the fact that unaltered males spray practically any surface they can back up against, roam, and get into savage cat fights if allowed out, and unspayed females can come into heat as often as every other week for eight to ten days—and yowl loudly during all of them to let you and the neighborhood male cats know it—every year thousands and thousands of unwanted kittens are put to death. Costs for spaying and neutering vary, but you can get information on finding low-cost facilities from local shelters, animal control agencies, or "Friends of Animals" (1-800-321-7387).

- If you want a purebred cat or kitten, realize that all breeds are not alike. They differ in personalities, energy levels, dietary and environmental requirements, maintenance levels, adaptability to children and other pets, and more. Find out all you can about the breed you're interested in, observe it at cat shows, and when you're sure it's the cat for you, buy it from a reputable breeder!

  HANNA'S HINT: If buying a kitten from a pet store, your best bet is to find one that works with local reputable breeders, as well as with local shelters, to help place animals.

JACK'S FACTS:
**Holy Cats!**
"One unaltered cat and her unaltered offspring can produce 420,000 cats in seven years!"
—Executive Director, Doris Day Animal League

## How to Recognize a Healthy Cat

Whether you're buying a kitten or cat from a breeder or adopting one from a shelter, you want it to be as healthy as possible. Optimally, kittens should be at least eight weeks old before being taken from their mom and littermates. If you are getting a kitten or cat from a shelter, try to find out as much as you can about its past and its personality.

### The Healthy Cat Scan
- Eyes should be clear of film or discharge—and look alert.
- Ears should be clean (white or light pink) and not sensitive to touch.
- Nose should be clean with no discharge.
- Mouth should have healthy pink gums, and no offensive odor.
- Coat should look healthy.

- Kitten fur should be fluffy and glossy.

  HANNA'S HINT: Use your hand to check the animal's coat. Start from the tail area—which should not feel greasy—and brush backward to the head, making sure the skin is a normal grayish white, with no reddened areas or little black flecks, which would indicate the excreta of fleas.

- Whiskers should be long and unbroken.
- Skin should be free of lumps, growths, or swellings—above and below the surface.
- Paw pads should be uncracked.
- Cats should be responsive, energetic, and curious.

  HANNA'S HINT: Some breeds, like the British shorthair, are naturally laid back; others, like the Somali, are anything but. Nonetheless, there's a big difference between an active cat and an aggressive one. Responsive, energetic, and curious does not mean biting, scratching, and hissing. So if your potential pet starts out on the wrong paw before you can say, "Here, kitty, kitty," you might want to rethink your selection.

---

JACK'S FACTS: **What's That in People Years?**

| CAT'S AGE | | HUMAN AGE | CAT'S AGE | | HUMAN AGE |
|---|---|---|---|---|---|
| 6 months | = | 10 years | 12 years | = | 64 years |
| 8 months | = | 13 years | 14 years | = | 72 years |
| 1 year | = | 15 years | 16 years | = | 80 years |
| 2 years | = | 24 years | 18 years | = | 88 years |
| 4 years | = | 32 years | 20 years | = | 96 years |
| 6 years | = | 40 years | 21 years | = | 100 years |
| 8 years | = | 48 years | 22 years | = | 104 years |
| 10 years | = | 56 years | | | |

---

## Trouble Signs and How to Read Them

Knowing what to look for in a cat is important. Once that cat becomes yours, knowing what to look out for is even more important. To avoid cat-astrophes, I suggest you familiarize yourself with the following feline symptoms and keep your vet's number handy.

### Your Cat Might Be Sick If . . .

- Its gums and tongue look pale.
- Its gums are red and puffy.

- There are skin lesions.
- It's coughing.
- It's sneezing.
- It has a fishy odor.
- It acts listless.
- It refuses food.
- It begins urinating in locations other than the litterbox.
- Its urination is frequent.
- Its urination is strained and urine is tinged with blood.
- There is recurrent diarrhea or constipation.
- There's loss of weight.
- Its thirst increases.
- Its coat has bald patches.
- Its eyes appear glazed or dull.
- Its scratching increases.
- Its skin feels oily.
- There is discharge from its ears.
- Its coat is sparse, matted, or dull.
- Its breathing sounds labored.
- Sudden or frequent vomiting occurs.
- Bumps or swellings can be felt on the inner side of its thighs.
- Stomach looks distended.

## Common Diseases

**ALLERGIES:** Can be caused by virtually anything! Airborne substances (pollen, room deodorizers, perfumes, cigarette smoke, even kitty-litter dust), contact allergens (fleas, flea collars, powders, soaps, carpet fresheners, oily-leafed plants, newsprint, cat beds), foods (any food—even one the cat has been eating for years). Most common symptoms for all allergies are itching, scratching, sneezing, skin lesions, runny eyes, diarrhea, and vomiting.

*Best Prevention Measures:* Minimize use of aerosol sprays; avoid foods with numerous artificial colorings; feed complete balanced nutrition foods as substantiated by AAFCO (Association of American Feed Control Officials) that meet or exceed NRC (National Research Council) requirements; consult with a vet *before* symptoms worsen.

**CHLAMYDIA:** A bacterial infection that affects the mucous membranes, usually around the eyes. Though it can cause a variety of symptoms, the most common is

JACK'S FACTS
## Cream of the Crop

The longest-lived domestic cat on record was a tabby named Puss who died the day after his thirty-sixth birthday in 1939 in Devon, England. The next-oldest was a female tabby named Ma, also from Devon, who died in 1957 at the age of thirty-four. (Kind of makes you wonder what—besides fabulous flavor and phenomenal calories—is in Devonshire clotted cream.)

conjunctivitis, starting in one eye and then spreading to another. Treatable with antibiotics, this disease can be transmitted to humans through contact.

*Best Prevention Measure:* Wash your hands after handling infected pet.

**DIABETES:** Occurs when the pancreas fails to produce adequate insulin, necessary to regulate the animal's blood sugar level. Symptoms include excessive thirst and increased urination.

*Best Prevention Measure:* Avoid feeding sugary treats and watch your pet's weight! Overweight cats (and dogs) are more prone to diabetes.

**FeLV (FELINE LEUKEMIA VIRUS):** A potentially deadly cat-to-cat virus—spread through saliva, urine, feces, and blood—that causes a breakdown in the animal's immune system, making it susceptible to other diseases which it might otherwise be able to overcome. In multicat households, mutual grooming, communal eating, and sharing litterboxes are common methods of transmission. NOTE: **This disease CANNOT be transmitted to humans or other species!**

*Best Prevention Measure:* In multicat households, an FeLV vaccination, though not 100-percent effective, is recommended.

**FIP (FELINE INFECTIOUS PERITONITIS):** A highly contagious viral disease that multiplies in the cat's white cells and circulates throughout the body, destroying the cells and releasing fatal toxins.

*Best Prevention Measure:* Vaccination.

**FIV (FELINE IMMUNODEFICIENCY VIRUS):** Like FeLV, this deadly disease also breaks down the cat's immune system, leaving it unable to fight off other infections. Transmitted through bodily fluids, it is often spread from cat to cat through open wounds, such as bites. NOTE: **Though the virus is related to HIV, you CANNOT contract AIDS from a cat with FIV!**

*Best Prevention Measure:* Keep your pet indoors, especially in areas where there is a large population of outside cats.

**FUS (FELINE URINARY SYNDROME):** Caused by urethral irritation and blockage (more often in males), and characterized by frequent strained voiding of small quantities of often bloody urine in locations other than the litterbox, this is one of the most common, painful, and treatable feline ailments.

*Best Prevention Measures:* Avoid all-fish diets and high-magnesium treats, such as shrimp. Ask your vet about foods that are acceptable for FUS management.

**HAIRBALLS:** Characterized by vomiting that doesn't seem to otherwise alter the cat's behavior, hairballs are caused by ingestion of hair that's swallowed as the cat grooms itself.

*Best Prevention Measure:* More grooming of the animal on your part. Also, you could put a pat of butter—or a dab of Petromalt—on your cat's toes or nose once a week. Your pet will lick it off, easing dry heaves—and cleanups.

WORMS: Any of the trouble signs listed on pp. 66–67 can indicate the presence of intestinal parasites, but not necessarily! If you're not a doctor, don't play one with your pet! (See "Cautions" section, p. 73). Take your cat and/or a fecal sample to your vet for a correct diagnosis and the correct medicine. The most common cat worms are hookworms, roundworms, tapeworms, and whipworms.

*Best Prevention Measures:* Proper diet, clean litterbox, flea prevention, regular fecal checkups for kittens and nursing queens. For outdoor cats, preventive heart-worm medication is recommended—especially during warm weather and in areas where there are mosquitoes.

## Diseases You Can Catch from Your Cat

TOXOPLASMOSIS: Caused by a parasite transmitted through nasal discharge or feces. If you accidentally ingest this parasite—through cleaning the cat's litterbox and not washing hands well afterward—you can develop mononucleosis-type symptoms. Not serious for healthy individuals, but extremely dangerous for expectant mothers.

CAUTION: *Pregnant women are at risk because the disease is transmitted to the fetus, where it can cause severe birth defects.*

*Best Prevention Measure:* Pregnant women should wear gloves and wash hands carefully after changing litterboxes. Better still, ask someone else to do it. Also, observe the same precautions around sandboxes and other areas that cats might use as potties.

RABIES: Any cat allowed outside can contract rabies and infect you.

*Best Prevention Measure:* Make sure your cat is vaccinated.

HANNA'S HINT: A bite from your pet, even if it has all its shots, can cause an infection and possible blood poisoning.

*Best Prevention Measure:* Keep your family's tetanus shots current and wash wounds with soap and water immediately, follow up with an antibiotic ointment.

RINGWORM: A highly contagious fungus (not a real worm) that can be transmitted to humans, as well as to other cats, by simple direct contact. The first symptom for both species is usually a patchy, moth-eaten look about the hair, accompanied by itching.

*Best Prevention Measures:* Wash hands thoroughly after handling your pet; keep cat's environment clean and sanitary.

CAT SCRATCH FEVER: An infection, believed to be viral, transmitted by the bite or scratch of a cat—even if the cat is a family pet and not ill! Naturally, not all scratches and bites cause the disease. Incubation period is usually three to ten days. There may be flulike symptoms, as well as redness, swelling, and tenderness in the area where the wound seems to have healed.

*Best Prevention Measure:* Be aware that when a cat's temper flares, so can its claws. Wash wounds with soap and water immediately; follow up with an antibiotic ointment.

## Handling Emergencies

THE PHONE NUMBER FOR THE NATIONAL ANIMAL POISON CONTROL CENTER IS (900) 680–0000 ($20 for the first five minutes, $2.95 for each additional minute), or (800) 548–2423 ($30 per case, as many calls as needed; credit card required).

Getting an injured cat to the vet quickly is often easier said than done. Even the most docile kitty will scratch or bite if in pain or confused. Gently restraining your pet by wrapping it in a towel, pillow case, blanket, or shirt is the safest way to transport it for medical attention. Additionally, if the animal is in shock, keeping it warm and calm is essential.

For external bleeding, use ice packs, cold compresses, pressure, and tourniquets. (Remember tourniquets are tied *above* the wound and must be loosened every five minutes!)

If something is stuck in your pet's throat—don't dig for it! Your best bet is to grasp your pet by its hind legs, hoist, and shake gently—and get to the vet as soon as possible.

If you suspect poisoning, call your vet or the National Animal Poison Control Center immediately.

### To Induce Vomiting

One teaspoon hydrogen peroxide 3 percent

or

One teaspoon salt (or mustard powder) dissolved in a cup of warm water

or

One-half teaspoon of salt tossed to the back of the cat's tongue

If vomiting does not occur within ten minutes, repeat. (Up to three times.)

HANNA'S HINT: With cat's mouth held open with your thumb and index finger, tilt the animal's head back and pour the solution in very slowly to prevent liquid entering windpipe.

CAUTION: *Never attempt to induce vomiting if your pet is inconscious, in shock, or has swallowed an acid, alkali, solvent, or sharp object!*

## Breeding Tips

Unless you are a breeder of cats, have a special reason for wanting to breed your cat or have potential owners waiting in line for a kitten from your cat's litter—don't breed! Bringing lives into the world is a big responsibility, and putting out a sign that says "FREE KITTENS" is not taking that responsibility seriously.

If you are planning to breed, consult with your vet before the mating to make sure your cat has all her vaccinations, or as soon afterward as possible to discuss diet, maintenance and what to expect when your pet's expecting. Pregnancy is a stressful period for everyone involved!

### JACK'S FACTS: Why I Nearly Had Kittens over a Late Date

When you're a zoo director, the birth of any animal in captivity is a cause for celebration. It is a means toward continuing propagation and preservation of that species. (And it's important to understand that animals in captivity really are our ambassadors to their cousins in the wild.) But sometimes the celebration can be embarrassingly premature, as I learned some years ago from two big sources—a couple of African bush elephants named Bomba and Coco. Elephant reproduction is still relatively rare in the United States, but at that time an offspring from these two would have been among the first few born in this country's zoos. Bomba and Coco were somewhat confused about the mechanics of mating, but we were hopeful. Eventually, a test said that Bomba was pregnant, the vet said she was pregnant, the ultrasound said she was pregnant, I believed she was pregnant and immediately opened my mouth to the media world and announced she was pregnant. Then the twenty-two-month gestation period passed. And passed. And passed! Bomba had gained seven hundred pounds, but there was no baby in sight. Upset? I nearly had kittens! The papers and TV stations ragged us (me) unmercifully. We still don't know what happened—did she reabsorb the fetus? Was she ever pregnant? Did she and Coco ever mate? What we do know is that Bomba bombed and that I have a real talent for putting my foot in my mouth. We also learned that not all couples are cut out to be parents. More than a decade later there is still no baby elephant, but Bomba and Coco are still with us at the Columbus Zoo.

## Compatible—and Incompatible—Household Pets

### *Cats*

If you're bringing a new cat or kitten into the household, it might not be love at first sight (for either of them) but they'll work it out. As a rule, the resident cat will be (forgive me) top dog.

**KEEP IN MIND**

- If you want more than one cat, it's easier to start with a pair of kittens than to introduce a new one at a later date.
- If you are taking on two adult cats, you'll have fewer personality clashes if they are of opposite sexes. Unless they are littermates, males tend to be hostile to one another. The same holds true, to a lesser degree, for females. But there are exceptions in all cases.
- If you have an older cat, a kitten is less likely to be perceived as a threat.

### *Birds*

See p. 42.

### *Children*

Cats and kids can certainly get along—with supervision.

**KEEP IN MIND**

- Young children might play too roughly with a very young kitten and seriously harm it.
- Though not as cute as kittens, older cats tend to tolerate—or at least are better equipped to escape—often thoughtless handling by children.
- Showing a child the proper way to play with a new pet right from the start will prevent lots of problems.

### *Dogs*

Yes, they can get along. It's best if they join the household together as youngsters, but if they're introduced properly—and neither has a prior history of hatred or abuse by the other species—they'll end up being friends.

**KEEP IN MIND**

- Aggressive dogs are less likely to take to feline additions to the household, and vice versa. (See Chapter 6.)
- Three little words: Separate Feeding Places.

### Rabbits, Mice, Hamsters, and Small Rodents

It's not advisable to try out potential dinner meals as playmates.

### Fish

As long as the aquarium is out of paws' reach.

### Reptiles

They're not going to play together. And if the reptiles need live mice for dinner, there are going to be problems.

## Cautions to Keep in Mind for Cats

- Don't give your cat chocolate! (A six-ounce bar of chocolate could kill a five-pound cat.)
- A single Tylenol (acetaminophen) tablet can kill a cat.
- Raw egg white can deplete your cat of important vitamins. (Egg yolk and *cooked* white are okay.)
- Some food preservatives, such as benzoic acid, that are harmless to humans can be toxic to cats.
- The taste and smell of antifreeze appeals to cats—but it can be lethal.
- Feeding canned tuna as a steady diet can kill a cat.
- Paints can be toxic, so keep cans closed. A lid left outdoors can gather rainwater, which your pet might sip.
- If your cat gets paint on its fur, do NOT remove it with turpentine! It can burn the cat's skin.
- If your cat steps on a floor still wet with household disinfectant, wash and dry its paws before it licks them.
- Hairball medication can interfere with necessary vitamin absorption if given right before, with, or immediately after meals.
- Do NOT use rodent poison in your home. (If the mouse doesn't get it, your cat might—or, your cat might eat the mouse that got it. Either way it could be deadly.)
- Pesticides can be toxic to your pet—even when ingested secondhand.
- If you let your cat outdoors, don't spray lawns or plants with chemicals that can be toxic to cats. (Read labels and ask garden stores for non-toxic alternatives.)
- Never feed your pet raw poultry or fish. (Salmonellae multiply rapidly.)

- Supplementing a nutritionally complete and balanced food with vitamins (unless directed to do so by a vet) can cause a depletion of necessary nutrients.
- Don't let your cat nap in closets where there are mothballs or camphor flakes; the fumes can cause serious liver damage.
- Leftovers unfit for human consumption can be just as unfit—as well as dangerous—for your pet.
- Milk is fine for kittens, but many adult cats are unable to digest it because of a lactose intolerance and can develop diarrhea, which can cause dehydration.
- Cellophane wrappers from cigarette packs or other products can be lethal if swallowed by your pet. (Digestive juices cause the cellophane to become sharp enough to cause internal bleeding.)
- Cats are climbers, so keep medicine cabinets closed. Even simple laxatives, aspirin, acetaminophen, hemorrhoid preparations, and other over-the-counter medications can be lethal for your pet.
- Be sure to leave fresh water for your cat daily. Cats cannot survive if they lose more than one tenth of their body water.
- Don't use fabric softeners on your cat's bedding. Chemicals can adhere to your pet's fur and cause intestinal problems when licked off.
- An everyday home remedy such as boric acid can be fatal if ingested by a cat.
- Windows without screens (even if open at the top) can use up all of your pet's nine lives in one fall.
- Be wary of plastic feeding dishes. They are porous (often retaining odors your cat might not like) and are easily scraped, permitting bacteria to form in the ridges.
- Never wash your pet's feeding dishes with strong disinfectants or bleaches; accidental residue could burn your pet's tongue or nose.
- Never give worm medicine to a cat with a fever (unless specifically instructed to do so by a veterinarian who is aware of the animal's condition).

### Dangerous Plants for Plant-Eating Pets

In the wild, undomesticated felines satisfy their innate desire for plant matter by obtaining it from the intestines of their prey. (In other words, the salad comes *within* the entrée.) Domestic cats instinctively seek out greens and grasses for a variety of reasons (to cleanse their intestines of hairballs or unwanted food; sometimes just for something to chew on), but some green choices can be hazardous to their health. (NOTE: The following list is not all-inclusive, and many plants are known by different names in different regions. When in doubt, check with your local veterinarian.)

| | | |
|---|---|---|
| Arrowgrass | Hemlock | Oleander |
| Asparagus fern | Jerusalem cherry | Peach leaves |
| Azalea | Jimsonweed | Philodendron |
| Bittersweet | Larkspur | Rhubarb leaves |
| Caladium | Laurel | Spider plant |
| Christmas pine trees | Lily of the valley | Wisteria |
| Dieffenbachia | Locoweed | |
| English Ivy | Mistletoe | |

## Cats by Breed

### The Shorthairs

PRO: Less grooming required on your part. Typically playful and outgoing.

CON: Some not suited for cold climates, cold weather, cold apartments. Voices tend to be loud.

CREATURE COMFORTS: A pillow or blanket—preferred in a location above the floor or out of household traffic. (If given the option or opportunity—your bed!) Toys, water and food dishes, litterbox, a scratching post.

DIET NEEDS AND TREATS: A complete or balanced cat food guaranteed to meet or exceed all NRC (National Research Council) requirements for growth and maintenance of adult cats and growing kittens. (Best if that evidence is based on AAFCO [American Association of Feed Control Officials] standards.) Check with your vet for brands with the best BV (biological value) protein sources—those most effectively utilized—for your particular pet. As for occasional healthy treats, *small amounts* of fruit, fresh or cooked vegetables, pieces of cheese, sardines (unless FUS is a problem), hard-boiled eggs, yogurt, freeze-dried liver, beef, or fish.

KEY: ➤◄➤◄➤◄➤◄ means all-around fine cat.

     ➤◄➤◄➤◄ means read description carefully for more pros and cons

     ➤◄➤◄ means think twice about the pros and cons

     ➤◄ means this cat deserves special consideration

## JACK'S FACTS: **Did You Know . . .**

- Cats are carnivores and cannot be vegetarians and thrive.

- Cats are the only animals besides camels and giraffes who walk by moving their front and hind legs together, first on one side and then on the other.

- Cats use their paws to express happiness. (No, they don't clap them!) They knead them against you, a throwback to when they were nursing kittens.

- Almost all solid-color cats—wild as well as domestic—are the result of a recessive gene that suppresses a tabby pattern. In fact, if you look at a black leopard in a zoo in the right light, you'll probably see shadow tabby markings.

- The average cat has stronger teeth than the average human.

- Cats mark favorite objects, people, things—even other cats—by rubbing the sides of their foreheads against them. (Their personal love fragrance comes from the temporal glands located on both sides of the forehead.)

- The gestation period for domestic cats is about two months (between 58 and 66 days); for wild cats it's almost twice that (about 108 days).

- Cats have short intestinal tracts. While it takes humans approximately two days to process food, it takes cats only about twelve hours.

- Dog food is nutritionally deficient for cats. (Cats require the amino acid taurine and must have it in their daily diet.)

- Declawing a cat leaves it virtually defenseless, physically imbalanced (cats walk on their claws instead of their paw pads), more prone to muscle weakness—and, because it must use its teeth in place of claws, potentially more dangerous to youngsters.

- Show cats may not be shown declawed.

- Cats sweat through their paws (not their pores).

- Almost all tortoiseshell cats are female as a result of a sex-linked gene.

- Cats have one of the keenest senses of hearing in the entire animal kingdom.

- A female domestic feline enters puberty between three and nine months of age—and can come into heat as early as three and a half months.

- Wildcats can purr only while inhaling. Domestic cats purr inhaling and exhaling.

- Shorthaired cats shed as much as longhaired ones; the long hairs are just more noticeable and usually shed in clumps.

- Most domestic cats sleep between fourteen and eighteen hours a day!

- Unlike humans (or dogs and other mammals), cats cannot store excess protein and must replenish their supply every day through food.

The symbol ⭐ means that there is something special you should know about this cat.

⭤⭤⭤⭤ **ABYSSINIAN:** Fast-moving, muscular, with the exotic look of an Egyptian animal god. Quiet, affectionate, and active. Elegant to look at. Easy to care for.

⭤⭤⭤⭤ **AMERICAN SHORTHAIR:** A tough, sturdy, intelligent classic pet—with a master's degree in mousing. Thick coat that can weather the cold. A non-finicky healthy eater (so watch those treats!). Gets along well with kids and other pets.

⭤⭤⭤⭤ **AMERICAN WIREHAIR:** Has springy, lightly curled, wiry fur—but its coarse coat requires no special grooming. Energetic, loves the outdoors, hunting, and climbing.

⭤⭤⭤ **BOMBAY:** An extrovert with a glossy, satiny coat that looks as good as it feels. A feline who enjoys hanging around the house, charming its owner, and being petted. Prefers quiet seniors to noisy families.

⭤⭤⭤⭤ **BRITISH SHORTHAIR:** Large, hardy, with an impressive coat that it tends to tend nicely by itself—thank you very much. Loathes water and believes in its own self-importance. Happiest when sleeping or eating.

⭤⭤⭤ **BURMESE:** A mischievous feline sound machine—Vocal (with a capital "V"), olympically active, outgoing, and intelligent. Minimum grooming with a damp towel will keep its sable brown coat shiny. Loves attention. A personality pet.

⭤⭤⭤⭤ **CHARTREUX:** Great for multipet houses, this feline is a large, gentle powerhouse. Hardy, soft-voiced, and not by nature a screamer or a scratcher. A companion for all seasons and all ages.

⭤⭤ **COLORPOINT SHORTHAIR:** Much like the Siamese (see below). Not recommended for multipet households.

⭤ ⭐ **CORNISH REX:** Curvy, long, and slender, this energetic eye-catcher has a tight, wavy, rippled coat without any guard hairs. This means it produces little dander and, though it still sheds, the Cornish Rex is a terrific feline pet for people allergic to other cats. Unfortunately, it's not an all-weather cat; it usually needs a sweater in cold climates.

➤◄ ⭐ **DEVON REX:** A slightly larger, more fuzzy version of the Cornish Rex—but the Devon Rex does have guard hairs, presenting the usual problems for the allergy prone. And, like the Cornish Rex, it doesn't fare well in the cold.

➤◄➤◄ **EGYPTIAN MAU:** A sleek and spotted, hardy predator that's strictly feline. Not thrilled with sudden temperature changes, this sweet-voiced cat is often temperamental. Not a kitty for little kiddies.

➤◄➤◄➤◄ **EXOTIC SHORTHAIR:** A low-maintenance version of the long-haired Persian. (Regular brushing is still a priority.) Exotic, intelligent and laid-back. A fancy feline with a down-to-earth personality. A fine pet.

➤◄➤◄➤◄ **HAVANA BROWN:** An adaptable, intriguing extrovert with a lustrous chocolate coat that is groomed easily. Mischievous, and sharing many traits of a Siamese, the Havana Brown is a great animal companion for an owner who doesn't mind giving a pet a lot of attention as well as being outwitted by it.

➤◄➤◄➤◄➤◄ **JAPANESE BOBTAIL:** Medium-sized, this feline is a minimal shedder with maximum energy, curiosity, and intelligence. A great mouser, considered a good-luck charm in its country of origin, the Japanese bobtail is a fun-loving, people-loving pet.

➤◄➤◄➤◄➤◄ **KORAT:** Aloof with strangers—but a-loving to its owners—the korat gets along with other household pets as long as they know who's boss. With its extraordinary agility and fabulous silver-blue coat, the Korat is a classy, cuddling companion.

➤◄ ⭐ **MANX:** Tail-less, adaptable, powerful—with a thick, double coat for all seasons—the Manx sheds. A lot! Regular brushing is essential. Though not a good pet for children, it makes a great animal companion for adults—and is ideal for single owners.

➤◄➤◄➤◄ **OCICAT:** Looks like a small, feral feline, but this spotted shorthair has the personality of a sweet, affectionate pussycat. Though prone to nervousness, they are gentle and undemanding pets.

➤◄➤◄ **ORIENTAL SHORTHAIR:** Very much like the Siamese (see below). Though the Oriental is more muscular and differs in color, it shares the same arrogance, attitude, and intelligence.

➤⋜➤⋜➤⋜➤⋜ **RUSSIAN BLUE:** A looker with a lush double-thick silvery blue coat that when brushed should stand erect. As a pet, the Russian blue is independent, resourceful, and content. Fond of family members but frequently shy of strangers.

➤⋜➤⋜➤⋜➤⋜ **SCOTTISH FOLD:** Well-behaved, affectionate, and an excellent mouser. A sweet and mellow pet. Longhaired varieties are also available. Adapts to urban and rural surroundings equally well.

➤⋜➤⋜ ★ **SIAMESE:** Upscale on the pet scale, the Siamese is intelligent, ingenious, ultrasleek, dauntless, affectionate—and VOCAL! (If you have thin walls and neighbors with short fuses, a Siamese might not be the cat for you.) They shed their short hair seasonally, but *substantially*, and should be brushed daily. Fine for households with kids and other pets. The Siamese never doubts its prime place in the home hierarchy.

➤⋜➤⋜➤⋜ **SINGAPURA:** Small, easy to care for, curious, and generally unafraid of new situations and sounds. Adaptable. Uncommon—but well worth seeking.

➤⋜➤⋜➤⋜➤⋜ **SNOWSHOE:** A fairly new puss on the cat scene, but becoming popular. It's a cross between an American shorthair and a Siamese. It's inquisitive but not standoffish, affectionate, and adaptable. A good all-around pet.

➤⋜ ★ **SPHYNX:** You don't have to worry about hair on the furniture or anywhere else—the Sphynx is hairless. (Actually it has a soft down, but it's almost invisible.) Though it is ideal for allergic individuals, the Sphynx does need lotions to guard against sunlight and dryness, sweaters to protect against cold, and, because it has no protective hair, scratches from other pets or mishandling could cause problems. A high-maintenance cat. Not for children or large, multipet households.

➤⋜➤⋜➤⋜➤⋜ **TONKINESE:** Outgoing, mischievous, a delightful combination of Siamese and Burmese (see above) but more flexible and adaptable than either. Good natured, they make wonderful all-purpose pets.

## The Longhairs

PRO: Beautiful to look at, delightful to stroke. Soft voices. Generally happier to be home than roaming.

CON: Regular grooming is essential. Prone to hairballs. Lush coats can be easy flea and tick havens. Seasonal shedding is a given.

**CREATURE COMFORTS:** Same as for shorthairs—with the addition of a wide-toothed grooming comb.

**DIET NEEDS AND TREATS:** Same as for shorthairs (see above). Check with vet to be sure food contains enough essential fatty acids and vitamins to keep coat in good condition. *Do not add supplements to a nutritionally complete food unless instructed to do so by a veterinarian.*

➤⋖➤⋖➤⋖➤⋖ ★ **AMERICAN CURL:** Outgoing, intelligent, great mousers, and available in longhaired and shorthaired varieties. (The "curl" has to do with their unique backward-curved ears.) Sweet temperament. They make fine family pets.

➤⋖➤⋖➤⋖➤⋖ **BALINESE:** Active, intelligent, long-haired, sweet-tempered relatives of the Siamese. A homebody that doesn't crave the outdoors, but does adore affection. Easy to groom and care for. Fine urban pet for all ages.

➤⋖➤⋖➤⋖ **BIRMAN:** The legendary "Sacred Cat of Burma," revered in times past because of its alleged ability to communicate with the goddess of Death, this white-pawed feline is thoughtful, elegant, and filled with positive, playful energy. Regular grooming is required, but worth it. A fabulous pet that loves company.

➤⋖➤⋖ **COLORPOINT LONGHAIR:** See Himalayan below.

➤⋖ **CYMRIC:** A longhaired version of the Manx see p. 78.

➤⋖➤⋖➤⋖ **HIMALAYAN:** A cat with the coloring of a Siamese, the flowing coat of a Persian, and the affectionate temperament of a swell pet (provided you don't have a dog in residence). Unfortunately, daily grooming is *required*.

➤⋖➤⋖➤⋖➤⋖ **JAVANESE:** Except for coloring, very much like the Balinese (see above) in all respects. Terrific pet choice.

➤⋖➤⋖ **KASHMIR:** Essentially a solid-color Himalayan (see above).

➤⋖ **LONGHAIR:** See Persian below.

➤⋖➤⋖➤⋖➤⋖ **MAINE COON:** A big bear of a cat (they usually go well over fifteen pounds) that is as responsive indoors as it is rugged outdoors. Gentle, loving, adaptable to all sorts of household situations, pets, and climates. A wonderful pet-and-a-half!

**≻≺≻≺≻≺≻≺** NORWEGIAN FOREST: Hardy, friendly, with a double-thick coat that's not only water-resistant but easily stays tangle free. A fearless feline that enjoys being a pet.

**≻≺≻≺** ORIENTAL LONGHAIR: A longhaired version of the Oriental shorthair (see p. 78).

**≻≺** PERSIAN: The ultimate longhair. Intelligent, demanding, unyielding in its belief that it deserves to be the center of the household universe (and usually gets its way). Brushing on a daily basis is a must. This is a high-maintenance cat. Not for anyone looking for a carefree kitty.

**≻≺≻≺≻≺** ⭐ RAGDOLL: Very sweet and very, very mellow. When you pet it, the ragdoll seems to go limp—like a ragdoll. A super companion for seniors, people with disabilities and shy, quiet children.

**≻≺≻≺≻≺≻≺** SOMALI: Very agile and lively. Essentially, a longhaired Abyssinian (see p. 77).

**≻≺≻≺** TURKISH ANGORA: Usually white, they do come in colors. Long, graceful, their silky coats do need daily grooming. They are affectionate and generally sociable. Not the best choice for a multipet household or one with rough-and-tumble children.

**≻≺≻≺≻≺≻≺** ⭐ TURKISH VAN: For anyone who lives on or near the water, this semi-longhair is the cat for you. Turkish Vans actually like water, and many (not all) are good swimmers, taking a dip at their leisure—in lakes, pools, tubs, and sinks. They are affectionate, smart, and seem to always enjoy a good backstroke from their owners.

## Celebrity Cat Owners and Their Cats

Whether you need inspiration or want to be a copycat, here is a kitty of famous names and the names they've named their felines to help you choose the right one for yours.

*Cleveland Amory:* Polar Bear
*Brigitte Bardot:* Crocus
*Jim Belushi:* Baal
*Daniel Boone:* Bluegrass

---

**JACK'S FACTS:**
## Town Without Kitty

Cats in a New Jersey town are required by law to be kept indoors or on a leash at all times. The name of the town is PIS**CAT**AWAY!

*Ray Bradbury:* Cactus Jack; Dingo; Ditzy; Nutty; Sophocles; Win Win; Tater; Gazza; Vic Vic

*La Var Burton:* Bootsy

*Roger A. Caras:* Eartha Cat; Sumfun Abigail

*Jimmy Carter:* Misty Malarkey Ying Yang

*Winston Churchill:* Nelson

*Bill Clinton:* Socks

*David Copperfield:* Dickens

*Katie Couric:* Frank

*Walter Cronkite:* Dancer

*Doris Day:* Miss Lucy; Mr. Lucky; Sneakers

*Bo Derek:* Coon Dog; Gina; Pissed Off; Jade; Penguin; She

*T. S. Eliot:* Admetus; Asparagus; Bustopher Jones; Demeter; Electra; George Push-dragon; Great Rumpuscat; Growltiger; Gumbie; Gus; Jellicle Cat; Jellylorum; Jennyanydots; Grizabella; Lady Griddlebone; Mr. Mistoffolees; Munkustrap; Pettipaws; Rum Tum Tugger; Skimbleshanks; Wiscus; Macavity; Mungojerrie; Old Deuteronomy; Quaxo; Rumpleteaser; Tumblebrutus

*John Lennon:* Alice; Elvis

*Michael Feinstein:* Bing Clawsby

*Roberta Flack:* Caruso

*Paul Gallico:* Chilla; Chin; Wuzzy

*Lisa Hartman:* Bear

*Bob Hope:* Bob

*Whitney Houston:* Marlin, Miste, Misteblu

*John F. Kennedy:* Tom Kitten

*Janet Leigh:* Turkey

*Jay Leno:* Cheeseler

*Joan Lunden:* Jay Leno; Kitty Kelly

*Ed McMahon:* Hershey Bar; Monty; Queen Tut

*Muhammad Ali:* Icarus

*Florence Nightingale:* Bismark; Disraeli; Gladstone

*Yoko Ono:* Charo; Misha; Sascha

*Jane Pauley:* Meatball

*Kenny Rogers:* Caboodle; Kit

*Willard Scott:* Ziggy

*Red Skelton:* Blondie; Freddy

*Liz Smith:* Mister Ships; Luke

*Suzanne Somers:* Chrissy
*Martha Stewart:* Teeney; Weeney
*Sally Struthers:* Joan Pawford; Kitty Dearest
*Elizabeth Taylor:* Charlie Brown; Jeepers Creepers; Cleo; Jill
*Shirley Temple:* Godzilla; Nicole
*Harry Truman:* Mike the Magicat
*Mark Twain:* Apollinaris; Beelzebub; Blatherskite; Buffalo Bill; Sour Mash; Zoroaster
*Vanna White:* Ashley; Rhett Butler
*Billy Dee Williams:* ChoCho

In the wildcat world of lions, tigers, leopards, and cheetahs, the claws-down cat woman is actress Tippi Hedren. She has made her ranch a home for several dozens of these felines, with names ranging from Alice to Zuru. (I've always wondered if her love of big cats had something to do with her role in *The Birds*.)

## Questions and Answers About Cats

### Shedding Light on Shedding

I was told when I got my Norwegian Forest cat, Fergie, that she would shed seasonally—in the spring. Well, we live in Wisconsin, and either Fergie thinks it's spring all year long (she's turned our furniture into FURniture!) or I was told a tall tale. She's healthy, eats well—is there something about the breed I wasn't told?

If Fergie is essentially an indoor housecat, and I'm assuming she is, what you weren't told was that artificial light can trigger shedding. For cats in the wild, and domestic cats who live outdoors, the natural lengthening of daylight signals the advent of spring, activating shedding of unnecessary heavy fur. Indoor cats are thrown off schedule by electric lights—as well as heating, TV, air-conditioning, and other human creature comforts. Combing and brushing your pet on a daily basis should control the problem.

### What's the Point?

What does it mean when they describe a cat as being "pointed"?

"Pointed" is terminology for a color pattern (primarily used to describe the Siamese, though other cats have a similar pointed pattern). The "points" are the animal's face, paws, and tail, which are darker than its body, and they come in many different colors, the most common being a "seal point" brown that shades to a pale tan or ivory body.

## Not Deafinitely

Is it true that white cats are always deaf?

They might not always listen to you, but they are *not always deaf*. It is true that white cats with blue eyes are more likely to be deaf than white cats with gold or green eyes, but there are exceptions in all cases.

## Cat Talk You Should Know

AGOUTI: individual hairs with alternating light and dark bands; found on tabbies

ALLOGROOMING: grooming done by another cat

AUTOGROOMING: self-grooming

BUN: blood, urea, nitrogen concentration test for kidney ailments

BV: biological value; the percentage of a nutrient absorbed, retained, and therefore presumably utilized by the cat's body

CATTERY: an establishment where cats are kept or bred

FIP: feline infectious peritonitis; a viral cat disease that grows in white cells and circulates throughout the body; when cells are destroyed they release toxins; contagious

FUS: feline urologic syndrome; a common lower urinary tract condition characterized by frequent strained voiding of small quantities of urine (see p. 68.)

HARLEQUIN: a mostly white cat with large patches of color

LOCKET: a white spot on a cat's chest

MITTED: a cat with white paws

NEUTERING: castration of male cats

QUEEN: a female cat

SPAYING: removal of uterus and ovaries of female cats

**SPRAYING:** performed by males (and females) from a standing position, facing away from the target, this is a deliberate act of marking territory, for a variety of reasons, and not to be confused with urination

**TABBY:** a cat with stripes, lines on face, and a tabby "M" on the forehead

**TIGER:** a tabby with narrow stripes running parallel down its sides

**TOM:** a male cat

**TORBIE:** a cat with patches of brown and red tabby; a tabby tortie

**TORTIE:** short for tortoiseshell in color; randomly patched with red, black, and cream markings

**URIS:** upper respiratory infections

**VAN:** a white cat with color patches only on head and tail

**ZOONOSES:** diseases that can be transmitted from cats to people

---

## JACK'S FACTS: Five Top Books for Cat Owners

*The Common Sense Book of Complete Cat Care* by Louis L. Vine (Warner)

*Understanding Your Cat* by Michael W. Fox (Coward, McCann & Geoghegan)

*The Revolution in Cat Nutrition* by Jane R. Bicks, D.V.M. (Rawson)

*The Tribe of the Tiger: Cats and Their Culture* by Elizabeth Marshall Thomas (Simon & Schuster)

*The Doctor's Book of Home Remedies for Dogs and Cats* by the editors of *Prevention* magazine (Rodale Press)

---

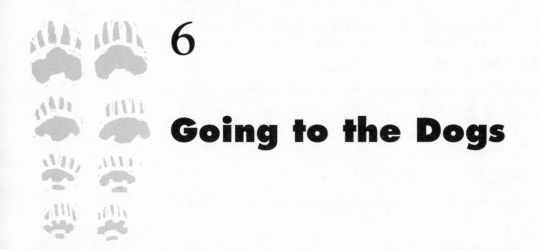

# 6

# Going to the Dogs

## Dogs as Pets

The dog has been man's (woman's and child's) best friend for over 14,000 years. And with good reason. Dogs are companions, coworkers, protectors, therapists, healers, buddies; they're part of the family in one-third of all American households; they perform amazing rescues, acts of heroism, feats of self-sacrifice, remarkable tricks—and yet are not above taking an occasional drink from the toilet.

Though opinions vary, the domestic dog is generally said to be descended from the wolf and the jackal or the fox. In ancient Rome, dogs were divided into six categories—house dogs, sporting dogs, herding dogs, war dogs, scent dogs, and sighthunting dogs (gazehounds). As time went on, man began breeding dogs in order to better suit their best friends' needs.

Today the AKC (American Kennel Club) recognizes 145 breeds, each part of a category, or group, based on the uses for which the breed was developed. There are now seven groups: Sporting dogs, Hounds, Working dogs, Terriers, Toys, Nonsporting dogs, and Herding dogs. (See the "Dogs by Breed" section, p. 101 for descriptions, advantages, and disadvantages.)

Bringing a dog into your life is a major commitment; ranking right up there with getting married, having a baby, and buying a home. If you know what you're letting yourself in for (before), it can be a joyous experience for all involved; if you don't—you've got problems.

Dogs have more social, exercise, and training requirements than any other household pets. You are not just mom or pop to this animal, you are pack leader, best friend; you are Supreme Stick Thrower, All Plentiful Food Supplier, Benevolent Belly Rubber, Lord of the Leash, The Fetchmeister. You are the center of their canine universe—and the hardest thing for them to understand is why they can't go everywhere with you.

### *What You Should Know*

- *Time:* Dogs need a lot of it from you—for socializing, for housebreaking, for training, for grooming, for walks, for exercise, for meals, for play, for vet trips, for cleanups.
  HANNA'S HINT: If you feel pressed for time in your life, it is not time to think about getting a dog.
- *Size:* Size counts in many ways when it comes to dogs as pets. If you have a small apartment, a large dog can be a big problem. (One tail-wagging greeting could cost you the china!) Also, if a dog is big and untrained, and you're physi-

cally not up to the task, both of you—to say nothing of others—are at risk. Plus, a dog of any size is going to take a sizeable bite out of your budget for many years; routine veterinary care, food, equipment, the unexpected (which you can expect to be expensive), so financial considerations should be considered.

HANNA'S HINT: Remember that all dogs start out as *little* puppies, so be aware of the adult size of the breed or mix that your getting before letting yourself in for a surprise that's too BIG for your apartment, your capabilities, and your budget!

- *Temperament:* Different breeds have different temperaments—ultraloving, lively, laid-back, super-protective, active, vocal, animal-friendly, a loner—just as different owners do. Read up on the characteristics of the breed you think you want and then think about how compatible you'll be.

  HANNA'S HINT: If you're getting a mixed-breed puppy from a shelter, try to find out what breeds are in the mix, and the typical characteristics of those breeds. Keep in mind that a breed trait is not a guarantee that an individual dog will exhibit it. I've known Labrador retrievers who wouldn't wade in a puddle to fetch a bone!

- *Sex:* As a rule (remember there are always exceptions) males are more macho than females. Even neutered males. Larger breeds usually require more discipline and a firmer hand in training. Females are gentler (as a rule) than males, but if they are not spayed, they come into heat twice a year, often scent-marking with urine, and sending out an all-points bulletin to every male dog in the neighborhood!

  HANNA'S HINT: Females generally make better-tempered and easier-to-handle family pets. But if you're not planning to breed, have your dog—whichever sex—neutered.

- *Looks:* Puppies are always cute, but when they grow up they can become pooches only their owners could love. Dogs come in all shapes and sizes, with fur coats that look like everything from flowing manes (Afghan hounds) to floor mops (komondors). And some seem to run around half-naked, which in the case of the hairless Chinese Crested they do!

  HANNA'S HINT: When picking a pup, be sure you have a pretty good idea of what it will look like grown-up. If possible, get to meet the puppy's mother (dam) or father (sire). If it's a mixed breed, take a good look at the *full-grown* ingredients in the mix. Just think of all the cute babies you've seen—and all the, well, un-cute adults.

## How to Recognize a Healthy Dog

Puppies, like kittens, should not be taken from their mother before they are six weeks old. If you are getting an older dog, you're entitled to—and should ask for—a certificate of health. The more you know about an animal before you make it your pet, the happier your pet will make you.

### The Healthy Pup and Dog Scan

- Eyes should be clear of film or discharge. (If a puppy has a teary eye—and no other signs of illness—it's probably just because his teeth are coming in.)
- Nose should be cool; no crusty deposits around nostrils.
- Ears should be clean—not red, swollen or sensitive to touch—and have no offensive odor.
- Mouth should have healthy firm gums and no offensive odor. (Young dogs' teeth should be smooth and white; teeth tend to darken with age.)
- Coat should look healthy, with no bare patches.
  HANNA'S HINT: Using your hand, brush backward from tail to head, making sure there are no black and white specks on skin, which would indicate the excreta of fleas.
- Skin should be firm and free of growths, scabs, scales, and any patches of redness.
- Dog should be alert, responsive and inquisitive.
  HANNA'S HINT: Toss a ball, gently, toward the pup. If it cowers or runs away, you might be wise to look away; overly timid or frightened pups can develop big-dog behavior problems.
- Dog should be curious about an unexpected noise, such as a handclap or a sharp sound made by banging a metal object, not cringe, cower, or ignore it. (See "Dogs by Breed," p. 101, for more tips on picking the right pet.)

JACK'S FACTS: **What's That in People Years?**

| Dog's Age | | Human Age | Dog's Age | | Human Age |
|---|---|---|---|---|---|
| 3 months | = | 5 years | 10 years | = | 56 years |
| 6 months | = | 10 years | 11 years | = | 60 years |
| 1 year | = | 15 years | 12 years | = | 64 years |
| 2 years | = | 24 years | 13 years | = | 68 years |
| 3 years | = | 28 years | 14 years | = | 72 years |
| 4 years | = | 32 years | 15 years | = | 76 years |
| 5 years | = | 36 years | 16 years | = | 81 years |
| 6 years | = | 40 years | 17 years | = | 86 years |
| 7 years | = | 44 years | 18 years | = | 91 years |
| 8 years | = | 48 years | 19 years | = | 96 years |
| 9 years | = | 52 years | 20 years | = | 101 years |

## Trouble Signs and How to Read Them

When a person is "sick as a dog," there's no doubt about it. But when a dog is sick, it's not as obvious unless you know how to recognize trouble signs. And the sooner they're recognized, the less trouble they'll cause for both you and your pooch!

### Your Dog Might Be Sick If . . .

- Its stomach looks distended.
- Lying down appears to be difficult.
- It's wheezing.
- It's panting rapidly (and not because of exercise or heat).
- Defecation is strained.
- There is increased thirst.
- It's shivering for no apparent reason.
- Its coat is sparse, matted, or dull.
- It has bald patches.
- Its tongue is swollen.
- Its eyes look yellow.
- It's scratching excessively.
- Its breath smells foul.
- It refuses food.
- It becomes ravenous and there is no weight gain.

- It's drooling excessively.
- Its ears develop an odor.
- Its headshaking is persistent.
- Its eyes appear bloodshot or dull.
- Its pupils appear dilated.
- Its ears are swollen.
- Its urination is strained.
- Its urine is tinged with blood.
- It rubs its rump along the ground.
- There is prolonged or projectile vomiting.
- It bites the air.
- Its breathing becomes rapid and shallow.
- It circles excessively.
- It has skin lesions.

JACK'S FACTS:
## World's Oldest Dog
According to *The Guinness Book of Pet Records*, an Australian cattle dog named Bluey, from Victoria, Australia, headed for the last roundup in 1939 at the age of 29 years and 5 months— which would have made him about 146 in people years.

## Common Diseases

**ALLERGIES:** Canine allergic reactions can be caused by virtually anything; you name it and I'll find a vet who knows a dog that's allergic to it. (In fact, there are reports of dogs that have actually been allergic to their owners!) Symptoms generally involve skin problems—itching, scratching and biting the skin, excessive licking, dandruff, scabs (though there may also be sneezing, tearing, and conjunctivitis). Allergens that affect cats (see p. 67) can also affect dogs. Fleas, though, are the most common cause of canine allergic dermatitis. And even the bite of a *single flea* can cause extreme itching in an allergic animal.

*Best Prevention Measures:* Flea control! Check with your veterinarian on what type of flea protection is best for your pet. Also, regular brushing and grooming.

**BLOAT:** A potentially fatal condition, also known as acute gastric dilation-torsion, that more frequently affects large dogs. Symptoms include dry heaves, extreme restlessness, drooling, and a swollen abdomen. Emergency veterinary treatment is required.

*Best Prevention Measures:* Never exercise your dog immediately after it has eaten; limit water intake after feeding.

HANNA'S HINT: If your dog tends to gulp water quickly, try offering ice cubes instead.

**BRUCELLOSIS:** A sexually transmitted animal disease that can cause sterility in both males and females. Symptoms of hair loss, depression, and painful joints may or may not occur. Bacteria spread through blood and vaginal excretions—and can infect people

*Best Prevention Measures:* Keep all dogs areas sanitized; wash hands after handling animals. If a female aborts, have her—as well as any males she's been in contact with—examined by your vet.

**CANINE DISTEMPER:** A potentially fatal viral infection spread through bodily secretions of many wild animals (raccoons, skunks, foxes, and other canids) as well as dogs, that is *airborne*—meaning that your dog does not have to come into direct contact with the carrier. It is commonly characterized by coughing, listlessness, vomiting, muscle twitching, yellow discharge from eyes and nose, among other symptoms.

*Best Prevention Measures:* Have your puppy inoculated at six weeks, or as soon as your vet recommends—and keep up with booster shots!

**CANINE PARVOVIRUS:** Contagious and deadly, this virus is spread by contaminated feces and is easily—and unknowingly—carried from place to place on automobile tires, shoes, and paw of pets. Vomiting and diarrhea, often tinged with blood, along with lethargy and appetite loss are among the disease's most common symptoms.

*Best Prevention Measures:* Vaccination!

**DIABETES:** See p. 68.

**EAR INFECTIONS:** Symptoms are usually recognized by excessive head shaking and a foul odor coming from the ears. When there is redness or dirt in the ears, ear mites are most likely the cause.

*Best Prevention Measures:* Clean your pet's ears regularly. At first sign of symptoms, see your veterinarian.

**HEARTWORM:** Spread by infected mosquitoes, this internal parasite is usually fatal—but it can be prevented. Symptoms include coughing, listlessness, and weight loss.

*Best Prevention Measures:* Have your dog tested—to make sure it hasn't already been infected—and then ask your veterinarian for heartworm-preventive pills. Also, keep your pet away from mosquito-infested areas.

KENNEL COUGH (TRACHEOBRONCHITIS): A contagious dog-to-dog viral infection that generally is complicated by a bacterial infection. Symptoms are dry hacking cough and sometimes gagging that results in a foamy mucus.

*Best Prevention Measures:* Have your dog inoculated *before* you bring it to a kennel.

LYME DISEASE: Caused by ticks, that can also infect humans, this disease can result in anemia, paralysis, and possibly death.

*Best Prevention Measures:* Examine your pet carefully when grooming and remove ticks as soon as possible by correctly using a pair of tweezers and pulling the tick straight out. If you live in a wooded or suburban area, ask your veterinarian about a Lyme disease inoculation, or alternative preventive, for your dog.

MANGE: Caused by mites, mange is characterized by itching, hair loss, dandruff, red skin, and similar dermatologic problems. Different mites pick on different parts of your dog. (See "Ear Infections" above.) And several types of mites can be transmitted to humans (see "Diseases You Can Catch from Your Dog" below).

*Best Prevention Measures:* Groom your pet regularly; ask your vet about preventive insecticides for your particular situation and dog.

RABIES: a danger for pets and their owners. Rabies is transmitted through the saliva of an infected rabid animal and fatal for dogs. Symptoms include light aversion, behavioral changes, drooling, muscle uncoordination, coughing, and indiscriminate biting.

*Best Prevention Measures:* Have your dog vaccinated!

WORMS: Virtually any of the symptoms listed on pp. 90–91 can indicate the presence of intestinal parasites—hookworms, roundworms, tapeworms, and whipworms—but only a vet and a stool sample can tell for sure.

*Best Prevention Measures:* Keep your pet's environment sanitary and remove feces frequently.

## Diseases You Can Catch from Your Dog

BRUCELLOSIS: A bacterial disease that may be transmitted to humans through the blood or vaginal excretions of infected dogs.

*Best Prevention Measures:* Keep animal areas clean; wash hands after contact with your pet.

**HOOKWORMS:** Like roundworms, eggs of hookworms are found in soil contaminated by feces of infected pets.

*Best Prevention Measures:* Same as for roundworms—keep conditions sanitary and hands well-washed.

**LEPTOSPIROSIS** and **RABIES:** Any dog allowed outside can contact these diseases and infect you. Don't take chances.

*Best Prevention Measures:* Vaccinate your pet!

**RINGWORM:** This is a fungus, not a worm, but it is highly contagious and can be transmitted to humans through simple direct contact. And children are most susceptible. The first symptom for people—and their pets—is usually a patchy, moth-eaten look about the hair accompanied by itching.

*Best Prevention Measures:* Keep dog's environment clean and sanitary; wash hands thoroughly after handling your pet.

**ROUNDWORMS:** Can be transmitted through soil contaminated by an infected dog.

*Best Prevention Measures:* Keep children away from areas where dogs relieve themselves and keep dogs away from areas—such as sandboxes—where children play, wash hands thoroughly after all pet contact.

**SCABIES:** A microscopic mite that burrows beneath the skin, causing an itchy bump, which then spreads. Scratching can cause secondary infections, such as impetigo.

*Best Prevention Measures:* Keep dog areas sanitized; wash hands after handling pets or pet waste.

**STREP THROAT:** A little loving licking from your pet may keep your family's strep throats bouncing back and forth. Dogs, although they evidence no symptoms, can act as carriers of the strep bacteria. And until the dog is treated, household members may continue to get sick. According to *New York Times* health expert Jane E. Brody, "Veterinarians who test a dog should be aware that in such cases the bacteria live in the dog's anus rather than the throat."

*Best Prevention Measures:* Wash hands and limit your dog's licking to its food dish.

## Handling Emergencies

Emergencies require immediate action, and knowing what immediate action to take can mean the difference between life and death for your pet. Keep in mind that an injured animal is confused, so it's up to you to keep calm.

Call your vet immediately so s/he is prepared to handle the emergency when you arrive. If your dog has been hit by a car, do not leave it alone. Animals that are seriously hurt will often run away in fright—worsening injuries and delaying potentially life-saving veterinary care.

Covering your pet with a blanket or coat can help in transporting it (as well as restraining it) and preserve body heat necessary to prevent shock. Carrying the animal on a flat board—or something that can be used as a firm stretcher, is best. A nose muzzle may be advisable; animals in pain are confused and can unwittingly bite even the most loving helping hand.

For profuse bleeding, apply a pressure bandage directly to the wound; if necessary use a tourniquet. (Tourniquets, definitely an emergency measure, are tied *above* the wound and should be loosened every five minutes.)

If you suspect poisoning (the dog is shaking, breathing heavily, having convulsions), call your vet, your local poison control center, or the National Animal Poison Control Center immediately. **Always keep emergency numbers by your phone!**

### *To Induce Vomiting*

One teaspoon hydrogen peroxide 3% (per 5 pounds of body weight)

or

One teaspoon salt (or mustard powder) dissolved in a cup of warm water.

or

One teaspoon of salt tossed on the back of the dog's tongue.

If vomiting does not occur within ten minutes, repeat (up to three times).

*After vomiting occurs,* there is a mixture called "The Universal Antidote" that may be used in emergency situations when veterinary counsel is unavailable. It is: Two parts burnt toast crumbled and mixed with one part milk of magnesia and one part strong tea.

CAUTION: *Never attempt to induce vomiting if your pet is unconscious, in shock, or has swallowed an acid, alkali, petroleum solvent, or sharp object.*

THE PHONE NUMBER FOR THE NATIONAL ANIMAL POISON CONTROL CENTER IS (900) 680–0000 ($20 for the first five minutes, $2.95 for each additional minute); or (800) 548–2423 ($30 per case, as many calls as needed; credit card required).

## Breeding Tips

Unless you are a professional breeder, unless you are fully aware of what you are letting yourself, your family, and your pet in for, and unless you are willing (and able) to raise any puppies you can't find homes for—don't breed!

That said, consult with your vet before the mating to make sure your pet has had all her vaccinations and is in good breeding health. Also, talk to seasoned breeders and make sure you're prepared for everything you should be prepared for—from understanding whelping behavior and whelping boxes to coping with postpartum stresses and potential puppy problems. (See recommended reading at the end of this chapter.)

## Compatible—and Incompatible—Household Pets

### *Dogs*

One good dog deserves another, and they'll usually become great buddies—that is, if they don't start off on the wrong paw. (Introducing them on neutral territory is strongly advised.)

**KEEP IN MIND**

- If you want two dogs, it's easier if they start out together as puppies.
- Dogs are pack animals and determining who is top dog is always an initial issue. To lessen the possibility of serious fights, veteran veterinarian William Carlsen of Los Angeles advises getting a second dog that's either two years younger—or older—than your resident pet. The younger dog will most likely submit to the older one. On the other hand, if the older dog is REALLY older, the kid could push it over the hill.
- Neutered dogs of opposite sexes get along best.
- Resident dogs need extra attention when a newcomer appears.
- Separate Feeding Places!

### *Cats*

They are comPETable. (See p. 72.)

### *Birds*

They don't have much in common, but they'll get along. (See p. 42.)

## *Children*

Some kids are better for dogs than others—and vice versa. (Read the breed-by-breed descriptions to determine what dogs might—or might not—be right for your kids.)

**KEEP IN MIND**

- Young children should not be left alone with large dogs (or little puppies).
- Children should be taught how to behave—and how not to behave—with a dog. (Lack of understanding on the child's part could have tragic consequences.)
- No matter how much responsibility a child swears that he or she will take for a new dog (walks, cleanups, feeding, grooming), don't count on it.
- Sharing a room is one thing, but a child who's allowed to share his or her bed with the dog can easily pick up fleas, ticks or other parasites.

## *Rabbits, Mice, Hamsters, and Small Rodents*

If these animals are kept in cages, most dogs can be taught to ignore (and not terrify) them. If, on the other hand, your children let their caged pets out for play periods, your dog should not be left alone with them.

**KEEP IN MIND**

- To a dog, free-range gerbils, hamsters, bunnies, guinea pigs, and mice may all look like squeak toys.
- To any of the terrier breeds, which were bred to hunt rodents, these small pets may look like prey.

## *Fish*

Some dogs will actually sit in front of a tank and stare at it. No one knows if they find this relaxing—or if it's just because there's nothing else to do.

## *Reptiles*

Dogs are curious about all living creatures, but not enough to intrude on your reptile home habitats.

### JACK'S FACTS: **Shedding Light on Shedding**

Dogs' hair grows in cycles, not continuously like human hair. When a dog's hair reaches a certain length, it stops growing and gets pushed out by new hair. In dog circles this process of shedding is called "blowing coat." In the dog's home it's called vacuuming time.

Smooth-coated shorthaired breeds, such as Dalmatians, bullterriers and beagles, drop dead hair on a daily basis. Though this is not actually shedding, you can't tell it by looking at the furniture. Fortunately, fallout can be minimized by regular brushing two or three times weekly. And if you think your problems are solved with one of the alleged non-shedding breeds— poodle, Portuguese water dogs, Kerry blue terrier, wheaten terrier, Welsh terrier—you're wrong. Dead hair has to go somewhere, so if you don't want it in your house or lying in state on your pet, you better brush up on your brushing. And your dog will appreciate it, too.

## Cautions to Keep in Mind for Dogs

- If you love your pet, don't give it chocolate. It contains caffeine and theo-bromine, which, depending upon the amount eaten and the size of your dog, could be lethal.
- Make sure soiled disposable diapers (as well as feminine-hygiene products) are safely disposed of so that your pet can't get them. If ingested they could cause serious intestinal blockage or lethal bacterial infection.
- Dogs, like cats (and small children), are attracted to the sweet taste of an-tifreeze containing ethylene glycol, which can kill them. Check your car for leaks, mop up spills immediately, and keep pet away from greenish puddles when out for walks.
- After wet-weather walks, dry your dog's paws to prevent fungal or bacterial in-fections.
- Clean and dry your dog's paws after winter walks; anti-icing compounds and salt can not only irritate pads but, if ingested by licking, can cause potentially lethal problems.
- Don't let your pet play with matches; the non-safety kind (and the striking sur-face on their boxes) contain phosphorus which can poison your dog.
- Mouse or rat poison can be equally deadly for your dog—even if it's ingested secondhand. (To a hungry dog, a dead rodent could look like an appetizer.)
- Keep puppies and dogs out of garden sheds, garages, or storage areas where there are pesticides.

- Leaving your dog in a parked car with the windows shut on a warm day may cause potentially fatal heat stroke. (Temperature in a car without proper ventilation can reach over 100°F on a mild 75° day.)
- Leaving you dog in warm weather for any extended period in an RV with the air-conditioning on and windows shut could be deadly if there is a power failure.
- Allowing your dog to ride in the car with its head out the window can result in ear infections.
- Keep all people medications safely out of your pet's reach; little pills of any sort can cause large—and often life-threatening—problems for pooches.
- Household disinfectants, bleaches, pine-oil products, and laundry detergents are all hazardous for your pet. (Good rule of thumb: If it's dangerous for children, it's dangerous for your dog.)
- Never use snail bait in your garden if there is *any* chance your dog can get at it.
- Just because your dog will eat anything doesn't mean you should let it; moldy foods—particularly spoiled dairy products and nuts—can cause life-threatening health problems.
- Do not tie up your dog if it is wearing a choke chain collar.
- Never use a pinch or prong collar on a puppy.
- Never give your pet small bones or chicken bones!
- Rawhide bones can swell and cause intestinal blockage if your pet swallows a large piece.
- Avoid imported rawhide bones; they may have chemical residues.
- Nicotine in tobacco, cigarette filters, and cigarette butts are all toxic hazards for dogs.
- Never use human toothpaste when cleaning a dog's teeth; dogs can't spit and the toothpaste can cause stomach upsets.
- Simple beauty products, such as nail polish, hair rinses, and deodorants, can cause ugly—and potentially lethal—health consequences in dogs.

## *Dangerous Plants for Plant-Eating Pooches*

If a plant can harm your cat, chances are it's not good for your dog, either. See p. 74 for a list of the most common potentially dangerous greens for pets.

JACK'S FACTS:
## Talk About a Dog-Owner Likeness

The person who was most responsible for publicizing one of the most naked pooches in dogdom, the Hairless Chinese Crested, and who bred them herself, was none other than the celebrated stripper Gypsy Rose Lee!

## Did You Know . . .

- Hairless dogs don't pant to cool off. Unlike other dogs, hairless dogs do have sweat glands, and when things heat up—they sweat!
- It is against the law in Pennsylvania to even *give away* a dog that's less than seven weeks old.
- A dog's mouth has fewer bacteria than a human's mouth.
- One out of every four dogs in America is overweight (and so is one out of every four Americans)!
- What is considered Paul Newman's sexiest feature (blue eyes) is a disqualifying fault in a bullterrier.
- Dogs should be bathed as infrequently as possible to prevent skin and coat from becoming too dry.
- Curly-coated dog breeds don't shed.
- A dog's sense of smell is more than a hundred times greater than that of a human.
- A dog can tell the difference between the sound of its master's footsteps and those of other people.
- Puppies don't hear until they are about twenty days old.
- A Skye terrier known as "Greyfriar's Bobby" kept a fourteen-year vigil at his master's grave in Edinburgh, Scotland. When he died the townspeople erected a seven-foot statue in his memory opposite the main gates where he'd kept watch.
- Very intelligent dogs usually need more training than others, otherwise these wise pups will amuse themselves at your home furnishing's expense.
- If you don't register a purebred puppy with the AKC, none of its descendants can ever be registered or compete in AKC shows.
- The Egyptians believed that names had magical powers and that a dog with a name enhanced its master's stature.
- The film actress Jean Harlow named her dog "Oscar" so she could always say that she had one.
- The smaller your breed of dog the earlier it matures.
- The founder of McDonald's, Ray Kroc, had a schnauzer named "**Burger**meister."
- A small dog will eat proportionately more than a large dog—if both are equally active.
- The dog is subject to more varieties than any other animals.

JACK'S FACTS: **Who Needs a Sweater?**

When it's cold outside, a lot of dogs need extra protection. Shorthaired breeds, small and large (yes, even fierce Dobermans) need help in subzero weather. In fact, even longhaired breeds might need extra protection—especially if they're old, ill, or have thinning fur. To find out what size to buy, measure your pet from the neck to the base of the tail. Most coats and sweaters correspond to the dog's length. If your local pet store doesn't have the outfit you want, check pet mail-order catalogues. . . . Or, you can take up knitting.

## Dogs by Breed

### Sporting Dogs

PRO: Likable, friendly, active, and, as a rule, not big barkers and good with children. Great for lovers of exercise and the outdoors. Most need room to run, but many of the spaniel types are happy in apartments as long as they get regular exercise.

CON: Generally need room to run and lots of exercise.

CREATURE COMFORTS: Leash, food, and water dishes; collar, bed, toys to fetch. Ideally, owners who enjoy hunting.

DIET NEEDS AND TREATS: A complete or balanced dog food guaranteed to meet or exceed all NRC (National Research Council) requirements for growth and maintenance of adult dogs and puppies—based on AAFCO (American Association of Feed Control Officials) standards. Check with your vet for brands that best meet your pet's particular protein needs.

HANNA'S HINT: Nutritional needs require adjustment and special attention during pregnancy, lactation, puppyhood, hot and cold weather, illness, hard exercise, stress, and old age. (But, do not add supplements to a nutritionally complete food unless instructed to do so by a veterinarian!) As for occasional healthy treats— freeze-dried liver, beef, or chicken; hard-boiled eggs; biscuits; and whatever veggies your pet might like (with the possible exception of raw onions and raw potatoes).

SIZE KEY:
- **T** (TOY) = *under 10 pounds*
- **S** (SMALL) = *approximately 10–25 pounds*
- **M** (MEDIUM) = *approximately 25–50 pounds*

**L**   (LARGE) = *approximately 50–100 pounds*

**G**   (GIANT) = *approximately over 100 pounds*

   *NOTE: These sizes are based on breed standards for males; females may be ten to twenty pounds lighter (but not necessarily).*

The symbol ⭐ means that there is something special you should know about this dog.

## SPANIELS

*Bred to pick up ground scents and flush birds out of hiding.*

**M** ⭐   AMERICAN WATER SPANIEL: A top-notch retriever, springs for game; uses tail as a rudder in water. May carry a grudge if mistreated.

**M**   BRITTANY SPANIEL: Can be aggressive.

**M-L**   CLUMBER SPANIEL: Loves families, kids, even apartment living.

**S-M** ⭐   COCKER SPANIEL: Merry, affectionate. Eyes and ears tend to need regular wipes.

**M**   ENGLISH COCKER SPANIEL: Same as Cocker Spaniel.

**M**   ENGLISH SPRINGER SPANIEL: Good in cold weather climates; sheds regularly.

**M**   FIELD SPANIEL: Calm and stable.

**M-L**   IRISH WATER SPANIEL: Good in cold climates. Loves family but is reserved with strangers.

**M**   SUSSEX SPANIEL: Strong and companionable. Much like other spaniels.

**M**   WELSH SPRINGER SPANIEL: His keen nose may lead him astray. Needs exercise.

## POINTERS

*Bred to locate game birds from body scents in the air—then stop and wait by "pointing."*

**M-L**   GERMAN SHORTHAIRED POINTER: Strong willed; can be high-strung.

**M-L**   GERMAN WIREHAIRED POINTER: More a field dog than an apartment pet.

**M-L**   VIZLA: Needs training; can be destructive if confined.

**L**        WEIMARANER: Likes being a family member.

**L** ★    WIREHAIRED POINTING GRIFFON: Points *and* retrieves.

### RETRIEVERS
*Bred to retrieve game birds from water.*

**L** ★    CHESAPEAKE BAY RETRIEVER: Very powerful. Can be tough around strangers.

**L**        CURLY-COATED RETRIEVER: Devoted. Needs room. Coat needs care.

**L**        FLAT-COATED RETRIEVER: More easygoing than his cousin "curly."

**L**        GOLDEN RETRIEVER: Ultra-gentle; loves every living thing. Hip dysplasia a frequent problem.

**L**        LABRADOR RETRIEVER: Needs lots of exercise but loves kids.

## Setters
*Bred to locate game birds from body scents in the air—then stop and signal by "setting."*

**M-L**    ENGLISH SETTER: Friendly, companionable, but not swift when it comes to training.

**M-L**    GORDON SETTER: Loves to run. Not a good apartment dog.

**L**        IRISH SETTER: Beautiful but not brilliant.

## Hounds
PRO: Gentle, friendly, loyal. Though hunting is in their genes, they are not naturally aggressive.

CON: Many will bay, bark, or howl. The larger breeds need LOTS of exercise or space.

CREATURE COMFORTS: Same as above. Some shorthaired breeds may need sweaters in cold climates.

DIET NEEDS AND TREATS: Same as above. For optimal nutrition, check with a veterinarian on what is right for your particular pet.

## Scenthounds
*Bred to hunt by scent.*

**M** ★    BASSET HOUND: May be difficult to housebreak.

**L-G**   BLOODHOUND: Extremely docile and affectionate, but is not happy cooped up.

**L-G**   SCOTTISH DEERHOUND: Big and shaggy, but easy-to-train and fine with kids.

## SIGHTHOUNDS

*Bred to hunt by sight.*

**L**   AFGHAN HOUND: Quiet, good apartment dog; coat needs extra grooming time.

**L-G**   BORZOI: Needs exercise. Loves the cold.

**L** ⭐   GREYHOUND: Needs sweater or coat in cold weather. Exercise is a given—greyhounds are the fastest dogs on earth!

**M**   IBIZAN HOUND: Not a barker. Loves family life and other pets. Often clicks teeth to invite play.

**G**   IRISH WOLFHOUND: We are talking large! Great with kids and other dogs. Prefers country living.

**M-L** ⭐   PHARAOH HOUND: Alert. Needs sweaters. Requires exercise, but enjoys apartment living.

**M-L**   SALUKI: Not a child's dog.

**L**   SCOTTISH DEERHOUND: Very similar to the Irish wolfhound.

**S**   WHIPPET: Much like the greyhound.

## OTHER HOUNDS

**L**   AMERICAN FOXHOUND: Needs space to exercise.

**S-M** ⭐ BASENJI: Doesn't bark.

**S-M** ⭐ BEAGLE: Adorable, but tends to yowl. A lot.

**L**   BLACK-AND-TAN COONHOUND: An all-weather pooch. Likes children, but prefers country living.

**S** ⭐   DACHSHUND (SMOOTH, LONGHAIRED, AND WIREHAIRED): Playful, family oriented. Not the easiest to housebreak.

**L**     ENGLISH FOXHOUND: Similar to the American foxhound.

**M**     HARRIER: Similar to English foxhound, beagle, and black and tan coonhound.

**M-L**   NORWEGIAN ELKHOUND: Independent. Loud barker. Sheds a lot, needs exercise. Can be very stubborn. Not good in warm climates.

**L**     OTTERHOUND: Loves the water, needs exercise. Shaggy but smart and devoted.

**S-M**   PETIT BASSET GRIFFON VENDEEN: Playful, eager to please. Has Basset and Griffon qualities.

**L** ★   RHODESIAN RIDGEBACK: Requires early training. Bred to withstand the elements, it can go without water for more than twenty-four hours—though not on a regular basis.

## Working Dogs

PRO: Bred to be useful in practical ways; their different abilities suit different human needs. Intelligent and loyal, they make wonderful guardians of people and property—and, in most cases, fine pets.

CON: Without proper training, their protectiveness can lead to unwanted aggression and problem behavior. They can be restless and unhappy if idle.

CREATURE COMFORTS: Same as above.

DIET NEEDS AND TREATS: Same as above. For optimal nutrition, check with your veterinarian for the foods best suited for your particular dog's age and lifestyle.

### DRAFT DOGS

*Bred to haul loads on sleds or wagons.*

**L** ★   ALASKAN MALAMUTE: Can be aggressive with other dogs.

**L**     BERNESE MOUNTAIN DOG: Not good for apartments.

**G**     GREATER SWISS MOUNTAIN DOG: Powerful, gentle, obedient—with an easy-care coat.

**M-L** ★  SAMOYED: Good watchdog; good with children. Not an easy pup to housebreak.

**M–L**  SIBERIAN HUSKY: Needs training and activities to keep out of mischief. Sheds—big time.

## PROTECTION DOGS
*Bred as herders, hunters, and guardians for people and property.*

**L** ⭐  AKITA: Can be aggressive. Not a child's pup.

**L** ⭐  BOXER: Slobbers, snores, but loves family life. May need a coat in frigid climates.

**G**  BULLMASTIFF: B-I-G—yet can adjust to apartment life. Born to guard.

**L** ⭐  DOBERMAN PINSCHER: Know thy breeder. Not for novice pet owner. One smart, tough, and fearless pup.

**L** ⭐  GIANT SCHNAUZER: A lot of powerful protection; not great with other pets.

**G** ⭐  GREAT DANE: Needs lots of exercise. Can be temperamental. Because of size, supervision around other pets and small children is necessary.

**G**  GREAT PYRENEES: Loving with families, other pets. Needs lots of grooming.

**G** ⭐  KOMONDOR: Looks like a giant dust mop with legs; corded coat should never be brushed. Devoted and bred to be a protection dog.

**L**  KUVASZ: Extremely strong instinct to protect children. Fearless.

**G**  MASTIFF: A gentle canine giant. Loves apartment-living and children, but an accidental nudge could send knickknacks and kids sprawling.

**M** ⭐  PORTUGUESE WATER DOG: More pal than protector. Has webbed feet and was originally bred to retrieve lost fishing tackle, herd fish into nets, and to act as a ship to ship—or ship to shore—courier. Comes with a nifty non-allergenic, non-shedding, waterproof coat.

**L** ⭐  ROTTWEILER: Not a dog for beginners. Great guard dog, loyal, but stubborn and in need of early training.

**M**  STANDARD SCHNAUZER: A one-family guard dog. Lively, affectionate—and stubborn. Needs daily grooming.

**RESCUE DOGS**

*Bred to save lives.*

**G**    **NEWFOUNDLAND:** Big, sweet, slobbery and trustworthy around children.

**G** ⭐ **SAINT BERNARD:** Comes in long- or short-haired versions. Docile and protective—if from a reputable breeder. Not for warm climates.

## Terriers

PRO: True grit! Spirited, lively, bred to kill vermin and hunt small game, they make good watchdogs and fun pets.

CON: They can be very independent, difficult to train. May be aggressive toward other household pets.

**CREATURE COMFORTS:** Same as above—with lots of exercise.

**DIET NEEDS AND TREATS:** Same as above. Check with your veterinarian about the diet most suited for your particular terrier.

**M**    **AIREDALE TERRIER:** Sweet, good with kids, and a great protector.

**M** ⭐ **AMERICAN STAFFORDSHIRE TERRIER:** Also known as the pit bull. Fearless, not for beginners—and illegal in some areas. Easily accepts new masters.

**S** ⭐ **AUSTRALIAN TERRIER:** courageous, full of energy. Slightly aggressive. Best for adults.

**S**    **BEDLINGTON TERRIER:** Looks like a lamb, but can fight like a lion with other pets.

**S**    **BORDER TERRIER:** Affectionate, obedient, easily trained—and tough.

**M**    **BULLTERRIER:** Friendly but stubborn, difficult to train. Bred to protect owner.

**S**    **CAIRN TERRIER:** Doesn't shed too much, good for apartment.

**S** ⭐ **DANDIE DINMONT TERRIER:** Long-lived, big-dog personality in small body. Breed prone to dermatitis in warm weather.

**S**    **FOX TERRIER (SMOOTH COAT, WIRE COAT):** The Energizer battery of dogs. They keep going and going . . .

**M**    IRISH TERRIER: Known as the "Daredevil," it will guard its human family in the face of virtually anything.

**S** ⭐ JACK RUSSELL TERRIER: Not recognized by the AKC at this writing—but definitely recognized by everyone familiar with the TV show *Frasier*.

**M** ⭐ KERRY BLUE TERRIER: Long-lived. Good watchdog. Not too fond of other dogs.

**S**    LAKELAND TERRIER: loves children and exercise.

**S** ⭐ MANCHESTER TERRIER: An easy-to-groom indoor pet—but a barker.

**S**    MINIATURE BULLTERRIER: An easier-to-handle version of its full-size cousin.

**S**    MINIATURE SCHNAUZER: An apartment-sized version of the standard schnauzer.

**S**    NORFOLK TERRIER: Sporty, not aggressive.

**S**    NORWICH TERRIER: Fearless, great companions.

**S** ⭐ SCOTTISH TERRIER: Confident, alert, strong. Essentially a one-person pooch.

**S**    SEALYHAM TERRIER: Good for apartment dwellers. Much like its Dandie Dinmont cousin.

**S**    SKYE TERRIER: Needs attention and grooming. Reserved with strangers.

**M**    SOFT-COATED WHEATEN TERRIER: Happy, sweet-tempered—a fine family pet.

**M** ⭐ STAFFORDSHIRE BULLTERRIER: Courageous, trustworthy, good with children—if pup is obtained from a reputable breeder.

**S** ⭐ WELSH TERRIER: Can be aggressive with other dogs.

**S** ⭐ WEST HIGHLAND WHITE TERRIER: Feisty. Independent. Difficult to train. Not for kids.

## *Toys*

PRO: A lot of pup bang for the buck! Bred to be people pals and suited to small living quarters and limited access to the outside. Long-lived and lovable; big-dog personalities in convenient pint sizes.

CON: Many of the toys have a lot of terrier instincts that are frustrated because of their size. Can be demanding, willful, and spoiled rotten. Many tend to be yappy.

CREATURE COMFORTS: Same as above. Most toy breeds need sweaters or coats in cold weather—and shorthaired and hairless breeds should be guarded against extended exposure to the sun. In fact, sunscreens are recommended.

DIET NEEDS AND TREATS: Same as above. Check with veterinarian for best diet for your particular dog.

HANNA'S HINT: Toy-dog owners tend to treat their pets with more treats than necessary. It's one thing to pamper your pup—but feeding it too many good things could pamper it to death.

T ☆ **AFFENPINSCHER:** Can become demanding of attention. And yappy.

T-S **BRUSSELS GRIFFON:** Needs early training. Very intelligent.

T-S **CAVALIER KING CHARLES SPANIEL:** Very intelligent, happy, and people-caring.

T **CHIHUAHUA:** Comes with or without a coat. A very portable pet.

T **CHINESE CRESTED:** Needs sweaters in cold climates; sunblock when out.

T **ENGLISH TOY SPANIEL:** Very sweet, very small.

T ☆ **ITALIAN GREYHOUND:** Needs protection against the elements, and loves to sleep under the covers with you.

T **JAPANESE CHIN:** Sensitive, but a good pet for any climate.

T **MALTESE:** A fearless little spaniel with manners. Needs grooming.

T **MANCHESTER TERRIER (TOY):** Same as Manchester terrier—only minimized.

T ☆ **MINIATURE PINSCHER:** The "Minpin" is a lot of pet in a little package—and a good watchdog, too.

**T**      PAPILLON: Needs lots of love, attention, and grooming.

**T** ⭐ PEKINESE: Prefers adults, city living, and adulation.

**T** ⭐ POMERANIAN: A little spitz that likes to rule—and is not particularly fond of kids.

**T**      POODLE (TOY): All the qualities of the poodle in miniature.

**S**      PUG: Lovable, adaptable, playful. One pup fits all.

**T-S**      SHIH TZU: Very friendly. A fine companion but needs lots of grooming.

**T** ⭐ SILKY TERRIER: Alert, but difficult to housebreak. Needs lots of grooming.

**T** ⭐ YORKSHIRE TERRIER: Sized for apartments. Stubborn, hard to housebreak, demands attention.

## Non-Sporting Dogs

PRO: They have, over the years, come to be bred specifically as pets. Good as pals and watchdogs, they adapt equally well to city and country lifestyles.

CON: It all depends on the individual dog-household match. Some are better with children and other pets than others. All require grooming, exercise, and training.

CREATURE COMFORTS: Same as above.

DIET NEEDS AND TREATS: Same as above. Because this group is so diverse, be sure to check with your veterinarian for the diet best for your pet.

**T-S**      BICHON FRISE: That's bee-*shahn* free-*zay*. And it's a pet for all.

**S-M**      BOSTON TERRIER: Lively, intelligent. Train early.

**M-L** ⭐ BULLDOG: Snores, slobbers, but does not shed and is a fine pet. Is prone to heart attack if subjected to sudden heat or left in unventilated vehicle.

**M-L** ⭐ CHINESE SHAR-PEI: Gets along with dogs and kids. All those loose skin and those folded down ears hark back to the days when it was a fighting dog. It would twist away from its opponent easily—and its tiny ears were difficult to bite.

**M** ⭐ **CHOW CHOW:** Has limited peripheral vision, a black tongue, and tends to be aggressive. Sheds a lot. Not for children or new pet owners.

**M** ⭐ **DALMATIAN:** Shorthaired but a shedder. Deafness runs in the breed. Fine family pet and good watchdog.

**M** **FINNISH SPITZ:** Loves kids, but tends to greet them by yodeling.

**S–M** **FRENCH BULLDOG:** Not big barkers. Easy to groom. Good watchdogs.

**M** **KEESHOND:** A sensible, friendly, fun family watchdog.

**S** **LHASA APSO:** Grooming a must.

**M** **POODLE:** If you appreciate intelligence, want protection, and enjoy hair-styling, this is your pooch. Its coat is non-allergenic, can be clipped in a variety of ways—or not.

**S** ⭐ **SCHIPPERKE:** Needs exercise, loves kids. Protective. Is not aware of the limitations of its size.

**S–M** **SHIBA INU:** Smaller cousin of the Akita. Alert and strong-willed.

**S** ⭐ **TIBETAN SPANIEL:** Has an independent "catlike" personality, is family-oriented and easy to groom.

**S–M** ⭐ **TIBETAN TERRIER:** Looks like a sheepdog, but doesn't shed like one.

## *Herding Dogs*

**PRO:** Intelligent, easy to train. Their inbred herding instincts make them fine watchdogs, companions, and pets.

**CON:** They all need grooming, exercise, and attention. And, because they are intelligent, they're more likely to get into mischief if unsupervised.

**CREATURE COMFORTS:** Same as above—with plenty of toys and activities to keep them busy.

**DIET NEEDS AND TREATS:** Same as above. Check with veterinarian for diet that best suits the needs of your dog.

**M** AUSTRALIAN CATTLE DOG: Likes to stay at your heels.

**M** AUSTRALIAN SHEPHERD: A family dog that loves herding and barks only when necessary.

**M** BEARDED COLLIE: A lot of coat, a lot of hair—but worth the vacuuming.

**L** BELGIAN MALINOIS: Easy coat care, bright, trainable.

**L** BELGIAN SHEEPDOG: Good all-around protection, search, rescue, therapy, and companion dogs.

**L** BELGIAN TERVUREN: Great temperament. Fine therapy and companion dogs.

**M** ⭐ BORDER COLLIE: A phenomenal herding dog that has "the eye," a trance-like gaze enabling it to creep up on a flock and get them to move without stampeding. Very bright.

**L** ⭐ BOUVIER DES FLANDRES: Not for apartments.

**L** ⭐ BRIARD: Described as "a heart wrapped in fur"—and it sheds! And matts!

**L** COLLIE: Not all collies are Lassie, but they need to be groomed as if they were.

**L** ⭐ GERMAN SHEPHERD DOG: Know your breeder. Socialize and train early.

**L** ⭐ OLD ENGLISH SHEEPDOG: Shuffles like a bear, but sheds like a dog. Coat protects from cold and heat.

**M** ⭐ PULI: Unkempt coat is its trademark.

**S** SHETLAND SHEEPDOG: Grooming a must.

**S** WELSH CORGI, CARDIGAN: A former member of the dachshund family.

**S** WELSH CORGI, PEMBROKE: The short-tailed corgi; member of the Royal family.

## Miscellaneous Class

Dogs not yet officially recognized by the AKC, but which may compete in AKC obedience trials and earn obedience titles. Though not eligible for championship points, they may compete at conformation shows in the Miscellaneous Class.

**M**      AUSTRALIAN KELPIE: A foxlike herding dog that loves to work.

**M-L**    CANAAN DOG: Israel's all-purpose search and protection pet.

**L**      SPINONI ITALIANI: Known as the Italian pointer, it looks like a shaggy hound.

## Other Unrecognized Breeds

**G** ⭐   ANATOLIAN SHEPHERD DOG: Sometimes called the Turkish guard dog. Much like the Great Pyrenees and Kuvasz. Friendly to families, but not other dogs.

**L**      BLUETICK COONHOUND: Bred to hunt raccoons. Gentle, but will bay a warning if a stranger comes around.

**M**      BOYKIN SPANIEL: Sort of a cocker-water spaniel mix . . . with a little Chesapeake retriever in the family tree. Very bright.

**L** ⭐   CATAHOULA LEOPARD DOG: Bred originally as a herding dog by the early settlers of Louisiana, this canine with its splotched leopard-like coat and unique turquoise eyes is also a formidable watchdog and raccoon hunter.

**T-S** ⭐ CHINESE IMPERIAL CHIN: Related to the Pekinese and Chow Chow, it comes in four sizes—Giant, Classic, Miniature, and Sleeve dog, which is only three inches tall and weighs about two pounds. The Chin is able to stand on its hind legs for long periods, and it's been written that the last empress of China had her fifty pets line up from the door to the throne and bow to her until she was seated.

**T-S**    CHINESE TEMPLE DOG: Related to the Chin above. Also available in four sizes.

**T**      COTON DE TULEAR: An affectionate little dog, with a heavy cottony coat, that likes outdoor activities as much as in-house snuggling.

**M**      ENGLISH SHEPHERD: Everything you'd want in a shepherd dog, but more dignified.

**M**    ICELAND DOG: A herder and protector. A member of the spitz family.

**T-S** ⭐ LITTLE LION DOG: Said to be the world's rarest purebred. Has a lion-like mane and a plumed tail. Adapts easily to urban or country living and plays well with kids and other pets.

**T** ⭐ MEXICAN HAIRLESS: Unusual in many ways. Completely hairless, it can lie in the sun and get a suntan and, when unhappy, weep tears. Looks like a chihuahua.

**G**    NEAPOLITAN MASTIFF: A smaller Italian version of the mastiff.

**L**    PICARDIE SHEPHERD: A French guard dog with a coat like a goat.

**L**    PLOTT HOUND: Brought to the U.S. in the eighteenth century to fight black bears. Recognized by the United Kennel Club of Britain.

**L**    REDBONE COONHOUND: A bloodhound and Irish hound mix used to hunt raccoons.

**L**    REDTICK COONHOUND: Related to the Bluetick coonhound. Different markings.

**S-M**    TELOMIAN: Looks like a small basenji, similar temperaments.

**M**    TENNESSEE TREEING BRINDLE: Bred from dogs used by the Cherokee Indians in the Appalachians in the early nineteenth century. People-loving hounds.

**L**    TIBETAN MASTIFF: Smaller than the Great Pyrenees and other mastiffs, but similar in temperament.

**T**    TOY FOX TERRIER: A toy version of a smooth-coated fox terrier.

**L**    TREEING WALKER COONHOUND: Popular American foxhound. Trees quarry.

**M-L**    TRIGG HOUND: A foxhound with lots of spirit.

**S-M** ⭐ XOLOXCUINTLE: The Xolo is a lot like the Manchester terrier—but is hairless, except for a tiny fluff on its head and tail. Because its body temperature is over 100°, people in Mexico still take it to bed with them for warmth.

**JACK'S FACTS: Titles Before and After**

In AKC dogdom, titles aren't bestowed or inherited, they're earned the old-fashioned way—by competing for them. Once a dog earns a title, it's put on that dog's AKC record before its name (prefix) or after its name (suffix).

**PREFIXES**

| | |
|---|---|
| CH | Champion |
| FC | Field Champion (Field Trials of Lure Coursing—different hunting, tracking, and retrieving tests for pointers, spaniels, retrievers, and hounds) |
| AFC | Amateur Field Champion |
| OTCH | Obedience Trial Champion |
| HCH | Herding Champion |
| DC | Dual Champion (already has a CH and an FC) |
| TC | Triple Champion (has CH, FC, and OTCH) |

**SUFFIXES**

| | | | |
|---|---|---|---|
| CD | Companion Dog | HT | Herding Tested |
| CDX | Companion Dog Excellent | PT | Pre-Trial Tested |
| UD | Utility Dog | HS | Herding Started |
| TD | Tracking Dog | HI | Herding Intermediate |
| TDX | Tracking Dog Excellent | HX | Herding Excellent |
| JH | Junior Hunter | JC | Junior Courser |
| SH | Senior Hunter | SC | Senior Courser |
| MH | Master Hunter | | |

The AKC now has a Canine Good Citizen program to reward responsible pet ownership. It's open to all dogs—mixed breeds, registered or not. Your dog performs ten simple activities—including allowing a stranger and strange dog to approach; walking calmly through a crowd; remaining confident when faced with distractions; sitting still for petting; demonstrating an understanding of the commands sit, down, and stay. If your pet passes the exam, he or she will get a CGC certificate. You can write to the American Kennel Club or check your local paper for the next Obedience competition offering Canine Good Citizen trials.

### Celebrity Dog Owners and Their Dogs

You're going to be calling your dog a lot, so you might as well pick a name that you'll like to hear, too. Here to help you are some famous names and some of the (*printable*) names they've called their canines; names that in many cases also tell you quite a bit about the owners who chose them.

*Joy Adamson:* Pippin
*June Allyson:* Heathcliff
*James Arness:* Matt, Miss Kitty
*Lauren Bacall:* Droopy, Harvey, Puddle
*Sarah Bernhardt:* Bull, Fly, Hamlet, Miniccio
*Marlon Brando:* Schlubber
*Edgar Rice Burroughs:* Rahjah, Tarzan
*George and Barbara Bush:* Millie
*Admiral Richard E. Byrd:* Holly, Igloo
*Jimmy Carter:* Bozo
*Calvin Coolidge:* Boston Beans, Calamity Jane, King Kole, Mule Ears, Oshkosh, Palo Alto, Peter Pan, Rob Roy, Ruby Rough, Tiny Tim
*Bill Cosby:* Black Watch Moonstruck
*Doris Day:* Audie Murphy, Barney Miller, Dillon, El Tigre, Heineken, Varmit
*James Dean:* Strudel, Tuck
*Bo Derek:* Bolero, China, Cif, Gunn, Harum Scarum, Hero, Ivory, Killer, Loch Lommond, Molly, Pamper, Peanut, Rob, Russia, Smoke, Snugger, Tough
*Phyllis Diller:* Phearless
*Bob Dole:* Leader
*Douglas Fairbanks, Jr.:* Marco Polo, Zorro
*F. Scott and Zelda Fitzgerald:* Bouillabaisse, Ezra Pound, Jerry, Muddy Water, Trouble
*Errol Flynn:* Man Friday
*John Forsythe:* Fallon, Krystle
*Charlie Gibson:* Dexter
*Kathie Lee Gifford:* Chardonnay, Chablis, Regis
*Jean Harlow:* Ocar
*Rutherford B. Hayes:* Grim
*Rita Hayworth:* Knockwurst, Lilac, Mink, Pookles
*Charlton Heston:* Arthur Pendragon, Brutus, Cleo, Drago, General Pompey, Heidi, Portia, Rameses, Tara, Tony, Wotan
*J. Edgar Hoover:* Cindy, G-Boy

*Bob Hope:* Recession, Snow Job

*Lyndon Johnson:* Her, Him, J. Edgar, Little Chap, Rover, Yuki

*Helen Keller:* Kamikaze, Kenzan Go

*Sally Kellerman:* Dylan, Roosevelt

*Gene Kelly:* Bambi

*John F. Kennedy:* Blackie, Buddy, Butterfuly, Clipper, Moe, Streaker, Wolf

*John F. Kennedy, Jr.:* Shannon

*Gypsy Rose Lee:* Bootsie, Mumshay

*John Lennon:* Merry

*David Letterman:* Bob, Stan

*Liberace:* Chop Suey, Chow Mein, Gretel, Lady Di, Minuet, Noel, Powder Puff, Prunella, Snuffy, Suzie Wong, Wrinkles

*Bob Mackie:* Amber, Pansy

*Leonard Maltin:* Scruffy

*Barry Manilow:* Bagel, Biscuit

*Garry Marshall:* Cindy, Linus, Lucy

*General George C. Marshall:* Bones, Nato

*Paul McCartney:* Martha

*Maureen McGovern:* Nicodemus Beebob Dickens, Rocky

*Glenn Miller:* Pops

*Mary Tyler Moore:* Dash, DisWilliam, Dudley, Maude

*Bill Murray:* Bark

*Martina Navratilova:* Killer Dog, Ruby, Yonex

*Richard Nixon:* Checkers, King Timahoe, Vicky

*Dorothy Parker:* Bunk, Daisy, Eikovon Blutenberg, Flic, Misty, Nogi, Rags, Robinson, Timothy, Wolf, Woodrow Wilson

*Dolly Parton:* Lickety Spitz, Mark Spitz

*Elvis Presley:* Brutus, Foxhugh, Snoopy

*Richard Pryor:* Brother

*Gilda Radner:* Sparkle

*Ronald Reagan:* Freebo, Fuzzy, Rex, Scotch, Soda, Taca, Victory

*Della Reese:* All Spice, Cajun, Cinnamon, Nutmeg, Spice, Sugar

*Don Rickles:* Clown, Jokier

*Joan Rivers:* Spike, Veronica, Lulu

*Edward G. Robinson:* Champ, Cigar

*Gene Roddenberry:* E.T.

*Roy Rogers:* Bullet

*Franklin Delano Roosevelt:* Blaze, Fala, Major, Marksman, President, Winks

*Diana Ross:* Tiffany

*Soupy Sales:* Black Tooth, White Fang

*Arnold Schwarzenegger:* Conan, Streudel

*William Shatner:* Kirk, Martika, Paris, Sterling

*Richard Simmons:* Ashley, Marty Wiener, Melanie, Pitty Pat, Prissy, Rhett Butler, Scarlett

*Frank Sinatra:* Leroy Brown, Maf, Miss Wiggles

*Gertrude Stein* and *Alice B. Toklas:* Basket

*John Steinbeck:* Charley, Toby

*Barbra Streisand:* Sadie, Sushie

*Jacqueline Susann:* Joseph, Josephine

*Albert Payson Terhune:* Argus, Explorer, Fair Ellen Gray Dawn, Lad, Lady, Sunnybank, Sunnybank Jean, Sunnybank Sigurd, Thane, Wolf

*James Thurber:* Christabel, Jeannie, Jennie, Judge, Medve, Muggs, Rex, Samson

*Mark Twain:* Don't Know, I Know, You Know

*Gore Vidal:* Rat

*Andy Warhol:* Amos, Archie

*Betty White:* Bandit, Binky, Bootie, Captain, Chang, Cricket, Dancer, Dinah, Simba, Sooner, Stormy, Toby

*Oprah Winfrey:* Arizona, Shane

---

JACK'S FACTS: **Names You *Can't* Call Your Dog**

Believe it or not, you can't call your dog "Dog." Not if you're registering it with the AKC. You also may not call it "Boxer" or "Rottweiler," because breed names alone are not allowed, nor are such words as "champ," "champion," "sieger" or any AKC title or show term (abbreviated or spelled out). Nor can the name include the words "kennel(s)," "stud," "male," "bitch," "dam," and "female." Though you may call your dog "George Washington," you may not call it "George Burns," because names of prominent living or recently deceased people are also prohibited, as are obscenities and words derogatory to any race, creed, or nationality. Additionally, a name may not contain more than twenty-five letters or include Arabic or Roman numerals. (The AKC reserves the right to assign Roman numerals in order to permit up to thirty-seven dogs of each breed to have the same name.) But don't despair if the name you had your heart set on is taken. The dog's registered name and the name that you actually call it are two different things—and it's the one that gets your pet to come to you that counts!

*For full details on AKC policies and guidelines for registration, you can write to the American Kennel Club, 5580 Centerview Drive, Suite 200, Raleigh, NC 27606–3390.*

## Questions and Answers About Dogs

### Size by Size

My cousin and I both got male German shepherd puppies from the same litter two years ago. Her pup was the runt and mine was the largest. But now, her dog, Rascal, is huge and my dog, Grizz, is just average. How did this happen?

It's not uncommon. "Runts," the little guys of the litter, if healthy, are probably just younger than their littermates. Dogs that are bred often mate over a period of several days, so some pups are conceived later than others. When they're born, they're naturally smaller. But, as you now know, they sure can make up for it on the outside.

### Overeager Eater

Our dog, Demo, is a two-year-old golden retriever but he gulps down his food like a starved bear, and regularly gets gas or hiccups or both. Is there anything we can do to slow him down?

This might sound strange, but I've seen it work. Put a few large (about four inches wide) clean rocks in his feeding dish along with his food. It will stop him from gobbling because he'll have to maneuver more to get to the good stuff.

### The Whole Tooth

Do I really have to clean my dog's teeth?

Let me put it this way, keeping your dog's teeth clean and free of tartar (which builds up to create plaque) can help prevent serious health problems—including liver, kidney, and heart ailments. Periodontal disease in dogs allows bacteria to build up in the space between teeth and gums, enabling nearby blood vessels to then carry that bacteria throughout the body where it may damage organs and even the nervous system.

Dogs fed soft food are more prone to problems than dogs who regularly eat dry food, crunchy biscuits, or chew on large knucklebones or hard synthetic ones—but they're not immune to trouble.

Most vets now recommend brushing your dog's teeth, which, of course, is easier said than done if your dog is fully grown with a mind and mouth of its own. (Starting in puppyhood is a LOT easier.) But you can get your dog used to it by using a specially flavored enzyme-enhanced dog toothpaste (never use human toothpaste on a dog), which can be found at pet stores or ordered through pet catalogues. Keep the experience positive. (Remember, patience is a virtue—and lack of it could make your dog "gum shy" and in dental denial for life.) Start by putting the toothpaste on a piece of gauze and get your pet used to having its gums and teeth massaged; after that you can use a soft toothbrush for regular twice-weekly brushings.

### Gravy-Ear Prevention

Our cocker spaniel, Gulliver, can't walk away from a meal without his ears getting stained with gravy from his food. It's a pain to clean him and the floor after every meal. Is there any way to keep his ears up?

None that Gulliver will appreciate. You're better off buying a high cone-shaped feeding dish—designed for hounds and other long-eared dogs—that's specially made to keep canine ears dry (and gravy-free).

HANNA'S HINT: Tall dogs such as wolfhounds, Great Danes and mastiffs, as well as other large breeds, are happier—and have less neck and back strain—if their food dishes are elevated.

### Boning Up on Bones

Whenever I give my bearded collie, Jemini, a rawhide bone, he runs around and tries to hide it. Sometimes he digs at our couch cushions and attempts to bury it there. Why does he do this? Is this normal?

Yes, it's normal and it's been going on for centuries (not in your living room, of course). Your dog is doing what his wolf ancestors have done for thousands of years—storing food surplus. When wolves bring down large prey, they can't eat it all at one time. But they know that if they leave it, scavengers will get it—so they bite off large chunks and bury them for the next day. It is this same behavior that your, obviously, well-fed pet is instinctively performing. Delay dinner for a few hours one night and I'll bet your Jemini will go digging for that hidden bone.

### Crate Starts

The people who gave us Tribble—a nine-week-old collie-shepherd mix—recommended that we use a crate to house-train her. This seems to us like putting a puppy in jail. Isn't there a better way to train her?

Not really. What looks like a jail cell to you represents a safe haven or a den, to a dog. And dogs, like wolves, will not soil where they sleep if at all possible. Make sure the crate is large enough for your dog to stand up and turn around in. (She's a pup now, but she'll grow fast.) Keep the crate, like a playpen, around where you are. Encourage your pup to go in it voluntarily by feeding her in it. Do not leave her in it for more than three or four hours at a time. (She still needs exercise.) Remember, the crate should never be used as punishment; it's to *prevent* the dog from doing something wrong. If you're not around to catch a dog "in the act" of misbehaving, you cannot correct if effectively. Be sure to let Tribble out often enough to relieve herself. Before long, she'll come to love the crate as much as you will. In fact, you'll realize that there's no better way, when you're not around, to keep Tribble out of trouble.

## Dog Talk You Should Know

**ACTION:** the dog's movement, coordination, or gait

**AKC:** American Kennel Club

**ANGULATION:** angles formed at the bone joints, mainly at the forequarters, stifle (knee) and hock (ankle)

**APPLE HEAD:** a domed top skull (*or a nickname for a dopey dog*)

**APRON:** longer hair—frill—below the neck

**BACK:** the topline of the dog from withers to tail

**BANDY LEGS:** legs that bow outward

**BARREL HOCKS:** hocks that turn out causing feet to turn in

**BARREL:** a rounded rib section

**BAT EARS:** erect, front-facing ears, rounded in outline

**BAY:** the deep, prolonged howl of a hound

**BEAUTY SPOT:** a distinct round spot of color on the top of the head

**BEE-STING TAIL:** short straight tail, tapering to a point

**BEEFY:** having overdeveloped hindquarters (*in other words, biggus buttus*)

**BELTON:** a color pattern in English Setters, essentially white hair intermingled with blue, lemon, liver, or orange color

**BENCH SHOW:** a show at which dogs are confined to benches or assigned stalls when not being shown in competition

**BEST IN SHOW:** award for dog judged best of all breeds

**BITCH:** a female dog

**BITE:** position of teeth when jaws are closed (see Overshot, Undershot, and Scissors)

**BLANKET:** a large color patch on back and upper sides

**BLAZE:** a white stripe running down the center of the face between the eyes

**BLOOM:** a coat's sheen in top condition

**BOBTAIL:** a tailless or docked-tail dog; also used as a nickname for Old English Sheepdog

**BOSSY:** having overdeveloped shoulder muscles (*sort of a pumped-up pup*)

**BRACE:** two of the same kind of dogs; a couple or pair

**BREECHING:** fringing of hair at the rear of thighs

**BRINDLE:** a color pattern of black with lighter tan or brown hairs

**BROKEN-HAIRED:** a wiry, rough coat

**BROOD BITCH:** a female used mostly for breeding purposes

**BRUSH:** a really bushy tail

**BURR:** the irregular formation visible inside the ear cup

**BUTTERFLY NOSE:** a partially unpigmented nose, spotted with flesh tones

**BUTTON EAR:** a forward folding earflap

**CAMEL BACK:** a humped or arched back

**CANINES:** the two upper and lower fanglike teeth (*and the dogs who own them*)

**CASTRATION:** removal of a male dog's testicles to prevent breeding

**CHARACTER:** appearance and temperament considered typical of a breed

**CHINA EYE:** a flecked or spotted light blue or whitish eye

**CHOPS:** the jowls or lower lips

**CLIP:** the style of coat trim

**CLODDY:** low, heavy, and thickset

**COBBY:** short-bodied; compact

**CONFORMATION:** shape and form of animal in accordance with a breed's standards

**CORKY:** lively

**COURSING:** the sport of chasing game by Sight Hounds

**CRANK TAIL:** one that is carried down and bent

**CROPPED:** describing ears trimmed or cut in order to stand erect

**CROUP:** the rump of the dog

**CRYPTORCHID:** a dog whose testicles have not descended into the scrotum

**CULOTTES:** longer hair on the back of the thighs

**DAM:** the female parent (*or what the owner says if the litter was unplanned*)

**DEWCLAW:** a functionless extra claw or "fifth toe," on the inside of the leg above the paw

**DEWLAP:** loose-hanging skin under the throat

**DOCKED:** describing a tail shortened by cutting

**DOG:** a male dog (as opposed to a bitch); also used for both male and female

**DOUBLE COAT:** a weather-resistant outer coat with a shorter, softer undercoat

**DUDLEY NOSE:** flesh-colored

**EARRINGS:** unclipped hair that dangles from ears

**EWE NECK:** the topline of the neck is concave

**FALL:** hair hanging over eyes or face

**FANCIER:** one active in the breeding or showing of purebreds

**FEATHERS:** longer hair on ears, legs, tail, or body (*frequently seen on bird dogs*)

**FIDDLE FRONT:** a bowed front, with forelegs and feet turned out, pasterns close

**FLAG:** a long tail, carried high and often feathered

**FLANK:** the areas between the last rib and the hip

**FLEWS:** pendulous upper lips, particularly at the corners

**FLUSH:** to drive (or spring) birds from cover

**FLYING EARS:** drop or semiprick ears that stand erect

**FOREQUARTERS:** the front end of the dog, from shoulder to feet

**FOUL COLOR:** an uncharacteristic breed color or marking (*or what a white dog turns after a rainy-day romp*)

**GAIT:** the leg rhythm while moving at various speeds

**GASKIN:** the lower or second thigh

**GUARD HAIRS:** the longer, stiffer hairs which grow through the undercoat

**HACKLES:** neck and back hairs that raise involuntarily in anger or fright

**HARD-MOUTHED:** leaving teeth or bite marks on retrieved game

**HAW:** a third eyelid

**HOCK:** the lower joint in the hind leg, similar to the human ankle

**HUCKLEBONES:** the top of the hipbones

**INCISORS:** the six upper and lower teeth between the canines

**ISABELLA:** fawn-colored

**JOWLS:** the flesh of lips and jaws

**KISS MARKS:** tan spots on cheeks and above the eyes

**KNEE JOINTS:** stifle joint

**LEAD:** another name for leash (*or what untrained dogs do on walks with their owners*)

**LINE BREEDING:** the mating of related dogs (but not in father-daughter, mother-son immediate family)

MANTLE: darker-colored marking on shoulders, back, and sides

MARCELED: having uniform waves in coat

MASK: darker color on the muzzle or around the eyes

MERLE: an intermixed or dappled blue-black gray with white coloring

MONORCHID: a dog with only one testicle in evidence

MUZZLE: the head from eyes to nose; a device to restrain dog from biting

NICK: a breeding that produces desirable puppies

OPEN BITCH: a female dog ready to be bred

OVERSHOT: the upper front teeth project beyond the lower ones when the jaw is closed

PADS: the shock-absorbing undersides of the paws

PASTERN: the area of the foreleg between the wrist and the paw

PEDIGREE: a written record of the dog's lineage going back at least three generations

PIG EYES: eyes set too close together (*a fault in dogs, a good thing in pigs*)

POINT: the frozen stance of a hunting dog to indicate the presence and location of game

PUT DOWN: to ready a dog for show; also, a dog unplaced in competition; (colloquially) to have a dog euthanatized

RACY: tall and lean

RAT TAIL: a hairless long tail

ROACH BACK: a convex back, not dissimilar to Camel back

RUFF: thick, long hair around neck (*think "Lassie"*)

SABER TAIL: curving in a semi-circle, like a cavalry sword

SCISSORS BITE: outside of lower incisor teeth touch inside of upper ones when jaw is closed

**SHELLY:** a narrow body, lacking sufficient bone

**SIRE:** the male parent

**SLEW FEET:** turned-out feet

**SPEAK:** to bark

**SPECTACLES:** dark markings around the eyes (*and the dog never misplaces them*)

**SPRING:** to drive or flush birds from hiding

**STANDOFF COAT:** a heavy coat that stands off from the body

**STARING COAT:** a coarse, dry coat

**STIFLE:** the joint of the hind leg between the upper and lower thigh; the dog's knee

**STOP:** the rise from the muzzle to the skull; the indentation between the eyes where the forehead meets the nose

**THUMB MARKS:** black marks on the pastern

**TICKED:** having small black or other colored hairs on a light coat (*what owners get when they see those hairs on the furniture*)

**TONGUE:** the barking of hounds on the trail; "to give tongue"

**UNDERSHOT:** front incisor teeth of the lower jaw project beyond the upper ones when the mouth is closed

**VARMINITY:** having a sharp, keen expression

**VENT:** the opening of the anus

**WALLEYE:** see China eye

**WHEATEN:** a pale yellow or fawn color

**WHELPING BOX:** a constructed box or bed designed for whelping

**WHELPING:** giving birth

**WHIP TAIL:** a pointed tail, carried stiffly and straight back

**WITHERS:** the highest point on the shoulders between the back and the base of the neck

JACK'S FACTS: **Five Top Books for Dog Owners**

*How to Be Your Dog's Best Friend: A Training Manual for Dog Owners* by the Monks of New Skete (Little, Brown)

*Dog Training by Bash* by Baskim Dibra with Elizabeth Randolph (Dutton)

*Good Owners/Great Dogs* by Brian Kilcommons (Warner)

*Dogwatching* by Desmond Morris (Crown)

*Good Dog, Bad Dog* by Mordecai Siegel and Matthew Margolis (Little, Brown)

# 7

# Mickeys, Minnies, and Other Rodents

## Mini-Mammals as Pets

They're cute, they're cuddly, they're fun—and, yes, they are rodents (see "This Just In . . . ," below), but as starter pets they're hard to beat for at least a dozen reasons.

### A Dozen Reasons to Consider Rodents

1. You don't have to walk them.
2. You don't have to housebreak them.
3. You don't have to train them.
4. They take up very little space in small apartments.
5. They travel easily.
6. They are relatively inexpensive.
7. They are quiet.
8. They don't whine, cry, or squawk when you put them back in their cages.
9. They don't mind being left alone.
10. They like children.
11. Children like them.
12. Buy one pair and you can have as many as you want for free!

JACK'S FACTS: **This Just In . . .**

Researchers from Italy and Sweden have recently released a report declaring that the guinea pig is not a rodent. In fact, the report goes on to suggest that, along with guinea pigs, rats, mice, squirrels, porcupines, hamsters, gerbils, and hundreds of other species long classified as rodents and descendants of a common ancestor (because of their self-sharpening and ever-growing specialized incisors with enamel only on the front) are, according to DNA evidence, of multiple lineages and only vaguely related. But at this time, in the scientific community, there are as many (if not more) opponents to this theory than there are supporters. So, until there is a definitive resolution, for the purposes of this pet guide, a rodent by any name—be it hamster, mouse, guinea pig, gerbil, or rat—is still a rodent.

## How to Recognize a Healthy Rodent

Rodents, be they mice, rats, gerbils, hamsters, or guinea pigs, should be young when you get them (around six to eight weeks). Older ones are often too set in their ways to be interested in people-pet bonding. But before you take any pet home, it's important to take a good look at it.

## The Healthy Mini-Mammal Scan

- Eyes should be clear of film or discharge.
- Animal should not blink excessively.
- Ears should be clean—free of dirt or specks—and dry.
- Coat should look healthy—smooth, glossy—free of bald patches.
- Skin should not be dry or scratched.
- Teeth should be barely visible.

HANNA'S HINT: A young rodent that's long in the tooth has problems you don't need.

## Rodent Raising 101

If you want friendly pettable pets, you have to get them used to being handled early—*but not the first day you bring them home!*

## Welcoming Your Pet Right

- Have a cage set up ahead of time and ready for your pet when you bring it home.
- Let the animal get used to its surroundings.
- Make sure your hands are clean before you handle your pet—and after. (If your hand smells like peanut butter, your pet might want a bite.)
- As with all caged animals, avoid sudden moves and let them approach you first.

## Compatible—and Incompatible—Household Pets

### Mice, Rats, Hamsters, Gerbils, Guinea Pigs

With the exception of hamsters, who seem to be happiest living alone, other rodent pets enjoy the company of their own kind.

**KEEP IN MIND**

- Before adding a new animal to an established group, clean the cage so all the animals will feel on neutral (unmarked) territory.

- Males generally do not get along with males.
- Spreading food around the cage at first will make things easier.
- If the animals fight, remove the newcomer and try again later.
- Give the group time to accept the newcomer.

## Cats
See p. 72.

## Dogs
See p. 96.

## Birds
See p. 42.

## Children
Mini-mammals are perfect laptop pets for kids, provided they are old enough to understand how to handle these little fellas *gently*.

### KEEP IN MIND
- Children often promise to take care of a pet and then forget when it comes to cage cleaning or any of the other un-fun stuff that pet owning involves.
- Unsupervised play with mice, hamsters, or gerbils could mean a loss of caged pets and an increase in your household rodent population.
- Children are often unaware of the danger other household pets could be.

## Fish
They'll get along as long as they stay out of each other's territory.

## Reptiles
Caution is advised, since for many reptiles these mini-mammals—white mice in particular—are meals!

## Mice Are Nice

One wonders if mice became housepets when someone decided "If you can't lick 'em, join 'em"—or, at least, breed them. Pet mice come in a palette of colors to complement any kid's room: white, blue, red, silver, cream, black, and even lilac.

Some in combinations of two or three colors, with silky straight or wavy hair, and eyes that are pure pink or midnight black.

PRO: They're self-grooming, don't need to be bathed. They're small (two inches with a two-inch tail) and easily tamed.

CON: They generally don't live beyond two years and are susceptible to fleas and mites. Male's urine odor is strong. They're nocturnal and therefore most active at night.

CREATURE COMFORTS: Cage with pullout bottom for cleaning or a five-gallon glass aquarium with a screened top; nesting material such as wood chips or shavings* or reprocessed paper litter (available at pet stores); a gravity-flow water bottle, food dish, exercise wheel, toys, a nesting house, non-toxic wooden sticks to chew on.

DIET NEEDS AND TREATS: Mouse seed mix or pellets, lab bricks, fresh vegetables, grains, an occasional piece of cheese (natch); small amounts of clover or dandelion leaves.

*Do NOT use cedar bedding for any rodents. It has been found to contain oils which, though masking cage smells, irritate the eyes and skin of many rodent pets. Aspen chips or shavings are recommended.

### What You Should Know

- Do not pick a mouse up by the tip of its tail.
  HANNA'S HINTS: You can hold its tail with thumb and forefinger close to where tail meets body; pick it up gently with thumb and forefinger behind its front legs; or, best of all, scoop it up supporting its feet.
- Mice must have something to gnaw on at all times because their teeth are constantly growing.
- Mice can stand on hind legs and on top of toys, so make sure that the walls of your pet's home are high enough to prevent a breakout when you're not around.
- Females are less odorous than males.
- Mice can breed at the age of two months.
- The gestation period for mice is three weeks.
- A female mouse (called a doe) is capable of breeding again the day after she has her litter—unless she is nursing.

- A male mouse should be removed from cage once the female is pregnant.
HANNA'S HINT: If you want a pair of mice, two males will fight, two females will
get along—and a male and a female will soon need a larger cage.

---

JACK'S FACTS: **You Call That a Rodent?**

The capybara, a member of the guinea pig family, is four feet tall, three feet wide, weighs up
to 100 pounds (over 200 pounds in captivity) and is the world's largest living rodent. Unlike
their cage-bound pet cousins, capybaras (also known as carpinchos or water hogs) are
aquatic. Shy and gentle, they head for water at the slightest sign of danger and—being expert swimmers and divers—they can remain underwater for several minutes. Quite a feat for
a rodent—and darn near impossible for a human.

---

## Rats Rate As Great Pets

Forget about "dirty rats" and "sewer rats." I'm talking about rats that have been
bred into high level of domesticity—serving as laboratory rats, show rats, and some
of the best pets people have ever owned.

PRO: They're intelligent, friendly, respond readily to humans, and are easily tamed.
They're small but not tiny (six to eight inches with an equally long tail), can recognize their names, perform tricks, and are as close to a dog as you can get in a
palm-sized pet.

CON: They live only for about three years. (If you're not into long-term pet commitment, this could be a positive thing.) Like mice, rats are also susceptible to fleas
and mites.

CREATURE COMFORTS: Cage with pullout bottom for cleaning or a ten- to twenty-
gallon glass aquarium with a screen top; nesting material such as *non-cedar* wood
chips or shavings (see note for mice above) or reprocessed paper litter; a gravity-
flow water bottle, food dish, toys, a nesting house, raw carrots, or non-toxic wood
to gnaw on.

DIET NEEDS AND TREATS: Specially formulated seed mix or compressed pellets;
nuts, bread, cabbage, apples, raisins. (See "Cautions," p. 137–138.)

### What You Should Know
- It is normal for rats to sneeze frequently. (*Though it is not necessary to say*
"Gesundheit.")

JACK'S FACTS:
**This Old Mouse**
The oldest caged
mouse on record is
Fritzy, a British subject
from Birmingham, En-
gland, who had its last
bite of cheese and
crumpets on September
11, 1985, at the age
of seven years, seven
months.

- Rats sleep a lot in the daytime.
- Rats will eat anything—but that doesn't mean you should let them.
- A pair of rats will keep each other company—two females are best unless you want to breed.
- Rats are fertile all year long.
- They can breed at about three months, gestation is about three weeks, and litters range between six and twenty-two babies (called pups).
- If handled regularly, rats will be eager for play with humans outside the cage.
- Unlike other rodents, pet rats rarely run away.
- They enjoy mazes and learning tricks (if food treats are the payoff).
- There are many different strains and colors available—including Dalmatian rats (spotted like the dog), Siamese rats ("pointed" like the cats) and numerous black-and-white combinations.
- Ceramic food dishes are advised because rats can easily gnaw through plastic.
- Older albino male rats, usually sold as snake food, are more difficult to tame.
- Male rats are larger than females, have coarse coats, and bear more of a resemblance to wild rats.
- Females are slender and sleek with wiry, but soft, fur coats.
- Once-a-week cage cleaning is usually all that's necessary—but it is necessary.

## Gerbils—Four Inches of Fun

They're larger than mice, smaller than rats, and they hop like bunnies!

PRO: They're lively daytime players; hardy, tamable, self-grooming, with potential life spans of three to four years.

CON: They will bite if startled or frightened; do not like being solitary pets; are susceptible to fleas and mites; tend to be too active for small children to handle.

CREATURE COMFORTS: A cage with pullout bottom for cleaning or a five- to ten-gallon aquarium with a screened top; nesting material such as non-cedar chips or shavings (see note for mice) or reprocessed paper litter; a gravity-flow water bottle, a ladder, exercise wheel, treadmill; non-toxic wooden sticks or raw carrots to gnaw on.

DIET NEEDS AND TREATS: Gerbil seed mix or pellet food; supplements of apple slices, corn, sweet hay, raisins, peas. (See "Cautions," p. 137–138.)

## What You Should Know

- Gerbils lick themselves clean, like cats, and should not be bathed.
- They are very social and are happiest when bought in pairs.
- Gerbils don't drink much water and urinate very little.
- Unless accustomed to being handled when young, mature gerbils may bite.
- Gerbils can breed when they are three months old.
- The gestation period is three and a half weeks.
- Gerbils have been known to be monogamous and may mate for life.
- Mature females will often defend territory and attack a male if it is placed in their cage.

## Hamsters—the Rodents with Relatives Everywhere

Virtually every hamster in this country is a golden hamster and descended from a single mother and her twelve offspring, which were discovered in Syria and brought here in 1930.

PRO: They're happy being alone; they don't overeat; they're amusing to watch on their treadmills or in a Habitrail environment; they're small (about five inches) and quiet.

CON: They're the rodents most likely to bite; if bored, they'll scatter litter everywhere; they're nocturnal and sleep during the day; they're susceptible to colds, mites, and lice.

CREATURE COMFORTS: A cage with a pullout bottom for cleaning—large enough for separate eating, sleeping, and eliminating areas; nesting material such as noncedar wood chips or shavings (see note for mice) or reprocessed paper litter; a gravity-flow water bottle, exercise wheel or Habitrail environment, treadmill, a sleeping box or nesting house, untreated hardwood sticks to chew on.

DIET NEEDS AND TREATS: Specially formulated hamster seed mix or pellets, nuts, seeds, raisins, carrots, apples, Brussels sprouts, turnips.

## What You Should Know

- The hamster's name comes from the German *hamstern*, to hoard—which is what these animals spend most of their lives doing. They stuff their cheek pouches with food to hide in a secure place—usually beneath the shredded paper or wood shaving in the cage.

- Until your pet is used to its cage and you, wear gloves when reaching into the cage.
- After cleaning your pet's cage, return some of the stored food to its location or your pet might get upset trying to find it.
- Limit moist food like lettuce, which can decay very quickly if hidden.
- Hamsters tend to urinate in the same spot every day. (*You're in luck if that spot is litter; you're not if the spot is your carpet.*)
- A full-grown hamster can fit through an opening the size of a quarter.
- An escaped hamster is not likely to return to its cage.
- A hamster can reproduce when she is just thirty-five days old! (Breeding is not recommended, though, until she is at least three or four months old.)
- Gestation is just sixteen days.
- Each litter can have seven to twelve hamsters.
- In only one year, a single pair can multiply into 100,000 hamsters!

## Guinea Pigs—Prime Primer Pets

PRO: They're cuddly, kitten-sized (about ten inches), gentle, easily tamed and relatively long-lived (about eight years).

CON: They're not the smartest rodents; they need to have their toenails clipped if they don't have access to rough surfaces; they're susceptible to fleas and mites.

CREATURE COMFORTS: A metal cage with a solid bottom, preferably one that slides out for easy cleaning. (Recommended cage size is two square feet for each guinea pig.) Bedding material such as a thick layer of non-cedar chips or shavings (see note for mice) or reprocessed paper litter; a gravity-flow water bottle; a slope to climb on; an outside hutch or run for grazing in warm weather.

DIET NEEDS AND TREATS: Vitamin C is essential for guinea pigs because, unlike other rodents, they cannot synthesize it. Guinea-pig pellets contain vitamin C, but C-rich treats such as kale, parsley, turnip greens, Brussels sprouts, collard greens, strawberries, and orange slices are recommended. And, of course, carrots sticks for gnawing. They also enjoy grasses, grains, and hay.

### What You Should Know
- Animal shelters often have guinea pigs for adoption.
- Guinea pigs are not climbers or jumpers.

- Guinea pigs do not have tails.
- They need a minimum of 10 mg. vitamin C daily. (Double that amount if pregnant or nursing.)
- Sneezing (unaccompanied by other symptoms) is normal in guinea pigs.
- A female guinea pig is called a sow and a male is called a boar.
- Though not recommended, guinea pigs can breed when only two months old.
- Gestation is approximately ten weeks.
- Babies are born with fur, teeth, and open eyes.
- Many antibiotics are toxic to guinea pigs.
- High-fat foods, such as nuts, are not recommended since guinea pigs have a tendency to "pig out" and become obese.
- They come with coats of many lengths and colors—Abyssinians have curly hair, Peruvians are long-haired, and silkies have hair that's medium-length.
- Guinea pigs can be neutered. (*NOTE:* Not all vets perform this surgery, but your local vet can probably direct you to one who is familiar with the procedure.)

---

**JACK'S FACTS: When Is a Pig Not a Pig?**

When it's a guinea pig! In fact, not only is a guinea pig not a pig, it's not even from Guinea. It is a species of cavy (*Cavia porcellus*), domesticated by the Indians of Peru—who prized it as an edible (not pettable) delicacy—long before the arrival of the Spaniards. Because cavies (as they're sometimes called) were imported into England from Guyana, and they do have piglike squeals, it is generally assumed that over the years the Guyana pigs of yore became your guinea pigs of today.

---

## Cautions to Keep in Mind for Rodents

- Feeding too many greens can give your pet diarrhea.
- Except for guinea pigs, don't feed oranges to your rodent pets.
- Wheels are great toys to keep rodent pets occupied, but make sure the one you buy is large enough for your pet when it's full-grown.
- Long rodent tails can get trapped and snapped off in wheels with wire spokes. (Look for spokeless or plastic wheels.)
- Steer clear of cedar bedding; the oils it contains can cause eye and skin irritations in small pets.

- Do not use shredded newspaper as bedding unless it uses *non-toxic ink*.
- Water dishes are great for dogs, but not rodents. They'll spill them, drop food in them, and often use them as toilets. (Buy a gravity-water bottle with a ball-bearing in the spout.)
- If you're making a cage, use only non-toxic material and steer clear of window screening which can trap wood dust.
- Avoid using wood as cage flooring—it soaks up urine.
- Hamster Habitrail environments are unsuitable for gerbils, who can gnaw holes through the walls.
- Do not put cages in direct sunlight.
- Keep your pets' homes out of drafty areas.
- Room temperatures should not be below 60° or above 90° Fahrenheit.
- When rodent pets are out, watch where you step—and make sure no other pets are around!
- If your guinea pig needs an antibiotic, makes sure your vet knows NOT to prescribe amoxicillin—it can kill your pet!

## Celebrity Rodent Owners and Their Palm-Size Pets

Some very big people had some very small pets. But, I've discovered, only a few have gone on record about them.

*Benjamin Franklin:* Amos (mouse)
*John F. Kennedy:* Billy, Debbie (hamsters)
*Gypsy Rose Lee:* Daisy, Jimmy, Samba, Sambo (guinea pigs)
*Theodore Roosevelt:* Admiral Dewey, Bishop Doan, Dr. Johnson, Father O'Grady, Fighting Bob (guinea pigs)
*Rudolph Valentino:* Ali, Babba (white mice)

In my travels I've been introduced to a lot of rodents with names I can't forget, so I'm listing them here in case you'd liked to keep them in mind, too.

*Gerbils:* Atom, Dot-Com, Micro, Minikin, Godzilla
*Guinea Pigs:* Mochadot, Titan, Swill, Roly, Poly, Tanker
*Hamsters:* Hamlet, Jambon, M.C. Hamster, Uncle Miltie, Encheese
*Mice:* Gotcha, Getcha, Betcha, Button, Ms. Pip
*Rats:* Artful Dodger, Loreena, Rizzo, Ivana, Heads, Tails

## Questions and Answers About Rodent Pets

### *Cheesy Dancers*

My uncle said that when he was a kid he had mice that waltzed. He's quite a joker, so I don't know whether to believe him. Have you ever heard of waltzing mice?

As a matter of fact—yes. But it's more of a birth defect than a ballroom-dancing feat. It occurs in mice with an inner-ear weakness that affects their balance and causes them frequently to stand on their hind legs and whirl around, giving the impression of waltzing.

### *Good Health in Small Packages*

My sister's guinea pig, Miss Muffin, is seven years old and has never been sick. Our dog, Jasper, on the other hand, is four and has been to the vet for skin infections at least three times and throws up or gets diarrhea at least once or twice a month. Are little pets less likely to get sick? Is it because they live in cages?

Little pets can get sick—just as big pets can—but because they're usually kept in a controlled environment it's easier to keep them healthy. Single pets, like your sister's guinea pig, are not likely to come down with communicable guinea pig diseases—such as coccidiosis (caused by parasites)—especially if the cage and food dishes are kept clean. But they can occur. (Excessive diarrhea, swollen belly, and lack of appetite are all warning signs.)

All small pets are subject to viral, bacterial, parasitic, and nutritional diseases. But keeping their living conditions sanitary, keeping a close eye on their coats for bald patches and redness, being aware of runny eyes, signs of diarrhea, and making sure that they're eating a complete and balanced diet according to their needs, should keep them happy and healthy throughout their lifetimes.

---

### JACK'S FACTS: **Five Top Books for Little Pet Owners**

*Guinea Pigs* by Katrin Behrind (Barron's)

*Hamsters* by Otto von Frisch (Barron's)

*Taking Care of Your Gerbils* by Helen Piers (Barron's)

*Gerbils as a New Pet* by Anmarie Barrie (T.F.H. Publications)

*A Petkeeper's Guide to Hamsters and Gerbils* by David Alderton (Tetra Press)

---

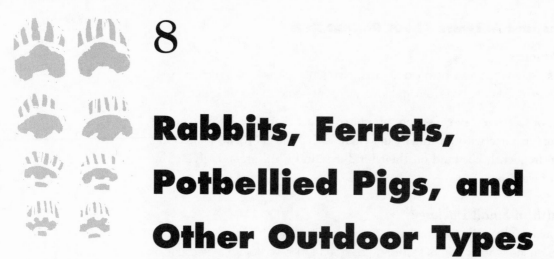

# 8

# Rabbits, Ferrets, Potbellied Pigs, and Other Outdoor Types

## Rabbits as Indoor Pets

When I was a kid, I had three female and two male rabbits. I raised them in outdoor hutches on our farm in Tennessee. They made great pets and they also made lots of rabbits. And no wonder. A female (doe) over the age of four months goes into heat just about every time she's with a male! Before long I had an intricate setup of forty rabbit hutches with runs and back doors, and about one hundred rabbits! (See p. 12.)

That's about ninety-nine rabbits too many for the average pet owner. (Believe me!) Especially if you're looking for an indoor animal companion.

But for the right people, rabbits make wonderful pets!

### *Seven Reasons to Consider Rabbits*

1. They can be kept in small apartments.
2. They don't have to be walked outside on cold and rainy days.
3. They can be litterbox-trained.
4. They are sociable and playful.
5. They enjoy sitting beside you—and will even purr when content.
6. Local animal shelters usually have a fine affordable selection.
7. There are over forty recognized breeds, in numerous color varieties, delightfully different personalities and sizes that range from two-pound dwarfs to twenty-pound giants.

### *What You Should Know*

- They have an average life span of seven to ten years, which means a substantial commitment to a pet.
- Like cats and dogs they should be spayed or neutered.
- Unneutered males will spray everywhere they can.
- Bunnies are delicate and not recommended as pets for young children.
- Pet rabbits must be let out of their cage for exercise and socialization with people at least a few hours every day.
- Unsupervised, rabbits can dig holes in carpets, chew furniture, clothing, and anything else they sink their teeth or claws into.
- Rabbits shed their fur every three months.
- Females weigh more than males.

## How to Recognize a Healthy Rabbit

The best way to recognize a healthy rabbit is to have a good idea of what more than one looks like. Before you make one a pet, check out local rabbit shows—4-H clubs, state or country fairs—and ask questions about the different breeds. For information on breeders and clubs in your area, you can contact the American Rabbit Breeders Association (ARBA), 1925 South Main Street, Bloomington, IL 61701.

## Hanna Quick-as-a-Bunny Health Scan

- Eyes should be bright and clear; no discharge.
- Ears should be clean and free of any dirt or foreign matter.
- Upper and lower teeth should close evenly. (Rabbit teeth grow continuously and must be ground down by chewing. If there is malocclusion—or "buck teeth"—they have to be clipped or ground down regularly or else they can prevent the rabbit from eating, causing it to starve.)
- Fur should look healthy and be free of matt or bald patches.
- Hindquarters should be clean, unsoiled by feces.
- Skin should be free of lumps, growth, or swellings.

## Breeding Tips

Male and female rabbits don't need any. And unless you're breeding for show or profit—don't. There are too many Easter Bunnies that never make it past spring break as it is.

JACK'S FACTS: **A Hare-Raising Difference**

When is a rabbit not a rabbit? When it's a hare. Hares and rabbits, though both members of the *Leporidae* family, differ in several ways. Hares generally have longer ears and hind legs than rabbits and tend to move by jumping rather than running. (Rabbits prefer to run rather than jump—unless, of course, it's for joy.) Another big difference is that rabbits are born blind and naked, while hares are born with fur and open eyes. And if you want to really get into splitting hares, I should mention that hares are wild and undomesticated, but the Belgian hare is domesticated because it's not a hare at all—it's a rabbit!

## Compatible—and Incompatible—Household Pets

### *Rabbits*

Two females will keep each other company, but add a male to the mix and you're in for . . . more rabbits.

**KEEP IN MIND**

- Rabbits are territorial, so if you're thinking of bringing home a buddy for your bunny, do it sooner rather than later. The longer you wait, the less likely your resident pet is to be pleased with a roommate.

### *Ferrets*

Ferrets were originally trained to drive rabbits from their burrows. Even without training, their games of hide-and-seek aren't those that you'd want played with your pet.

### *Cats*

Though rabbits aren't rodents (they're lagomorphs), they look an awful lot like meals to most felines.

**KEEP IN MIND**

- If you want both, introducing a kitten to a grown rabbit would be the way to go.
- Also, know that cats can terrify rabbits—even when they're protected in a cage.

### *Birds*

See p. 42.

### *Dogs*

It's not impossible for them to get along, but if the dog is a hunting breed, aggressive, or untrained, there are going to be problems. In any event, strict supervision is essential. (See Chapter 6.)

### *Children*

Children tend to expect more from rabbits than rabbits are capable of giving.

**KEEP IN MIND**

- Though domestic rabbits rarely bite, there are exceptions.

- Young rabbits must be handled gently. (Picked up by the withers and then scooped up, supporting the hindquarters.)

## Fish

All clear. Rabbits are not known as big swimmers—with the possible exception of the rabbit alleged to have attacked former President Jimmy Carter's fishing boat (most likely a member of the little known *Estherus Williams* species).

## Reptiles

If you have a large reptile, especially one that enjoys live entrees, I don't think détente should be expected—and play dates are out of the question.

---

JACK'S FACTS: **Let 'Em Eat What?**

I know this sounds strange, but it's true. It is all right to allow your rabbit to eat its feces. This is because gnawing animals have two types of excrement. One type is the product of an initial predigestion, soft and containing nutrients, that the animal can eat again to sustain itself. (This is what enables them in the wild to nourish themselves as well on a piece of wood as on a vegetable.) The second type is a hard excretory product that they never consume—and you get to clean up.

---

## Trouble Signs and Common Diseases

A single pet rabbit is less likely to get sick than one in a hutch, but knowing what to watch—and watch out—for is the best way to ensure a healthy pet.

COCCIDIOSIS: A common but serious parasitic disease characterized by loss of appetite, diarrhea, bloated belly, rough or dull coat, droopy ears, sitting in a hunched position.

*Best Prevention Measures:* Keep pet's cage clean; ask your vet about giving Sulfaquinoxaline sodium as a preventive.

DIARRHEA: This could be bloat or the parasitic disease coccidiosis (see above) or simply an upset tummy from too many greens, or the wrong greens for your pet (see list of potentially dangerous plants, p. 74). In any event, contact your vet for the proper antidiarrhetic dosage.

HANNA'S HINT: If an antibiotic is called for, be sure to mention to your vet, in case s/he is not used to treating rabbits, that you've read that amoxicillin can be deadly for rabbits. There are other, safer antibiotics available.

**EAR CANKER:** Caused by mites which burrow into the ear, causing ear scratching, itching, scabs, and droopy ears—and your pet is not a lop-eared rabbit.

*Best Prevention Measures:* Keep pet's cage clean; check ears regularly for dirt or discharge.

**HAIRBALLS:** Nope, they don't just afflict cats. Rabbits shed fur about every three months, and every other shedding is heavy. Since they groom themselves like cats, rabbits can ingest a LOT of fur, which can seriously gum up their systems. Their droppings will decrease in size, their stomachs will increase in size, but if you pet or stroke them you'll discover these animals are quite thin—and quite possible starving.

*Best Prevention Measures:* Brush and comb your pet regularly. Try the Petromalt hairball remedy recommended for cats on p. 69. Timothy hay is good roughage and can help as a preventive, as can alfalfa and exercise. Check with your vet on what other measures you can take that are suitable for your pets age and breed.

**SCRATCHING AND ITCHING:** Usually caused by mites, but if left untreated can cause sores, bald patches, and serious skin problems. Check with your vet for the best method of treatment.

*Best Prevention Measures:* Clean cage; keep other household pets flea- and mite-free.

**SNUFFLES:** Starts with sneezing. Could be a cold, could be nothing. But if your pet is rubbing its nose a lot and you see nasal discharge, call your vet.

*Best Prevention Measures:* Keep your pet's cage out of drafts.

## Cautions to Keep in Mind

- Keep rabbits off lawns that have been sprayed with pesticides or fertilizers.
- Never put rat poison in an area where your rabbit roams.
- Rabbits under five months of age should not be fed leafy greens.
- A cage with an all-wire floor could cause your pet to develop sore hocks or abscesses on its feet, especially if it enjoys thumping.
- Supervise your pet in any area where there are exposed cables, phone, or electrical wires it could sink its teeth into.
- Don't pick a rabbit up by its ears.

**JACK'S FACTS:**
**Red-Wetter Daze**
Rabbits can be perfectly healthy and have bright red urine. Unless your pet evidences other symptoms—loss of appetite, squinty eyes, straining at voiding, lethargy, fever, etc.—it is probably just having a red-wetter day.
**NOTE:** If it continues for more than a day, or if it doesn't seem normal for your pet, call your vet.

- If you do keep your pet (even part-time) in an outdoor hutch, make sure the enclosure has a sheltered nestbox and protection from wind and rain.
- Don't let your rabbit nibble rhubarb leaves, buttercups, or privet hedges; they are all potentially toxic. (See p. 74 for other hazardous plants.)
- Keep sugar treats away from your pet; too many can harm its digestive system.
- Never leave books, important papers, pencils, or pens on the floor when your pet is out and about.
- Be sure your rabbit has sufficient water and shade when outdoors.
- Never leave your rabbit unattended outside, even if it's in a fenced yard. (Cats can climb and dogs can jump.)
- Make sure water is fresh daily; stale water is unhealthy for your pet.
- Avoid buying more food than your pet can eat in six weeks; spoiled pellets can be hazardous to its health.
- Never feed your pet moldy hay or grasses.
- Make all dietary changes gradually to avoid digestive upsets.
- Introducing more than one fresh vegetable at a time to a rabbit's diet can cause diarrhea.
- Never store opened food in warm, moist areas.
- When you're not around, make sure other pets cannot terrorize your rabbit in its cage; they could literally frighten it to death.
- Never add vitamin supplements to a nutritionally complete pelleted food unless advised to do so by a veterinarian.
- Do not use cedar chips or shavings as bedding materials. They contain volatile oils that can irritate eyes, skin, and possibly cause serious liver damage to your pet.
- Apple-tree twigs are good roughage, but make sure they are not from a tree that has been sprayed with pesticides.

### JACK'S FACTS: **What a Woolly Wabbit**

Angora rabbits, usually white, look like large, silky cotton balls with appetites. Their fur is generally used to spin into wool, and you can make a sweater from your pet's fur if you like matching outfits. But even if you don't, Angoras still make fine pets—that is, if you're up to the extra grooming that's required. The length of their coat is about three inches, so they tend to look larger than they actually are, which is generally around six to nine pounds. Of course, when you discover that the saved wool you comb and brush from your pet is enough for one short-sleeved sweater a year, you might want to take up knitting after all!

## Rabbits by Breed

PRO: All breeds are essentially good-natured, friendly, affectionate, and litter-trainable—although individual personalities vary. They come in dwarf, small, medium, and giant sizes. Rabbits also come in three different fur types: *Normal* (about one-inch long, underfur dense, coat quickly returns to normal when stroked from tail to head); *Rex* (only about ⅜ inch, with top and undercoat the same length; plush velvetlike fur, found only on Rex rabbits, which are not yet available in all sizes); *Satin* (about one-inch long, characterized by its remarkable luster and intense color, currently found only on medium-sized rabbits).

CON: They shed, they need supervision outside of their cages, their personalities change as they mature. (See "What You Should Know," p. 141.)

CREATURE COMFORTS: As a house pet, your rabbit should have a cage with a floor that is at least partially solid—a piece of Plexiglass—or one made with galvanized wire that won't hurt your pet's feet. A three-by-three-foot cage with a removable tray for easy cleaning is recommended for pets that will spend most of their days confined. Non-plastic, heavy food dish, water dish, gravity-flow water bottle, non-cedar bedding materials, litterbox, hard plastic infant toys, or clean frozen-juice cans.

DIET NEEDS AND TREATS: Nutritionally balanced rabbit pellets are best, but you can add fresh vegetables (slowly) to your pet's diet as treats—broccoli, carrots, carrot tops, celery, clover, dandelion greens, kale, parsley, spinach, watercress—along with alfalfa and timothy hay. Commercially prepared treats should be offered in moderation. Fresh water is a necessity.

## Most Popular Giants

CHECKERED GIANT: White body with black ears, nose, and circles around the eyes. Also black spots on cheeks, sides, and hindquarters with a wide stripe down its spine. (Available in black and blue varieties.) Weight ranges between twelve and fifteen pounds.

FLEMISH GIANT: Powerful, long, and big—the world's largest. Flowing arched back with thick hindquarters. (Available in light gray, steel gray, sandy, blue, white, fawn, and black varieties.) Can weigh up to twenty pounds!

GIANT CHINCHILLA: Large, long, and lustrous, weighing between twelve and sixteen pounds, its coat is a luxurious gray ticked with black.

## Most Popular Medium Sizes

**CALIFORNIAN:** Plump, firm, and white, with nicely marked dark ears and nose, weighing between nine and twelve pounds.

**CHAMPAGNE D'ARGENT:** One of the oldest breeds. Name does not come from color, but from the province breed is said to have originated in. (In fact, the name means "silver rabbit from Champagne.") Well-rounded, with large hindquarters, weighing between nine and twelve pounds.

**ENGLISH LOP:** The ears have it, being a minimum of eighteen inches from tip to tip! These flop-eared sweet things tend to sweep their lop siders into everything from water dishes to litter and can make a bit of a mess, but they are delightful pets, weighing between nine and ten pounds.

**FRENCH LOP:** A thickset, Gérard Depardieu type with ears that hang vertically (soulfully) close to the cheeks. The outer part of the ears are markedly convex, slightly resembling horseshoes. Like their English relatives, the French Lop weighs between nine and ten pounds.

**NEW ZEALAND WHITE:** A well-rounded body and personality, weighing between nine and twelve pounds, and all white. (It also comes in recognized black and red varieties.)

**REX:** These velvety-furred rabbits come in white, black, blue, brown, golden, fawn, or mixtures of orange and silver or blue with a tan undercoat. Weight ranges between approximately eight and twelve pounds.

**SATIN:** An American breed with nine recognized varieties (black, blue, Californian, chinchilla, chocolate, copper, red, Siamese, and white) all said to have been developed from a litter of chocolate Havana rabbits in the 1930s. Weight ranges from eight to twelve pounds. All Satin coats are more lustrous than those of other rabbits, with the exception of the Tan.

## Most Popular Small Sizes

**DUTCH BLACK:** A compact bunny, smooth, rounded, and sleek, with white forehead, nose, shoulders, chest, and forelegs, and black eyes, ears, and hindquarters. Weight ranges from three and a half to six and a half pounds. (Other varieties include the Dutch blue, chocolate, tortoise, steel gray, and gray.)

ENGLISH SPOT: Cute and quirky colored—a white body with black, blue, chocolate, gray, gold, lilac, or tortoise spots. The spots on its head also appear on its nose, ears, cheeks, and as circles around the eyes—and then there's a spine marking that trails from ear base to the tip of its tail. Though considered a small breed, it can weigh between five and eight pounds.

HAVANA: An ever-popular breed, with ultralustrous, medium-length dense fur. Glossy chocolate-brown, with dark toenails, it's a pettable pet. Weighing between four and seven pounds, the Havana (standard in its chocolate color) is also available in blue.

SILVER MARTEN (BLACK): Glossy, extremely dense jet-black fur, with silver-tipped guard hairs. Large for a small, with weight ranging from six and a half to nine and a half pounds. Though most popular in black, silver martens come in blue, chocolate, and sable varieties.

TAN: Known for the unsurpassed luster of its outer hair, its tan undercolor is combined either with black, blue, chocolate, or dove gray. Weight generally ranges between four and seven pounds.

## Most Popular Dwarf Varieties

NETHERLAND DWARF: The smallest of all rabbits—with the widest variety of colors—it weighs two and a half pounds (or less) when fully mature.

POLISH: An itty-bitty delight. Pure white and under three pounds.

OTHERS UNDER THREE POUNDS: AMERICAN FUZZY LOP, BRITANNIA PETITE, DWARF HOTOT, HOLLAND LOP, and JERSEY WOOLLY.

HANNA'S HINT: If you have an aversion to rodents, and limited space for pets, these dwarf varieties of lagomorphs might be just what you're looking for!

## Ferreting Out the Truth About Ferrets

They're members of the *Mustelidae* family, related to minks, ermines, polecats, weasels, badgers, skunks, otters, and other fur-flaunting wild animals, but don't hold that against them; as pets, they're somewhere between cats and dogs. But as anyone who has ever gotten between a cat and dog knows, that could be trouble. Ferrets are definitely not for everyone.

## *What You Should Know*

- At this writing, ferrets are illegal in California, Massachusetts, Hawaii, Washington, D.C.; many cities in Texas, including Dallas, Fort Worth, San Antonio, and Beaumont; Bloomington and Burnsville, Minnesota; Tulsa, Oklahoma; and Salt Lake City, Utah.
- You need a permit to own a ferret in New York, New Jersey, Rhode Island, and parts of Minnesota.
- Just because your local pet store sells ferrets, doesn't mean they are either legal or permitted without a permit. (Check with your local Wildlife Agency, Department of Fish and Game, Department of Natural Resources or humane society.)
- They need vaccinations against rabies and canine distemper.
- They *need* to be spayed or neutered.
- Unspayed females can die when they go into heat if they are not bred.
- Unneutered males will mark territory with a smelly slime.
- Ferrets are not recommended as pets for children.
- Ferrets require cautious handling—be careful: ferret bites really hurt!
- They have an average lifespan of six to ten years, which is a commitment that deserves serious consideration.

## How to Recognize a Healthy Ferret

If there is a ferret club in your area, I'd strongly advise checking with them on the best places to obtain a healthy ferret. Though many local human shelters become the recipients of unwanted ferrets, there might be a reason why these ferrets were rejected by their owners. Although I am strongly in favor of rescuing animals, I think you should know if you're letting yourself in for more pet care than you care to handle.

### *Fast Ferret Health Scan*

- Eyes should be clear and alert; free of discharge.
- Ears should be free of blackish spots or scabs.
- Whiskers should be long and unbroken.
- Coat should be soft, no bald spots.

## Breeding Tips

Breeding ferrets requires a lot of experience and work. Most veterinarians recommend that the average pet owner leave this type of multiplication to the experts—and I couldn't agree more.

## Compatible—and Incompatible—Household Pets

### Ferrets

Ferrets do get along with other ferrets—of either sex—provided both sexes are neutered.

### Rabbits

Nope. (See p. 143.)

### Cats

Ferrets have been known to get along with cats if they're introduced as kittens—but there are no guarantees. (And I wouldn't advise leaving them alone together.)

### Dogs

They can get along, depending on your dog's breed, personality, training, and size—but if your ferret is out of its cage, human supervision is advised.

### Mice, Hamsters, and Small Rodents

No, no, and no. Ferrets were originally bred to ferret them out (along with rabbits), and it was not just a game of hide-and-seek.

### Children

Ferrets are not advised as pets for children, and they could be dangerous to toddlers and infants.

**KEEP IN MIND**
- Children *must* be taught how to handle pet ferrets if they share a household.
- Never leave a child alone with a ferret.
- With proper introductions, instruction—and supervision—a responsible older child and a ferret can become friends.

JACK'S FACTS:
**Spay for Life**
It is estimated that 90 percent of all unspayed female ferrets who are not bred will die during their first year of life!

## Birds

Ferrets and birds do not make good buddies. (A caged canary that can be reached by a free-roaming ferret is essentially a sitting duck.)

## Reptiles

Not ferret-friendly—and vice versa.

### KEEP IN MIND

- As small and cute as ferrets are, they are still carnivores and capable of killing prey that's many times their size.

## Fish

If your tank is out of paw's reach—and covered—your fish should be all right. But ferrets can get into a lot of mischief, so if you don't want your favorite tropical specimens to become sushi, keep your ferret on a leash when out of its cage.

JACK'S FACTS:
**Adopt-a-Ferret**
If your child wants a ferret, but you don't, there are adoption alternatives. Check with nearby ferret clubs or local humane society and rescue services.

## Trouble Signs and Common Diseases

ADRENAL GLAND DISEASE: Characterized by hair loss, itching, and flaky skin, it is a condition where the adrenal glands on the kidneys become enlarged. A special blood test is necessary and surgery is recommended.

EPIZOOTIC CATARRHAL ENTERITIS (ECE) OR MYSTERY GREEN SLIME VIRUS: A failure in the ferret's intestinal tract that causes twenty-four-hour vomiting and then green diarrhea. Highly contagious among ferrets, it can be cured by preventing dehydration and preserving nutrients. Once recovered, ferrets develop an immunity (or are subject only to mild relapses).

INSULINOMAS (PANCREATIC CELL TUMORS): Very low blood sugar, evidenced by extreme lethargy, rear leg weakness, and pawing at the mouth. Medication and/or surgery is recommended. Early detection increases survival chances.

LYMPHOSARCOMA (LSA): Characterized by weight loss, enlarged lymph nodes behind the front legs, and lethargy, this common ferret cancer is deadly—but there is hope for survival if diagnosed early.

## Cautions to Keep in Mind

- Ferrets love to steal and hide small objects (earrings, paper clips, car keys) under furniture and other unreachable places around the house.
- Because they are burrowing animals, ferrets can do nasty things to nice carpets.
- Ferrets should not be allowed to roam outside without a harness and lead.
- If you walk your ferret outdoors, ask your veterinarian about the advisability of heartworm medication.
- If you forget to wash or change your ferret's bedding twice a week, your nose is going to remind you.
- Ferrets are susceptible to heat exhaustion and stroke, so be sure to keep your pet's cage out of direct sunlight.
- Don't keep the temperature of your pet's room above 80° F.
- Uncovered outlets, cables, phone cords, and electrical wires can be hazardous to a free-roaming ferret.
- Do not feed your pet chocolate.
- Foods that contain sugar, milk or are high in fiber are potentially harmful ferret treats.
- Do not add vitamin supplements to a nutritionally balanced food—unless advised to do so by a veterinarian.
- Foods that contain high levels of vegetable protein—soyflour, soybean meal, corn or wheat gluten—are not good for your ferret.
- Ferrets can squeeze through tiny one-inch holes.
- Ferrets have nails like dogs and should not be declawed.
- Safety gates will *not* keep a ferret from reaching a baby.
- Vaccinations may cause adverse reactions in some ferrets, so it is advisable to remain at the vet's office for at least twenty minutes after your pet receives its shots.

### JACK'S FACTS:
### Fast Food
Because of their fast metabolisms, whatever ferrets eat passes through them every three to four hours!

## Are Ferrets for You?

PRO: They're friendly, quiet, apartment sized, playful, intelligent, litter-trainable, live six to ten years, enjoy hanging on your shoulder, living with or without other ferrets.

CON: They're fiercely independent, unpredictable, *need* to be neutered, have strong spray odor, require grooming, are illegal in some states, require licenses in other states, don't get along with many household pets (see p. 151) and are not recommended for children.

**CREATURE COMFORTS:** Though ferrets don't mind living alone, they do work and play well with other ferrets of either sex. A tall wire cage (that locks securely and is easily cleaned) large enough for ferrets to climb around in; double-decker models are preferred; ferret hammock, ramps, food dish and gravity-flow water bottle; litter-box, bedding, ferret toys, play tunnels.

**DIET NEEDS AND TREATS:** Nutritionally complete ferret food. Occasional snacks of flaked or puffed corn, wheat or oat cereals (dry).

## Ferret Specifications

**SIZE:** Males about fifteen inches; females fourteen inches

**WEIGHT:** Males three to five pounds; females one and a half to three pounds

**COLORS:** albino, sable (most common), siamese (a lighter sable), butterscotch, cinnamon (this color ferret said to be most docile), silver mitt, sterling silver

**LONGHAIRED ANGORA FERRETS:** orange, black, pastel, and albino colors

---

**JACK'S FACTS: Ferret Relatives on the Brink**

Though the popularity of ferrets as pets is on the rise, the ferret's closest wild cousin, the black-footed ferret, still remains on the brink of extinction. Intensive captive breeding with hopes of reintroducing this species back into the wild is continuing, and despite setbacks (including decimation of its natural prey, the prairie dog), wildlife professionals believe there is hope for success. Nonetheless, at this writing, the black-footed ferret retains the dubious distinction of being "the most endangered mammal in North America."

---

## Miniature Potbellied Pigs as Pets

Originally from the jungles of Vietnam and China, these mini porkers were introduced to the United States as pets around the mid 1980s. Unique, bright, and clean, they quickly became popular, eye-catching, and hip animal companions, and were soon crowned by the media as "Yuppie Puppies."

## *Potbellied Pluses*

- They're viable pets for asthmatics or anyone allergic to cats and dogs.
- They can be litter-trained or housebroken.
- They can be taught cute tricks.
- They're compatible with children and most other pets.
- They can be kept indoors or outdoors with proper shelter.
- They can be walked on a leash.
- They are virtually odor-free.

## *What You Should Know*

- Some residential zoning laws prohibit keeping potbellied pigs as pets.
- Locating a companion animal veterinarian who is familiar with pigs can be difficult in urban areas.
- Hoof-trimming is necessary because minipigs do not wear them down enough on carpets, wood floors, or linoleum to keep up with nail growth.
- They require soil or soft dirt to satisfy their natural rooting instincts—or else they'll dig where they must and quickly turn your lawn or living room into a pigsty.
- They require supervision around children and other pets (and vice versa) until everyone gets acquainted.
- Males need regular tusk-trimming.
- Their canine teeth should be removed for safety's sake. (Everyone's safety.)
- A fully grown male can weigh ninety-five pounds and live for eighteen years.

## Breeding Tips

Before you even consider it, speak to professionals who'll explain why it's not something that average pet owners should attempt without A LOT of pre-planning.

## How to Recognize a Healthy Potbellied Pig

Let me state right off, a fat pig is not a healthy pig. Just because potbellied pigs have potbellies doesn't mean they should be obese. Too much weight is just as unhealthy for a pet pig as it is for a human or any animal companion.

JACK'S FACTS
**Pigs-a-Poppin'**
The Potbellied Pig Registry, created in 1988 to track the bloodlines of the nation's newest pet, had found 23,000 in 1995. At this writing (a year later), experts estimate that there could be about one million pet pigs in the U.S.

### The Quick Pig Health Check

- Eyes should be clear, free of discharge.
- Ears should be erect, clean, and free of any sores.
- No fat rolls on face.
- Body should have no offensive odor.
- Skin should be free of scaly patches, crusts, or lesions.
- Ribs should not be seen, but able to be felt easily.
- Jaw should be visible and not hidden by jowls.

## Trouble Signs and Common Diseases

Most pet owners know when their pet is ailing, but sometimes we don't realize there is a problem until too late. The following trouble signs should not be ignored.

### Your Pig Might Be Sick If . . .

- there are noticeable changes in its behavior.
- its breathing is rapid.
- it remains lying down for more than eight hours.
- diarrhea continues for more than a day.
- constipation is unrelieved for more than two days.
- skin looks bumpy.
- blood appears in stool.
- food is refused for more than twenty-four hours.
- gait is unsteady or labored.

### Common Health Problems

ATROPHIC RHINITIS: Upper respiratory tract infection characterized by sneezing. In severe cases there is nasal bleeding, eye discharge, and possible distortion of the snout or twisting of the upper jaw. May be carried by dogs, cats, and rodents.

*Best Prevention Measure:* Vaccination!

MANGE: Caused by mites and characterized by itching, hair loss, dandruff, red skin, and similar dermatologic problems.

*Best Prevention Measure:* Regular grooming and bathing.

PNEUMONIA: An upper respiratory infection, often characterized by coughing, that can be mild or severe depending upon the strain.

*Best Prevention Measures:* Dry and draft-free housing; no fraternization with un-known pigs.

SEBORRHEA: Overactivity of the sebaceous (oil) glands on the skin, causing crust-ing and scaling.

*Best Prevention Measure:* Regular brushing and grooming.

HANNA'S HINT: As thick-skinned as you might think potbellied pigs are, they're prime candidates for sunburn and frostbite. Sunblock is recommended; snow play is not.

## Going Whole Hog for Potbellied Pigs

PRO: They are bright, trainable, non-shedding, non-allergenic, and bond happily with humans.

CON: They need attention, training, vets who know their needs, hoof-trimming; they are considered livestock in many areas and may be illegal to own (see "What You Should Know," p. 155).

CREATURE COMFORTS: A bed if indoors; a shelter and run if spending time out-doors; food and water dishes; soft-bristle grooming brush; a special area to indulge its natural rooting instincts; a litterbox (if not housebroken for the outside); har-ness and leash for walks.

DIET NEEDS AND TREATS: A commercially prepared, nutritionally complete, and balanced food; regular mealtimes; fresh water; fresh fruit and vegetable treats.

### *The Skinny on Potbellied Pets*
- Their expected lifespan is twelve to eighteen years.
- Their expected height is twelve to eighteen inches.
- They weigh in at anywhere between thirty and ninety-five pounds full grown.
- They have a great sense of smell, which compensates for their poor eyesight.
- Vaccinations are required. (Pigs do not need rabies vaccine and Lyme disease vaccine is not approved for pigs. Ask your vet about possible adverse reactions to any shot—*before* your pig gets it!)
- Don't feed your pig dog or cat food—it's too high in protein and calories.
- Taking your minipig for walks on concrete will cut down on the need for hoof-trimming.

- Pigs reach puberty at about six months of age; spaying or neutering is recommended before your pet starts rooting around for company.
- Training your pig gently, but early on, to accept you (and your family members) as the Head Honchos in the home pen will prevent pigheaded dominance struggles later on.

## The Scoop on Pet Skunks

Skunks bred as domestic pets can be animal companions—but not for everyone. (Personally, I don't recommend them for anyone.) They are high-maintenance, not suitable for children, or for multipet households—particularly those that include mice, rats, or birds (which omnivorous skunks in the wild tend to view as dinners). You must remember that just because an animal is bred in captivity does not make it domesticated; that's a process that takes thousands of years.

### *Sniffin' Out the Facts*

- Pet skunks are illegal in many states and counties. (Check with your local wildlife agency.)
- Some states allow you to keep a pet skunk only if you have captured it on your property. *(Good luck!)*
- Pet skunks are sold descented—but they still have a musky smell and NEED to be spayed or neutered. CAUTION: Unspayed females may die if not mated during their heat cycle. Unneutered males become aggressive when mature. Also, they bite during mating, which could be a painful problem if they mistake the socks you're wearing for a gal pal.
- The expected lifespan of a hand-reared skunk is five to ten years (though there are reports of some that have lived twice that).
- They can be litter-trained—if they approve of where the litter box is placed.
- They have very sharp teeth and will bite, especially if frightened or hit. (Skunks do not take spankings lightly—and have been known to retaliate by soiling their owner's bed or favorite chair.)
- They need vaccinations. (Check with your veterinarian.)
- They will come when they're called *if* they think there is food involved. (To a skunk, an electric can opener sounds like a dinner bell.)
- Aside from your basic black and white, skunks come in colors that range from browns and grays, to snow white, blonde, and even lavender—with two, four, even six stripes (sometimes spots, too) and different-shaped tails.

- They're usually quiet, but if they're frightened or angry they'll outscreech a Siamese in heat!
- They are nocturnal, and more active in the evenings.
- Though domestic skunks don't hibernate during the winter months, they do slow down and tend to be lethargic.
- They need a large cage with a nesting box to provide privacy, as well as dishes for water and food.
- Diet consists mainly of vegetables, with small portions of boiled or broiled chicken or turkey, high-fiber cereals, lamb and rice-based low-protein dog food, an occasional dog biscuit. (Check with a vet on best diet and treats for your particular pet.)
- Foods with preservatives, such as MSG, chocolate, high-protein cat food, and raw beef, should not be given to pet skunks.

## Pet Names and Some Celebrities Who Claimed Them
*Fred Astaire:* Thumper (rabbit)
*John F. Kennedy:* Zsa Zsa (rabbit)
*Abraham Lincoln:* Pig (pig) (*Not inspired, but those were simpler times.*)
*Luke Perry:* Jerry Lee and Violet (potbellied pigs)
*Vincent Price:* Phew (skunk)
*Ginger Rogers:* Harvey (rabbit)
*Theodore Roosevelt:* Maude (pig); Peter (rabbit)
*Mae West:* Lil (rabbit)

And some other memorable pet names, whose owners' names I've forgotten:

*Rabbits:* Hopper, Bun-Bun, Buckaroo, Bugs, Roger, Quicken
*Ferrets:* Flash, Festor, Toupee, Epaulet, Terminator
*Potbellied Pigs:* Keg, Rasher, Hitchcock, Orson, Preggers
*Skunks:* Pew, Skedaddle, Nosetradamus, Odorable, Stinkerbell

## Questions and Answers About Rabbits, Ferrets, Potbellied Pigs, and Other Outdoor Types

### Ferret Bathing
Is there any trick to getting a ferret to like a bath? My little one-year-old, Fleetwood, hates it!

Your little Fleetwood is not alone. I've yet to meet a ferret that *likes* a bath. Generally, they get to tolerate it. It's best if you start when the ferret is very young, before it develops negative attitudes about grooming. A good idea is to not let it splash around in the tub (they're ferrets, not fish). Besides, you don't have to totally submerge the little critters to get them clean. Sponge-bath style works fine, and no more than twice a month is necessary. Your local pet store should carry a ferret shampoo (if not, a cat shampoo will do). Towel-drying, some sweet talk, and a couple of kisses should make the experience a lot better—for both of you.

### What You Can Get from Your Rabbit

My ten-year-old son wants a rabbit as a pet. If I buy him one, is there anything he can get from it?

Aside from a lot of pleasure, not much. In fact, the only disease I can think of would be ringworm (see p. 94). This is a parasitic disease that's characterized by patchy hair on your pet (young animals are especially susceptible). The best preventive is having your son wash his hands after handling the rabbit and keeping the rabbit's living quarters clean. If you notice scratching and hair loss on the rabbit, call the vet; if you notice it on your son; call the pediatrician. It's curable for both.

### Digging for Love

I know pigs have a great sense of smell, but what is it about truffles that sets them digging? They don't seem to have any unusual odor to me.

If you were a sow, they would. According to Diane Ackerman, in her book *A Natural History of the Senses*, researchers have discovered that truffles contain twice as much androstenol (a studly male pig hormone) than most male pigs. So when the female puts her snout to the ground, suddenly she's in pig heaven. Convinced that the hog of her dreams is hiding down there, she starts digging like mad only to discover that her hunk-to-be is nothing more than, well, a mushroom. Undaunted (and obviously unspayed) she'll try again and again. Frustrating for her, but lucky for everyone who enjoys truffles.

## Rabbit, Ferret, and Potbellied Pig Talk Owners Should Know

ALOPECIA: loss of hair

BARROW: a castrated male pig

BOAR: a male pig used for breeding purposes

BREED: a race or class of rabbits which is distinguished by fur color, markings, shape, size, and growth

BUCK: a male rabbit

BUCKTEETH: teeth that protrude beyond others; usually hereditary

BUNNY: a colloquial term for a baby rabbit, which is usually called a kit

CINNAMON: a ferret color of rich reddish-brown in which the underfur is white

COBBY: short and stocky rabbit type

DESCENTING: removal of ferret's anal scent glands to prevent it from releasing its strong-smelling spray

DEWLAP: a loose fold of skin hanging from the throat

DOE: a female rabbit

DWARF: rabbit weighing no more than three pounds when full-grown

FLY BACK: fur which returns to normal when stroked from tail to ears (*round-trip fur*)

GIANT: rabbit weighing twelve to sixteen pounds when full-grown

GIB: a neutered male ferret

HOB: an unneutered male ferret

HOCK: the section of the hindleg between foot and hip, thickly padded with fur

JILL: an unspayed female ferret

JUNIOR: a rabbit not yet six months old

KINDLE: to give birth to a litter (*what happens when two rabbits re-light that old flame*)

KIT: a baby ferret or rabbit

MARKED: a rabbit with a fur pattern of two or more colors

MEDIUM BREED: rabbit weighing nine to twelve pounds when full-grown

MOLTING: shedding fur

**RACY:** a slender rabbit body type, alert and active

**REGISTRATION:** official examination and recording of rabbit pedigree by ARBA registrar

**REX:** rabbits with short, plush fur

**SABLE:** a ferret coat color in which the markings and mask resemble that of a raccoon

**SATIN:** rabbits with extremely lustrous coats due to transparent hair shaft

**SENIOR:** a rabbit over six months old in a breed under ten pounds; over eight months old in a breed over ten pounds

**SOW:** female pig

**SPRITE:** a spayed female ferret

**STRAIN:** a line of rabbits within a breed evidencing distinguishing characteristics

**TRIO:** a buck and two does

**UNDERCOLOR:** fur color next to skin

**WHITE-FOOTED SABLE:** a sable-colored ferret with four white feet, sometimes with a white throat patch

---

JACK'S FACTS: **Five Top Books on Rabbits, Ferrets, and Potbellied Pigs**

*Ferrets as a New Pet* by Greg Ovechka (T.F.H. Publications)

*Rabbits as a Hobby* by Bob Bennett (T.F.H. Publications)

*A Petkeeper's Guide to Rabbits and Guinea Pigs* by David Alderton (Tetra Press)

*The Complete Guide to Ferrets* by James McKay (Swan Hill Press)

*Potbellied Pigs: Mini-pig Care and Training Manual* by Kayla Mull and Lorrie Boldrick (All Publishing, CA)

---

# 9

# Leapin' Lizards—
# Reptiles and Amphibians

### For Goodness Snakes

For anyone with limited space and unlimited curiosity about another species, snakes make fascinating pets. Before making one your pet, though, be sure to read up on all that you're letting yourself in for. (See "Five Top Books for Owners of Cold-Blooded Pets," p. 181.) Buying a captive bred snake from a reputable pet store or breeder is the recommended route for beginners. Unless you are a seasoned herpetologist, snaring a snake on a trip to the country to keep as a *city* pet is not a good idea (you can literally scare the you-know-what out of a garter snake, and, boy, will you know it). And, be forewarned, attempting to snare one from another country could land *you* in a cage!

### *The Cold-Blooded Facts*

PRO: They're quiet, don't require play with humans (or other snakes); come in magnificent color varieties; require simple housing; have the hypnotic appeal of an exotic pet.

CON: They are confirmed carnivores and the larger the snake the larger the preferred entrée (which could mean a mouse or a rat) and some prefer their meals alive; attention must be paid to maintain proper cage temperature; they won't come when called or perform tricks.

CREATURE COMFORTS: A converted aquarium with a Peg-Board top, a plastic storage box with enough airholes for proper ventilation, or a store-bought plastic cage all make fine vivariums. (Recommended sizes are ½ square foot of floor space per foot of snake for reptiles up to six feet; ¾ square foot of floor space for snakes six to nine feet long—and a minimum increase of 24 percent for each additional snake.) Experts recommend *not* using wire mesh or screening on cages because snakes can rub their noses raw on it. Also, a cage floor covering of newspaper, gravel, outdoor carpeting or shredded aspen chips. (See "Cautions," p. 168.) Plus a water bowl, a hiding place (cereal box with hole in it, an inverted clay flowerpot with a drainage hole), some rocks, tree branches, or a log. A heater or light to keep cage at 80–85° Fahrenheit, a thermometer to check cage temperature, and an in-cage gradient that allows the snake to decide when it wants to be warmer or cooler. Habitat should be kept clean and draft-free.

DIET NEEDS AND TREATS: Forget the veggies—all snakes are carnivores. Depending on the size and species of your snake, foods range from live insects, crickets, fish, rodents, birds, rabbits—even other snakes—to frozen (but completely thawed) or fresh-killed versions of the same. (CAUTION: If not devoured rapidly—or at least within an hour—living prey should be removed from the cage. Live mice or rats can injure and even kill captive snakes.) Most adult snakes can go for several weeks without food, but in captivity fare best on medium-sized meals once a week. Young, growing snakes should eat more often.

## Most Popular Pet Snakes

**BOA CONSTRICTORS:** They are large, generally docile; non-poisonous; ovovivipa-rous (meaning they give birth to live young); related to anacondas (which are "water boas" and much more unpredictable in temperament). Length varies ac-cording to species (average large adult red-tails may reach ten to fifteen feet) and there are quite a few species to choose from. They have no fangs, but do have strong jaws and long teeth that they use to penetrate the skins of their prey. Most captive breeds prefer freshly killed or frozen (but completely thawed) rodents or chicks. Well-cared for, boas can live more than twenty years.

HANNA'S HINT: Tree boas and others often referred to as "specialized" are high-maintenance, not particularly people-friendly, and should be kept only by seasoned herpers.

**PYTHONS:** Cousins to the boas, available in dwarf and giant varieties, they are oviparous (meaning they lay eggs instead of birthing live young). There are many different species of pythons, some more suited than others to being kept as pets. Captive bred blood pythons (adults five to six feet), adjust readily to caged condi-tions, as do Burmese pythons (adults eighteen to twenty feet). Ball pythons (three to four feet) get their name from coiling into a ball when threatened (a hiding box is essential). African or rock pythons can live up to thirty years in captivity, but even when "tame" need careful handling. Children's pythons are small (adults less than three feet long), have generally good dispositions, but they are *not* meant as playthings for youngsters.

HANNA'S HINT: Speak to owners, herpetologists, and read everything you can on pythons before making any one a pet.

**KINGSNAKES:** Among the most popular snakes as pets, there are half a dozen differ-ent species and almost three dozen subspecies to choose from. In captivity, they happily dine on freshly killed or frozen (thoroughly thawed) rodents. In the wild, they also eat snakes—including venomous species, such as copperheads and rat-tlers, as well as bird and reptile eggs. The average-size adult is three to four feet long. Estimated captive life spans are often more than fifteen, sometimes twenty years.

**MILK SNAKES:** Slimmer members of the Kingsnake family and popular as reptile pets. Brilliantly colored, they are happy in dry cages equipped with a hiding place and burrowing materials. Owners vouch for their good dispositions—and life spans of more than fifteen years.

**RED RAT SNAKES A.K.A. CORN SNAKES:** Hardy, popularly bred snake pets with good temperaments. Happy in dry, creature-comforted cages (see p. 164) with diets of freshly killed or frozen (thoroughly thawed) rodents (though in the wild they constrict their prey), they are brilliantly colored and available in variations of black, white, and yellow as well as red.

HANNA'S HINT: Most species and subspecies of captive bred rat snakes fare well as reptile pets.

**GARTER SNAKES:** They're active night and day, vary in adult length from fifteen to thirty inches (though there are some species that grow to four feet long), eat live or dead insects, worms, frogs, salamanders, and minnows, and do very well in cages that are kept dry.

HANNA'S HINT: Yes, garter snakes are non-venomous, but that doesn't mean they won't bite. If frightened or startled, they often will bite, and the wound will probably bleed more than you expect because garter snakes have an anti-coagulant factor in their saliva.

**OTHER SNAKES:** There are over 3,000 species of snakes living today. It would be impractical (if not practically impossible) to list them all, especially since the vast majority do not make good pets. But if you're interested in learning more about herpetology, raising snakes as companions (or breeding them), I'd suggest you check out the books recommended at the end of this chapter as well as contact The Herpetological Society for your state or region (local libraries can help find addresses) for more specific information, especially pertaining to laws regarding the keeping of reptiles and amphibians in your area.

## Trouble Signs and Common Snake Diseases

If your snake looks sick, it probably is sick—unless it's shedding (see p. 167). Snakes, unlike kids and some other pets, don't fake illness for attention.

**INTESTINAL DISEASES:** If your snake refuses food for a long period or stools look different (much looser, lighter, darker, have specks in them) worms might be the problem, but cannot be detected without fecal examination and should only be treated by vet-approved worm medication. Virtually all digestive problems are treatable if caught early.

**MOUTH ROT:** Evidenced by a yellowish area in the mouth that produces a cheesy substance that builds up along the teeth and can eventually prevent the mouth from closing. Appetite fails and veterinary care is recommended.

**RESPIRATORY INFECTIONS:** Snakes are subject to viral and bacterial infections, including pneumonia. Signs of trouble are usually mucous in the mouth, bubbling nostrils, and open-mouthed breathing. Consult vet about possible need for antibiotics.

*Best Prevention Measures:* Keeping cage clean and at proper humidity and temperature levels.

**SKIN PROBLEMS:** Mites attach to the skin and are bloodsucking parasites, usually found on snakes that have come from infested locations or owners who haven't housed or handled them properly. They can be very dangerous. Consult your vet about the best method for eliminating them from your particular snake. Skin blisters can occur if an environment is too damp. Snakes can also develop Dirty Cage Syndrome, which is caused by a buildup of droppings.

*Best Prevention Measures:* Thoroughly clean cage every week or two; keep at proper humidity and temperature levels. See "Cautions," p. 168.

**SKIN SHEDDING:** This is not a disease—it's a fact of snake life. Every one to three months, snakes shed their skin. Before this reptile molt occurs, the eyes are cloudy for several days. Then, a few days after the eyes clear, the old snakeskin is rubbed loose. Food is often refused during shedding. Sometimes animals that are stressed or dehydrated do not shed their skin completely.

*Best Prevention Measures:* Keep humidity levels up; gently spray your pet with water as soon as the eyes clear.

**JACK'S FACTS:**
## Don't Swallow That Milk Snake Myth!

No matter what you've heard, milk snakes do not milk cows! No one knows when the myth started or who started it (probably someone who was drinking more than milk at the time), but the belief that this kingsnake cousin slithers up the rear legs of cows and milks them is as far-flung as it is far-fetched!

---

**JACK'S FACTS:**

## You Can Pick an Anaconda, but Never Pick Its Nose!

I seem to be in the habit of learning things the hard way. And when snakes are involved, the hard way can be a painful experience. The experience that stands out in my mind happened when I was running the Central Florida Zoo and got involved in a movie deal that involved a fourteen-foot, 120-pound anaconda. I was helping out on location, with some animal close-ups that were being shot in a local pond, when I noticed a loose piece of skin dangling from the snake's nose. Not very attractive, even for an anaconda, so I went to pick it off. A well-intentioned move—but dumb. Without warning the snake just sucked up my finger and clamped down on it.

The next thing I heard, beside my own scream, was my friend Stan Brock, former cohost of Marlin Perkins's *Wild Kingdom,* shouting, "Don't move your finger, or you'll lose it!" Move it? Was he kidding? It was being held in a vise of 220 sharp and unyielding reptilian teeth. So I kept screaming while Stan and Herbie Sullivan, our herpetologist (who was there to give snake advice—which I, obviously, hadn't heard) tried to pry my finger loose.

Meanwhile, some guy from a local newspaper was taking pictures! Stan finally got him to put his camera down and get something to jam in the snake's mouth, which he did, enabling them to hold the snake's jaws open and me to retrieve my finger, which—though pretty well shredded—was miraculously still attached to my hand.

At the hospital, they insisted on giving me shots against infection, even though anacondas are not poisonous. My finger healed pretty quickly, but because of the shots I couldn't sit down for a week. And if that wasn't adding insult to injury, there is always the fact that the film was called *The Forgotten Wilderness* and I've yet to meet someone who remembers it.

---

## Cautions

- Don't keep reptiles on cedar shavings (the volatile oils can irritate their mucous membranes).
- Aquarium gravel can cause skin irritations and mouth infections in snakes and is not recommended for reptile vivariums.
- Be aware that live prey may trigger defense reactions instead of vital feeding responses in captive snakes.
- When supplying your basking lizard or turtle with a vitamin D supplement, make sure that it is vitamin $D_3$ (not vitamin $D_2$ as for mammals), which is es-

sential for correct calcium and phosphorus absorption necessary for bone and shell formation.

- Live mice have been known to seriously injure and even kill captive reptiles.
- Cleaning cages with coal tar or phenol cleansers (i.e. Lysol, Pine-Sol) can be hazardous to your reptile's health, as those substances are toxic to snakes.
- When cleaning a cage with bleach, make sure it is diluted as advised on the label for use on woodwork.
- Just a few hours of insufficient humidity in its environment will kill a lungless salamander.
- Large salamanders and large frogs will eat smaller members of their own species, so they should be kept separately.
- Cage temperatures of over 85° Fahrenheit can kill most salamanders in a matter of hours.
- Be sure that insects gathered as food for any amphibians or reptiles have not been sprayed with pesticides.
- Household water softeners may contain residual chemical salts that are lethal to newts and salamanders.
- If the temperature in a turtle's tank is low, it may be too cold for eating yet too warm for hibernation, and the turtle can die.
- Not all vets are familiar with reptile and amphibian illnesses. Before your pet gets sick—before you even buy it—ask your local animal hospital, humane society, or herpetological society for help in finding a herp veterinarian in your area.

## Breeding Tips for Reptiles and Amphibians

There are so many variables within the myriad species involved that I suggest you seek professional herpetological advice before putting your pets through the necessary stresses of reproduction.

## Compatible—and Incompatible—Household Pets

### Children

Not all children are right (or ready) to raise cold-blooded pets, and not all reptiles and amphibians are right for children to keep as pets. Age, conscientiousness, and available care time are all factors that need to be considered—by both parent and child.

**KEEP IN MIND**

- The pet might belong to your child, but when he or she is not around it will be up to you to care for it—so be sure that you're up to it, too!
- The only true "low-maintenance pet" is one that belongs to someone else.

### Birds
See p. 42.

### Cats
See p. 72.

### Dogs
See p. 96.

### Rodents and Other Mini-Mammals
See p. 130.

### Rabbits, Ferrets, and Potbellied Pigs
See p. 151.

### Creepy-Crawly Critters
Though some might keep them as pets, cold-blooded pets would like them for dinner.

### Fish
They'll stay in their tanks, so if your other pets stay in theirs—no problemo!

## Salamanders and Newts

There are over one hundred species of salamanders in the United States, all belonging to the order *Caudate*, the tailed amphibians. That's far too many to even attempt to mention here by individual name, but for a best-bet pet in that category, the Red Eft newt—which is a small salamander (about three inches)—would be the one to pick. (The Red Eft is the juvenile form of the Red-Spotted Newt, but is so totally different in markings and habits—being completely terrestrial until breeding size—that it has been given a separate name.)

## Salamander Specs

PRO: Quiet, undemanding, no grooming required.

CON: Mostly nocturnal; cages must be kept moist but clean; cage temperatures must be monitored carefully; not cuddly or playful.

CREATURE COMFORTS: An aquarium with a glass top (raised just enough to allow air to circulate) or a plastic sweater box with small holes drilled through the top. Humidity and moisture are essential. Rotted wood, or damp gravel covered with wood bark for lining cage bottom. Pieces of wood, leaf-litter, moss, flat stones for hiding places. A water dish (*except for woodland salamanders, which are completely terrestrial and might drown.*) Cage temperatures should be cool, 60–70° Fahrenheit depending on species. (*Temperatures above 85° Fahrenheit can kill most salamanders within hours.*) Aquatic species, such as the Axolotl, do best when kept in simple non-chlorinated water-filled aquariums, unadorned with anything except a layer of pebbles.

DIET NEEDS AND TREATS: All salamanders are carnivorous (and all newts are salamanders), so diets—depending on size of your pets—should include worms, insects, small spiders, crickets, store-bought Tubifex worms. Vitamin powders are available for sprinkling on foods.

## Lizards You Can Live With

Lizards are a lot like people—and vice versa. There are your diurnals (day persons) and your nocturnals (night persons). Some are vegetarian, some are meat-eaters; some are bright, some are dull; some prefer living in trees (high-rises), others enjoy camping at lakesides, or basking in warm sand. Virtually all enjoy spacious accommodations and a warm environment.

## Chameleons (Green Anoles)

PRO: They're fun to watch because they change color (depending on lighting, background, temperature, and mood); they can be trained so you can hand feed them; easy to care for.

CON: Their favorite foods are flies and other little bugs that you'll have to provide (plentiful in summer, but hard to come by in the winter); short life spans.

CREATURE COMFORTS: A converted aquarium, with branches and living plants to climb on, fine gravel; ventilation to prevent too much humidity—but a lid secure enough to prevent escape; a light bulb or other heating device to keep temperature close to 85° Fahrenheit.

DIET NEEDS AND TREATS: Small insects, crickets, grasshoppers; water droplets from plants that you mist daily.

**KEEP IN MIND**

- Males are territorial and two in the same enclosure will fight.
- They are good jumpers and climbers—and faster than you think.
- Very young children, if allowed handling privileges, can accidentally be hazardous to a chameleon's health.
- You can usually determine the sex of your chameleon by putting a mirror in front of it. If it puffs up under its chin upon seeing its reflection and looks like it's about to attack, it's a male. If it ignores the reflection (*or puts on lipstick*) it's a female.

## Geckos

PRO: Attractive, active, colorful; most species easy to train; exotic-looking, not difficult to care for.

CON: Physically delicate; careful handling necessary for small species; most are nocturnal; not recommended for amateurs.

CREATURE COMFORTS: Escape-proof cage (see "Keep in Mind" below); nooks and crannies in which to hide—rocks, broken pots; floor coverings of gravel, newspaper (with non-toxic ink), sand; plants for arboreal species to climb (some enjoy sections of thick bamboo); access to water for drinking or damp areas for egg laying.

DIET NEEDS AND TREATS: All geckos are carnivorous; enjoy small crickets, flies, mixed insects sprinkled with vitamin and mineral supplements. Some species enjoy a sweet—artificial hummingbird nectar, a sugar cube. Also, if breeding, a cuttlefish or powdered calcium supplement should be added to the diet.

**KEEP IN MIND**

- Many gecko species have toe pads that enable them to climb glass and even to walk upside down across ceilings—making an escape-proof cage a must!
- Don't panic if while holding your gecko's tail it comes off; it will grow back.

• Established pairs or resident groups may not tolerate the addition of newcomers (of either sex) to their turf.

## Iguanas

PRO: Beautiful, impressive, lizards with attitude, style, and class. Can be taught to come when called for food.

CON: Need extensive enclosures. Can reach lengths of five to six feet as adults. Though they rarely bite, they have very sharp claws and use them if improperly handled. Require regular care—plan on at least three-quarters of an hour daily.

CREATURE COMFORTS: A medium-large terrarium (as iguana grows, space needs will increase), the bottom lined with sand, rounded gravel, soil (or other non-toxic materials); facilities for climbing, sloping branches for lounging; heat/light lamp for basking; water dish; shade/hiding area. (Cage should incorporate a thermal gradient that allows iguana to vary its body temperature at will.)

DIET NEEDS AND TREATS: Essentially herbivorous, iguanas do enjoy some insect food while young. Shredded fresh vegetables and fruits (lettuce, carrots, apples, sprouts) are preferred. New fresh vegetables and fruits should be added to diet in moderation and slowly. Vitamin and mineral supplements are recommended, particularly calcium (or cuttlebone powder) and are easily sprinkled on foods.

### KEEP IN MIND
• Feeding your iguana outside its cage can keep its cage cleaner inside.
• Iguanas enjoy daily mistings—but not damp conditions.
• Feeding your pet after it has had time to bask in heat and light is best.
• When purchasing a young iguana, look for one that is bright green, active, and attempting to bask in the heat source. (Avoid thin, lethargic dark iguanas, which may be ill or carrying salmonella bacteria.)
• The size of your pet is determined more by the amount of food it eats and the temperature of its environment than by its age.
• In cold climates, a backup heat source should be provided in the event of power outages.

## Blue-Tongued Skinks

PRO: Intelligent, filled with personality, docile, curious, friendly, hardy.

CON: Some species are quite expensive; even without defined teeth they have a powerful bite and tend not to let go. Not recommended for children or amateurs.

CREATURE COMFORTS: Terrarium enclosures should have maximum floor space—three to four square feet recommended—with a substrate of mulch (aspen bedding, cypress mulch, wood bark), sphagnum moss, or leaf litter for burrowing; a shallow water dish; a hide box and several other places to sneak behind or under. A screen or perforated cover to provide good ventilation and a heat light to provide a basking area (or an undertank heater or thermostatically controlled heating pad) that can warm up to 90° Fahrenheit, as well as a shady area for thermoregulation at will.

DIET NEEDS AND TREATS: Animal and plant foods, snails, insects, small pieces of finely ground chicken, cooked shrimp, diced or mashed vegetables (sweet potatoes, cooked peas, corn, green beans), bits of fruit (grapes, strawberries, melon); water-soaked monkey biscuits or iguana pellets. Supplements of calcium as well as other vitamins and minerals are recommended.

**KEEP IN MIND**
- Blue-tongues do better when housed alone (they are very territorial).
- Cage substrate, floor bedding should stay dry.
- Young skinks eat daily or every other day; adults can manage on once- or twice-weekly feedings.
- Young skinks shed more often than adults, which shed approximately every six weeks.
- Appetites decrease before shedding and increase right after.


## Friendly Frogs and Toads

All frogs and toads are *anurans*. (*Though that sounds as if they're aliens on a* Star Trek *episode, it merely means that they are all tail-less amphibians.*) The difference between frogs and toads is somewhat arbitrary, but essentially the smooth, slimy, slick high-jumpers that hang out in moist areas are frogs, while the larger, drier, leap-challenged, and warty ones are toads. (Another difference: Frogs have to return to water to reproduce; toads don't.)

### The Green Scene
PRO: They're hardy, quiet, interesting. (*Look, not all frogs are Kermit, okay?*)

CON: They're not pettable pets. (NOTE: Amphibians should be handled as little as possible. Their skin is permeable, a supplemental breathing organ, and the oils found naturally on our hands may be harmful to them.)

CREATURE COMFORTS: Varies with size and species of frog or toad, but most fare well in large, tall vivariums with a lot of plants and hollow branches. Frogs need warm water (with gravel base) to frolic in and out of, and more moisture in their habitat. Both frogs and toads need moss or leaf-litter substrate, hiding places, rocks, logs, live or artificial plants. Heater, full-spectrum light, or undertank heat pad to keep vivarium at comfortable warmth for daytime (70–80° Fahrenheit depending on species) and cooler (usually 60–65° Fahrenheit) at night.

DIET NEEDS AND TREATS: Most frogs are carnivorous, preferring live (at least wriggling) insects, worms, flies, crickets, spiders, centipedes, and mealy worms. (They can be bought at pet stores if you're not into catching your own.)

### KEEP IN MIND
- Large frogs need larger meals—like mice.
- When feeding your frog crickets, it's best to fatten them up with nutrients and vitamins before putting them in your pet's cage. (Mix vitamin powder with tropical fish flakes, mash in a piece of pulpy fruit, and serve on a jar lid.)

## Let's Talk Turtles and Tortoises

Turtles have been around a long time. In fact, their ancestors were around before the dinosaurs, some 200 million years ago, and turtles today are relatively unchanged from the way they were 150 million years ago. (*With the exception, that is, of Ninja Turtles.*)

These shelled reptiles, whether they are called turtles, terrapins, or tortoises, are aquatic, semi-aquatic, or terrestrial, all belong to a group known as *chelonians*, which are shelled reptiles (*shelled shrimp are something else entirely*) and interesting companions for compatible owners.

### *Slow and Steady Pets*
PRO: Quiet, non-demanding, happy living alone; some types can recognize and become attached to owners.

CON: Long-term commitment (box turtles may live forty or more years!); though inexpensive to come by, veterinary care and food may run $20 or more a month; at least one hour a week is required for cage cleaning; may harbor salmonella from a contaminated breeding location, or from eating contaminated food.

CREATURE COMFORTS: For semi-aquatic turtles, a well-vented vivarium where there is enough water (deeper than the turtle is wide), filter, water heater, and thermometer; a dry section for basking (flat, smooth rocks, a log or artificial platform to climb on) with a heat lamp above it. Terrestrial species, particularly box turtles, need large vivariums, floor enclosure coverings of peat moss, wood shavings (not pine or cedar), orchid bark, shredded newspaper (non-toxic ink); a shallow water dish large enough for soaking; hiding places (wooden box, flowerpot with hole, logs); heat lamp for basking (keeping temperature underneath at about 85° Fahrenheit); cool areas so turtles can thermoregulate at will.

DIET NEEDS AND TREATS: Most aquatic and semi-aquatic species are carnivorous, enjoying earthworms, whole feeder goldfish, snails, crickets, mealworms, as well as occasional lettuce, fruits, tofu, small bits of lean beef. Terrestrial species are mostly vegetarian, but will eat some crickets, mealworms, and other insects. All pet turtles and tortoises should receive supplements of vitamin $D_3$ and calcium, which can be sprinkled on food.

**KEEP IN MIND**
- Turtles drink the same water that they soak and poop in, so water dishes should be changed daily.
- You can prevent a common vitamin A deficiency, characterized by swollen eyelids and appetite loss, by regularly placing a drop or two of cod-liver oil on your turtle's favorite foods.
- If you have an outdoor enclosure for your box turtle, and the weather is warm, fifteen minutes of exposure to real sunlight is said to be the equivalent of many hours under an artificial lamp.
- If turtles are too cold, they won't eat.
- You can endanger a turtle—and yourself—by taking it from the wild without first securing a permit from the local Department of Wildlife.

## Did You Know . . .
- Snakes have no limbs.
- Snakes have no external ear opening.

- The eyelids of snakes are fused and do not move.
- Male snakes have two penises (called a hemipenes)—and can copulate with either one.
- Because of the flexible arrangement of the bones in their lower jaw, snakes can swallow prey whole—even when it's larger than their head.
- A reptile's body temperature is the same as its surroundings.
- The king cobra's favorite meals are other snakes.
- The ancient Greeks used snakes as symbols for worshipping the god of medicine; today intertwined snakes remain on the medical caduceus as the symbol of medicine.
- Of the more than 100 species of snakes native to the U.S. and Canada, only five are poisonous to humans—the rattlesnake, the copperhead, the cottonmouth, the coral snake, and the water moccasin.
- The snake's long forked tongue is harmless. (It acts as a sensor by bringing in particles from the air that contain information about what is nearby.)
- When aroused, snakes of all species shake their tails—but only rattlesnakes have a noisemaking rattle on theirs.
- Rattlesnakes can be killed by their own poison—but cobras cannot.
- All frogs sleep with their eyes open.
- Though they are terrific swimmers, if frogs don't have access to land they will drown.
- A frog's bulging eyes can see in almost any direction.
- Most frogs breathe through their skin, mouth, and lungs.
- Frogs do not drink (*not even on weekends*); they absorb water from their surroundings through their skin (osmosis).
- Frogs often retract their eyes, one at a time, when swallowing food.
- Frogs swallow their food whole, so they're only limited by the size of their mouth . . . and, of course, the speed of their prey.
- Some tadpoles not only don't grow larger, but actually shrink and become smaller frogs.
- You can hypnotize some frogs by placing them on their back and gently stroking their belly.
- The way to tell a salamander from a lizard is the salamander's lack of claws and scales.
- Gecko lizards' eyelids (like snakes') are fused and transparent, so they use their long tongues to wipe dirt from their eyes.
- Gecko lizards' eyes move independently of each other.

JACK'S FACTS:
## Now That's Power Lifting!

The North American box turtle can support a weight two hundred times greater than its own (which means, theoretically, that a five-pounder could easily help you move the piano). A man with proportionate supporting power could lift two large African elephants! (The question, of course, is why would he want to?)

- Gila monsters hold reserve food supplies in their tails.
- Sale of very young red-eared slider turtles (the most popular and well-known turtle pets) that are under four inches in length has been banned in the United States since the 1970s because of salmonella-poisoning concerns.
- Any sudden disturbances causes a turtle involuntarily to force air out of its windpipe, producing a hissing that sounds like a reptile.
- The Columbus Zoo is one of the world's largest turtle-breeding centers.

### Herpetological Pet Names and Some Celebrities Who've Claimed Them

*Alice Cooper:* Angel; Eva Marie Snake (boa constrictors)
*Shelly Duvall:* Iggy, Stiggy, Stutz, and Twiggy (iguanas)
*Michael Jackson:* Muscles (boa constrictor)
*Robert F. Kennedy:* Shadrack (salamander)
*Mary Pickford:* Don Juan (iguana)
*Ginger Rogers:* Fred (turtle)
*Theodore Roosevelt:* Bill (toad)
*Slash:* Pandora, Clyde (boa constrictors)
*Robin Williams:* Carl (turtle)
*Tennessee Williams:* Mr. Ava Gardner (iguana)

And other cold-blooded pet names that I've warmed up to:

*Snakes:* Boa Derek, Monty Python, Slitha, Herp Alpert, Hiss Honor, Elvis
*Lizards:* Lounger, Skinker, Liza, Zorba (the Gecko), Karma Karma (chameleon)
*Frogs:* Big Mac (African bullfrog), D'Artagnan (poison arrow frog), Buttafucco (giant toad), Prince (green tree frog), Satchmo (horned toad)
*Turtles:* Shelly, Myrtle, Speedo, Doorstop, Picasso (painted turtle)

## Questions and Answers About Reptiles and Amphibians

### Turtle-to-Kid Trouble

My son keeps a pet turtle in a tank in his bedroom. I know he takes Pokey (that's the turtle) out and lets it climb on him while he does his homework. Pokey crawls over my son's hands and his books. Can my son get anything from it?

Not the answers to his homework, that's for sure. But turtles do carry bacteria (as do all animals, even humans) so to avoid trouble just make sure that your son washes his hands thoroughly after handling Pokey—and, no matter how fond they are of each other, to refrain from kissing. Though cases of salmonella-infected turtles are rare these days (usually caused by having been fed raw chicken), you can, if concerned, have Pokey tested for it by a veterinarian. And be sure to assure your son—and Pokey—that it is treatable.

## *Prey Tell*

My friend has a boa constrictor and when I hold it, it doesn't squeeze me very tightly. He feeds it frozen mice, but in the wild don't boas crush their prey? Do they lose their strength in captivity?

No, they don't lose their strength in captivity—and they don't "crush" their prey in the wild. A boa doesn't have fangs, but it does have teeth and strong jaws, and gets its food by striking its prey's head quickly and then coiling around it. Each time the prey—be it a rodent, bird, or large lizard—breathes out, the coils of the boa tighten around its chest. This prevents the prey from breathing and it suffocates—a method of killing that is known as constriction.

## *Iguana Don't Wanna*

My three-year-old iguana, Rootie, is very intelligent and friendly, and often eats out of my hand. But all my attempts to train him to use a litterbox when he's out and about have failed. Do you have any suggestions?

Well, "give up" comes to mind. I, personally, don't know of any housebroken iguanas, and if your iguana don't wanna . . . well, just be happy he's happy doing business as usual.

## **Reptile and Amphibian Talk Pet Owners Should Know**

**AMPHIBIANS:** cold-blooded, non-scaly vertebrates, mostly four-legged, living on land and in or near water—frogs, toads, newts, salamanders

**ANTIVENOM:** an antitoxin to a venom

**ARBOREAL:** tree-dwelling

**ARTHROPODS:** insects, crustaceans, spiders; any of a major group of segmented invertebrates having jointed legs

**BIFURCATED:** forked

**CLOACA:** a chamber in most vertebrates (not mammals) into which intestinal, urinary, and reproductive tracts empty

**COLD-BLOODED:** body temperature is related to the temperature of the environment

**DIURNAL:** active during the daytime

**HEMIPENES:** the paired mating organs of male lizards and snakes; the "double penis"

**HERPETOLOGY:** the branch of zoology dealing with reptiles and amphibians

**KEELED:** ridged

**NOCTURNAL:** active at night

**OVIPAROUS:** egg-laying

**PREHENSILE:** adapted for grasping

**REPTILES:** cold-blooded, scaly vertebrates—turtles, lizards, snakes, alligators, and crocodiles

**SUBSTRATES:** substances used to line the bottom of a cage or vivarium

**THERMAL GRADIENT:** a devised measure providing temperature variation enabling reptiles and amphibians to regulate their body temperatures at will

**THERMOREGULATION:** the ability to adjust body temperature by seeking out the proper ambient heat or coolness to suit metabolic needs

**VIVIPAROUS:** bearing live young

## JACK'S FACTS: **Five Top Books for Owners of Cold-Blooded Pets**

*The Care of Reptiles in Captivity* by Christopher Matison (Blandford Press)

*Iguana Iguana: Guide for Successful Captive Care* by Fredric L. Frye (Krieger Publishing)

*Snakes: The Keeper and the Kept* by C. Kauffield (Doubleday)

*Reptiles of the World* by Raymond Ditmar (Macmillan)

*The Proper Care of Snakes* by Armin Geus (T.F.H. Publications)

Plus: *Reptiles Magazine*, P.O. Box 58700, Boulder, CO 80322, (303) 666-8504. A monthly publication with an extensive variety of herpetological articles and all the latest information on the care and keeping of reptiles and amphibians.

# 10

# Something Fishy Going On

## Taking the Plunge

Underwater pets can be as companionable, beautiful, and fascinating as any others on earth, but before taking the plunge into aquatic pet owning, you have to start out by providing the right environment for their survival

THE TANK: A twenty to thirty gallon tank is best for beginners. Aside from giving your finny new friends a pleasantly roomy environment, it provides you with better viewing. Also, a long, low tank is better than a short, high one for providing fish with optimal oxygen. And it's easier to keep the water chemistry stable in larger tanks than smaller ones (where small chemical changes can cause a bigger imbalance).

- Glass tanks are better and cheaper per gallon than acrylic tanks, and harder to scratch.
- If buying a tank second-hand, don't buy one that is scratched; algae grows easily in scratches and will spoil the look of your tank (to say nothing of your looks at your fish).
- Before setting up a used tank, make sure it doesn't leak. (Fill and let stand outside for several days.)
- Clean the tank with water, or a mild pure-bleach solution that you can rinse thoroughly. (NEVER use soaps or detergents—unless specifically for aquariums!)

THE HEATER: Some fish like warmer water than others, but unless you do live in the tropics (and even then), you're going to need a heater and a thermometer to make sure that the tank temperature is right for your fish.

- The heater should keep the tank at its target temperature, without fluctuating, no matter what the outside room temperature is.
- For most freshwater and saltwater fish, a tank temperature of around 77° Fahrenheit (25° C) is recommended.
- Submersible heaters are best; they remain completely under the water and can be placed horizontally along the tank bottom for more uniform heat.
- Traditional heaters must be unplugged for water changing; the glass tube containing the heating coils may crack when refilling the tank.
- Stay away from heaters that are too large for your tank size. (*You could wake up with twenty gallons of bouillabaisse.*)

- Many aquarium owners recommend using two parallel small heaters to minimize disaster in the event that one fails.
- Check your tank thermometer daily.

**THE FILTER:** All fish tanks must have biological filtration to decompose and filter out the toxic ammonia that fish produce as waste products. Typical filters will do this, as well as trap other particles, such as dirt, plant leaves, or uneaten food, so they can be removed from the tank before also decomposing or undermining biological filtration.

- A combination of under-gravel and outside-power filters works very well, but for beginners an under-gravel filter is sufficient.
- Debris must be cleaned from a filter regularly, otherwise it becomes ineffective.
- Filter should be large enough to service the needs of your size tank. (And if it's a little larger, it's even better.)

**AIR PUMP:** This produces bubbles that provide water oxygenation. If you have an under-gravel filter, an air pump will force water through it via the uplift tubes.

- A submersible water pump that works with an under-gravel filter can perform the same function as an air pump, making an additional one unnecessary if there already is good water circulation. (Check with your pet store if you're unsure about the equipment you have.)

**GRAVEL:** Two to three inches of gravel is recommended for the bottom of your tank. Aside from adding beauty, it's essential if you're using an under-gravel filter. It also serves as a substrate or growing medium for plant roots.

- All gravel should be washed before using the first time. (Rinse in a bucket of warm clean water, drain, and rinse again until water is clear).
- Gravel from unknown source (or someone's old tank) should be boiled for ten to fifteen minutes. (CAUTION: Nowadays, most gravel sold for aquariums is plastic-coated—DO NOT BOIL.)
- Dark gravel highlights most fish colors better than light gravel.

**HOODS AND LIGHTS:** Hoods reduce water evaporation and unexplained disappearances of fish (especially in households with cats). Lights are necessary for seeing your fish and for growing plants.

- Combination light-hood units (with one or two fluorescent light tubes) are fine for fish-only tanks, but generally not enough for those with living plants.
- Fluorescent lights are preferable to incandescent bulbs, which could give off too much heat for your pets.
- If possible, aquarium bulbs that provide "full-spectrum" lighting should be used, as they are good for both fish and plants.

**PLANTS:** Aside from decoration, plants provide necessary hiding places for your fish.

- Plastic plants are the easiest to care for—and they won't die.
- Real plants consume excremental substances, to a limited extent act as fish food, and provide oxygen—but they can also hide parasites.
- Find out what plants are best suited for the temperature, lighting, and denizens of your tank.

**THE NET:** Because fish don't answer to their names, every owner needs at least one net—and two are better.

- Nets with wide mesh are not good for really tiny fish; and nets with really fine mesh may be difficult to use because of their water resistance.

**THE BUCKET:** A regular bucket to use exclusively for adding and removing water from your tank.

- Changing 25 percent of your tank's water every two weeks is recommended to prevent stress on the fish caused by toxic buildup, although many aquarists have found that a 30 percent water change once a month is sufficient.

**TANK ACCESSORIES:** Decorating your pets' tank is fun, but make sure that whatever you add—be it a sunken ship or treasure chest—is safe for your fish.

- If you want to add an attractive piece of wood to your tank, make sure that you boil it first to kill off any hazardous bacteria or chemicals. (Also, extensive boiling will make wood sink—which is a definite plus in a fish tank.)

WATER: Last but first in importance in fish tanks is the water. It can come straight from the tap, but if it contains chlorine you must be sure to remove that chemical before filling your tank or your fish may die. This can be done with dechlorination tablets, which are available with instructions at most pet stores. (Letting water stand for two or three days to allow the chlorine to evaporate will also work.)

- You should also determine whether your water is hard or soft, and choose fish that are best suited for it. (You can get pH-test kits from local pet stores and advice on types of fish from local aquarium clubs.)
- For most fish, a pH of between 6.5 and 7.5 is healthy.
- If the fish you want and the water you have are incompatible, there are chemicals that can change its natural hardness or softness.
- Saltwater fish are more sensitive than freshwater fish to changes in their water-world.
- What is often called New Tank Syndrome is when the water turns gray and cloudy (this is caused by bacteria) or green and cloudy (caused by algae). For the gray bacterial problem, make sure the filter is clean and working properly, and change a quarter to half the water daily until the water returns to normal. For the green algae problem, reduce the amount of light in the tank, partially change the water, and keep a check on the nitrate concentration, which algae thrive on.

## How Do You Recognize a Healthy Fish?

Check out your potential fish's tank and swimming companions. An unhealthy-looking environment—or sickly pals—do not bode well for any fish.

### The Healthy Fish Scan
- Eyes should be bright and clear—not sunken.
- Belly should not be sunken.
- Back should not be overly ridged.
- Fins should be away from the body, not clamped against it.
- Movement should be smooth, even, with gentle fin motion.

## JACK'S FACTS: "THE CYCLE"

Doug Warmolts, assistant director of the Living Collection at the Columbus Zoo, believes that most fish deaths, most beginner aquarium failures, are a direct result of not understanding the nitrogen cycle. As he explains it, once you have completed setting up and filling your aquarium, you need to establish your "biological" filter. The first step is to add a few small fish (three for a ten-gallon aquarium). This will be all you should add for the next four weeks. Soon after adding the fish, changes in your water chemistry will begin.

Buy a test kit that can measure pH, ammonia, and nitrite. This way you can monitor "the cycle" and determine its completion. The goal is to allow two types of helpful bacteria to grow on the gravel, which in turn will break down the toxic wastes of the fish. This takes time (about four weeks) and there is no easy way around it. Patience is an important part of being a good aquarist. The following chart illustrates the cycle:

"THE CYCLE"

FISH FOOD→ →FISH
↓
Fish Waste Products
↓
Ammonia ($NH^3$) *TOXIC*
*Nitrosomonas* Bacteria
Nitrite ($NO_2$) *TOXIC*
*Nitrobacter* Bacteria
Nitrite ($NO_3$)

↙           ↘

*Proper Maintenance*          *Buildup of Excess* TOXIC
Regular Water Changes          Insufficient Water Changes
Correct Feeding                Overfeeding
Good Fish Population           Fish Overpopulation
                               Dirty Filter

When the cycle is complete, there will be enough helpful bacteria to break down wastes as new fish are introduced. (DON'T FORGET: Uneaten food is waste, too.)

- Gill covers should not stick out at a wide angle. (Sign of labored breathing and possible illness.)
- Dorsal fin (the top one) should be upright and in use.
- Body should have no missing scales.
- Skin should have no white spots. (Nor should any other fish in tank have them.)
- Body surface should be free of blemishes which could indicate the presence of parasites.
- All fins should be in good condition.

HANNA'S HINT: Be sure *you're* sure of how many fins your particular fish is supposed to have before you suspect it's missing any.

## Trouble Signs and How to Read Them

If your fish has spent the afternoon floating at the top of the tank, it is most likely not sick; it is more likely dead. But since you can't hear fish sneeze, or cough, or complain, the best way to tell if they're feeling unwell is to observe them.

### *Your Fish Might Be Sick If . . .*

- it swims sideways.
- food is refused for more than two days.
- fins clamp close to the body.
- it sinks or swirls.
- there is noticeable scratching against plants or tank decorations.
- it becomes very active when it normally isn't.
- formerly active, it becomes lethargic or still.
- its belly is distended.
- it gasps at the water surface.
- its gills look purple.
- lesions or white patches appear on its skin.

## Common Diseases

DROPSY: Fish becomes bloated, scales stand out at an angle to the body, and the eyes bulge. May be caused by internal bacteria or external stresses.

*Best Prevention Measures:* Check water pH and temperature regularly; don't overfeed fish or overcrowd tank.

FIN OR TAIL ROT: Stress-related bacterial disease caused by lowered resistance, frequently brought on by injury, chilling, overcrowding, or poor water quality. There are viral and bacterial forms of this ailment—check with local aquarium society, vet, or pet store to determine proper treatment.

*Best Prevention Measures:* Don't overcrowd tank; check pH and temperature regularly; reevaluate diet.

FUNGUS: Characterized by tufts of cottony filaments adhering to fish—usually following an injury. Also attacks fish with lowered resistance—spreading from tail to fin to entire body. Check with your local aquarium society, vet, or pet store for medication and treatment best suited for your type of fish.

*Best Prevention Measures:* Quarantine injured fish; don't overcrowd tank; make sure all species are compatible.

ICH (ICHTHYOPHTHIRIUS MULTIFILIIS): Highly communicable parasitic disease characterized by small white blisters on fish, which often cause them to scratch against objects in the tank. When parasites fall off, they attach to gravel or tank and multiply, then attach to other fish. Quarantine time is longer for saltwater fish than for freshwater fish. Check with your local aquarium pet store for remedy that's best for your tank.

*Best Prevention Measures:* Keep your tank clean and water temperature from fluctuating.

VELVET: Fish develops a plushy coat of whitish, gold flecks, causing fins to clamp and a shimmy type of movement. Anti-parasitic medicine is available. Check with your local aquarium society, vet, or pet store for the right dosage and treatment for your fish.

*Best Prevention Measures:* Keep tank pH and temperature regulated; regular and thorough tank and filter cleaning.

## Breeding Tips

Fish are either live-bearers or egg-layers. If they are live-bearers, a male and a female need no instructions. When the female is pregnant, she'll swell slightly—with pride and with baby fish (called "fry")—and you'll see a dark spot near her vent. In about twenty-five days, when she is ready to drop her fry, her lower abdomen will become much larger. If she is not put in another tank, and immediately removed after the fry are born, the fry often become dinner before they become

full-sized fish. If you want these fry to survive, ask your aquarium store about a breeding trap and how to use it, what to feed the newborns, and when to release them into the tank.

Some fish (anabantids, or "labyrinth fish") are bubble-nest builders, building protective nests of bubbles for eggs and babies; others, like some cichlids are mouthbrooders. But to breed egg-laying fish successfully, you really need a separate tank and guidance from seasoned aquarium breeders. (To find out more about how to go about it, check out the books and resources listed at the end of this chapter.)

## Compatible—and Incompatible—Household Pets

As long as you keep a lid on your tank—and explain to children that it's not the place to float their bath toys—fish can get along with everyone.

## Cautions to Keep in Mind When Keeping Fish

- Bargain fish may carry diseases that can infect your entire tank.
- Rapid pH changes in tank water causes hazardous stress in fish.
- Water that is overly high in nitrates can stunt your fish's growth and shorten its life.
- Using a heater that is much larger than the size recommended for your size tank can cost you a tankful of fish.
- If your municipal water uses chloramine as a sterilizing agent, you *must* remove it with special dechlorinating compounds. Unlike ordinary chlorine, it will not evaporate from water by itself—and it is poisonous to fish.
- Real coral and seashells will leach substances into your tank that may be hazardous to your fish.
- Water-temperature fluctuations of more than 2° Fahrenheit in a day can weaken a fish's immune system.
- A tank that is not level, where the weight is unevenly distributed, has an increased risk of breaking.
- Plants that came from a store tank that had fish in it may carry disease and should be carefully disinfected before being added to your tank.
- If the fish you add to your tank are incompatible with the current residents, you jeopardize the well-being of all of them.

- If you purchase a fish that's just recently arrived at the pet store, adding it to your tank without a quarantine period could endanger the health of your other fish.
- Insufficient hiding places in a tank can cause stress in fish, making them more susceptible to disease.
- Medicating fish that aren't diseased as a preventive measure can actually weaken their immune system.
- Spraying room deodorizers or other aerosol sprays near your aquarium can be hazardous to the health of your fish.
- Never buy fish from tanks with green, blue, or yellow water, which indicates the presence of medicines.
- Acrylic tanks may be hazardous to Placo catfish, as they may chew into the tank material and ingest toxins.
- Putting too many fish in a tank will soon cause you to have less of them.

## Did You Know . . .

- It is estimated that 80–90 percent of all diseases in captive fish could be prevented by avoiding stress.
- Providing your fish with sufficient hiding places will actually *increase* your chances of seeing them because they'll feel more secure in the tank.
- Bonefish have tongues that can exert a crushing power of sixty pounds.
- A school of piranhas can strip a full-grown horse down to a skeleton in minutes, readily eat their own family members, and are considered delicacies in many parts of South America.
- Weather loaches will jump out of aquariums at the approach of a storm.
- Climbing perch, members of the anabantid fish group, are said to be able to climb trees and live out of water for two days.
- Iridescent sharks are not sharks—they're catfish.
- Some cory catfish can survive in tanks with low oxygen because they're able to swallow air from the surface and absorb it through their intestines.
- The Paradise fish, named after the Bird of Paradise, because of its color, was the first tropical fish ever kept by hobbyists.
- The flathead catfish of the Mississippi valley may attain weights of 150 pounds.

JACK'S FACTS:
## Drunk as a Fish

The Brazilian hiccup fish swallows huge gulps of air that, when released, sounds like a hiccup. Full grown, these fish reach a length of twelve feet— and their hiccups can be heard for a mile!

## The Fish Story

**PRO:** Fish are fascinating and calming to look at; you can start with a few pets and keep expanding; they don't shed on the furniture, require shots, walks, or litter-boxes—and feeding takes just a few minutes once or twice a day.

**CON:** Tank must be cleaned once a month—optimally, every two weeks (figure half an hour); preventing algae formation is a constant responsibility; regular temperature monitoring, filter-cleaning, and maintenance are essential.

**CREATURE COMFORTS:** All the equipment mentioned above in "What You'll Need" section. Also, to decrease the likelihood of stress on your fish caused by toxic buildup, 25 percent of the water should be changed every other week. (Some aquarists feel that monthly changes of 30–40 percent of the water works equally well.) And to keep all your creatures comfortable, the rule-of-thumb for how many fish should be in a single tank is "no more than one inch of fish per gallon of water."

**DIET NEEDS AND TREATS:** Most can get by on processed food, which comes in flake, stick, or pellet form, and is available for omnivorous, vegetarian, and carnivorous fish. But fish owners being pet owners will also want to treat their aquatic pals with occasional freeze-dried, frozen, or live bloodworms, daphnia, brine shrimp, tubifex worms (or Tubilina, tubifex worms freeze dried with spirulina). For exotic species with specialized diets, check with local aquarium societies or pet stores.

HANNA'S HINT: Fat fish are dead fish. Overfeeding has probably been responsible for more fish deaths than oil spills and sushi bars combined! (*Well, at least in home aquariums.*) The old adage "Feed your fish only what they can eat in three minutes" is good advice—and may save your pets' lives.

GETTING NEW FISH INTO THE SWIM OF THINGS: Place the water-filled bag in which you brought the fish home into your tank for about fifteen to thirty minutes, allowing the temperature to equalize. Then, add ¼ cup of tank water to the bag every fifteen minutes for about an hour. (If the bag gets too full, throw that water away—you don't want that in your clean tank.) Transfer fish to tank with a net and throw bag with store water away. Many aquarists keep new fish for a week or two in a small quarantine tank before adding them to the larger tank population. Since this is not always an option, use extra care when selecting new fish—and monitor them closely for the first few weeks.

Keep in mind that schooling fish fare much better in a tank if there are several of their own species present for them to interact with. Check with your pet store, local aquarium society or club on the number recommended for each species and your size tank.

## *Fish by Fish*

NOTE: Aquarium fish for brackish water (intermediate between fresh water and salt water, found naturally in gulfs, estuaries, deltas, and lagoons) and saltwater (or marine) fish, of which there are thousands of aquarium-suitable species, are more difficult for beginners to keep because there is more involved in keeping them healthy. For this reason, with a few exceptions, they are not covered here. But if those are the fish you're interested in, you can find out about them from the books and societies mentioned at the end of this chapter.

### MOST COMMON FRESHWATER AQUARIUM SELECTIONS

ANGELFISH: Beautiful, medium-sized, and mellow cichlids, but require a tank that is taller and longer than a ten-gallon aquarium—and plants for hiding behind. Be forewarned that they will eat fish small enough to be easily swallowed.

BARBS: Best kept in schools, especially the tiger barb, which is notorious for nipping the fins of other fish if not swimming with its own kind. Cherry barbs are colorful and small (up to two inches); clown, rosy, and black ruby barbs are all mid-sized (up to four and a half inches); checker and spanner or T-barbs are easygoing but long (can get up to seven inches.) For extra-long tanks only, there are tinfoil barbs—they can get up to more than twelve inches.

BETTAS (SIAMESE FIGHTING FISH): Do not work and play well with others in a communal tank. They're aggressive; two males will fight. (In fact, a male will fight with any fish that even looks like another betta; many people put a mirror on the side of the tank to fool the fish into fighting with itself.) They can be kept in large bowls or tanks without filtration, if given frequent, partial water changes, but a heater needs to be provided unless the room remains a constant 75° Fahrenheit.

CHINESE ALGAE EATERS: These tank-cleaners do eat algae, but they also can endanger slow-moving fish by grating against them, making them vulnerable to infections. They are often thought of as small fish (two to three inches) because so many die within a relatively short time after purchase; survivors, however, can get up to a foot long.

CLOWN PLECOS: Small (under four inches) algae-eating suckermouth catfish; require sinking food intended just for them (commercially sold pleco wafers or zucchini that has been blanched or weighted so it sinks); good for all size aquariums.

CORY (CORYDORAS) CATFISH: Small, hardy schooling bottom feeders (under two and a half inches); require special sinking foods—pellets or frozen bloodworms.

DANIOS: Most active of all the schooling fish; different patters of blue markings enable many owners to identify individual fish. Zebra, leopard, and pearl danios are the species most beginners enjoy. Size usually under two and a half inches. (Giant varieties may grow to four inches.)

DISCUS: Like angelfish, discus need tanks taller and longer than ten gallons; they have other specialized needs—warmer tank temperatures and more acidic water—that make them not good choices for beginners.

GLASS CATFISH: Beautiful, small (no more than six inches), but delicate. Beginners are better off with cory catfish (see above).

GOLDFISH: Anyone who thinks that if you've seen one goldfish you've seen them all hasn't seen many goldfish. There are more than one hundred different varieties! Some don't even look like goldfish. They range from the common carplike goldfish to fish that look as if they're from another planet—the lionhead, veiltail, and the water bubble-eye are a few examples. They are cold-water fish (*not ice cold but cold*), and they don't do well in fish tanks with tropical species. Additionally, they can grow quite large. But, they are long-lived (averaging about ten years) if not overfed, and can be kept in unheated tanks with regular water changes. (Selectively bred varieties may have special needs.)

GOURAMI: Members of the anabantid group, but not as aggressive as the bettas or paradise fish, and all enjoy live food. Blue gouramis (which, oddly enough, also come in gold and silver varieties) get up to about six inches and do best in tanks with larger schooling fishes. The thick-lipped gourami (about three and a half inches) is fairly timid and suitable company for smaller tank-mates. The kissing gourami is peaceloving and fun for beginners, though it can grow up to a foot long. Males challenge each other by pressing their lips together and "kissing." (It's actually a very macho pushing competition—they just have a strange way of showing it.) Dwarf gouramis are exceedingly beautiful, timid, and small (grow only to two inches) and are suitable companions only for smaller, peaceful species.

GUPPIES: Live-bearers that are peaceful, sociable, and not fussy about food. They come in dozens of varieties, different shapes, and unusual colors. As a rule, they do best in water that has at least one uniodized teaspoon of salt for every five gallons.

HATCHETS: Related to pencil fishes and tetras. Not particularly hardy or recommended for beginners. They require soft, acid water (low pH). Their aquariums should be kept covered as hatchets have a tendency to shorten their life spans by launching themselves out of the tank.

JURUPARI: May grow as large as a foot, but slowly. This is a cichlid that's easy maintenance and will help clean your tank by sifting through the gravel for food.

LOACHES: Long-bodied, bottom-feeding scavengers that will eat whatever other tank residents leave over. But they need their own special sinking foods, too. (See Cory Catfish.) A good member of most tank communities.

LONG-WHISKERED CATFISH: You know how cats like fish? Well, these catfish like 'em too. If the other fish in the tank are less than half their size, they'll see them as breakfasts, lunches, and dinners. And they can get really big! Know what you're getting into before you let a pictus, channel, or shovelnose catfish into your tank.

MOLLIES: Black mollies (which grow up to three inches) and sail-fin mollies (which grow to six inches) are live-bearing fish which are recommended to beginners because they're relatively inexpensive, in plentiful supply, and compatible with other fish.

OSCAR: The popular big fish in the cichlid family, it grows to over a foot quickly. Aggressive, it dines on other fish regularly and is not recommended for beginners or average communal tanks.

OTOS (OTOCINCLUS) CATFISH): Smallest and daintiest of algae-eating tank cleaners; capable of cleaning algae from live plants without damaging them. (Food requirements same as for clown plecos.)

PARADISE FISH: Predatory, aggressive, males fight ruthlessly with each other. Not a fish for a community tank, but do well in a separate tank. They are jumpers, so a cover is necessary—but they can survive in temperatures as cool as 60° Fahrenheit.

PENCIL FISHES: Relatives of the hatchet fish. They need soft, acid water—much like tetras. Pretty, but hard for beginners to keep . . . alive.

**PIRANHAS:** These fish are not recommended as pets. They require a regular diet of feeder fish, which are costly and may carry deadly parasites; they are schooling fish and become stressed when kept alone; they can reach lengths of over twelve inches. And even if you have a large enough tank to house several piranhas, you have to be absolutely sure they are well-fed or they will kill and cannibalize each other. No fish deserve that kind of preventable abuse. (*Enough said?*)

**PLATIES:** Related to swordtails, these are also often called "Moons" or "Moonfish." Short and thickset (about two inches full-grown), they generally prefer tanks where there is one teaspoon of salt for every five gallons. They can interbreed with Swordtails and Swordtaile/Platy strains are available.

**PLECO (PLECOSTOMUS) CATFISH:** Algae-eating suckermouth catfish. Good for cleaning tanks, but do require food intended just for them; can get too large for small aquariums (sometimes up to a foot long).

**RAINBOW FISH:** Lots of color and action in these mid-sized schoolmates; best when kept in groups of six or more.

**RASBORAS:** Hardy, colorful schooling fish known for their stop-and-start swimming. Harlequins stay small (under two inches); clowns are mid-sized (up to four inches) and scissor tails can get long (up to six inches).

**SPINY EELS:** They look like gray linguini and are extremely hardy. But they are also aggressive and not always tank-team players.

**SWORDTAILS:** Related to platies, swordtails (which grow to about four inches) come in numerous colors and fin varieties. They seem to thrive best in tanks where there is one teaspoon of salt for every five gallons. Tuxedo swords are popular, but not as hardy as green swords, which are actually multicolored. Males are likely to nip at each other, so one in a tank is best. Also, keep the tank covered—these fish like to jump.

**TETRAS:** Beautiful schooling fish, but many varieties require soft, acidic water with a low (below 7) pH—among them are the neon, cardinal, flag, blue neon, loreto, black phantom, and red phantom tetra. Hardier tetras that do not require a special acidic pH are the small black, glow light, jewel, flame, and red-tailed pristella; the mid-sized penguin, hockey-stick, diamond, and emperor tetra; and the large (up to four inches), strikingly colored congo tetra.

**THOMAS' DWARF CICHLID:** Stays small and gets along with schooling fish in a communal tank. Needs hiding places.

**WHITE CLOUD MOUNTAIN MINNOWS:** Schooling fish that can be kept in unheated tanks (down to 55° Fahrenheit); can live in tropical tank if not kept above 75° Fahrenheit. Grow to 1½ inches.

**ZEBRA OR CONVICT FISH:** (See Danios above.)

---

**JACK'S FACTS:   It's a Girl . . . It's a Boy . . . It's a Girl**

One of the strangest facts of life for several species of marine fish, particularly the wrasses and groupers *(to say nothing of their owners)*, is that they begin lives as females and then change into functional males. Aside from "Huh?" the name for this is "protogyny." But just to show that Mother Nature is an equal opportunity employer of quirks, the reverse also happens (though less frequently). In a pattern known as "protandry" *(which means "What the heck is going on here?")* fish that are born males grow up to be moms. Sort of gives a whole new meaning to the expression "there are a lot of other fish in the sea."

---

## Questions and Answers About Fish

### Waiting to Exhale

Why are the members of the anabantid fish group called "labyrinth fishes"—and what sets them apart from other fish?

The anabantids can gulp air at the surface of the water and absorb oxygen directly through the labyrinth organ (a mass of mazelike chambers near the gills), enabling them to live in water with too little oxygen for gill-breathing fish—as well as to survive out of water for several hours breathing only through their labyrinths (as long as they're moist).

### Life-Guard Tactics

I have a fairly large saltwater aquarium, but I've been very unlucky in adding new members to my community. I tend to be an impulse buyer, but it's turning out that many of my impulse pets become fish food—even though I was told they would get along with my resident fish. Do you have any suggestions for how I could protect them?

I'm against arming fish with automatic weapons, so I'd suggest a technique that researchers have used. Put your new fish in a large jar, after it has been acclimated to the water's salinity and temperature, and place it on the bottom of the tank. Observe the reaction of your resident fish to the newcomer. If they ignore the fish, chances are it has a good chance. On the other hand, if the jar is attacked—well, chances are it doesn't have a chance. So don't chance it.

## Fish Talk You Should Know

ANAL FIN: the fin on the fish's underside behind the vent

AQUARICULTURE: maintaining an environment within the confines of an aquarium and then breeding and cultivating a species; captive propagation of a species

BARBELS: the long feelers about the mouth of catfish that resemble whiskers

BRACKISH WATER: partway between freshwater and marine

BREAST FINS: see Pectoral fins

BRINE SHRIMP: sometimes sold as sea monkeys; grow to 1/4 inch and used as live fish food

CAUDAL FIN: the tail fin that provides the chief propelling power in swimming

DORSAL FIN: the fin on the fish's back

FIN RAYS: spines which branch out toward the outer part of the fins

GENERA: plural of genus; a classification consisting of more than one species

GONOPODIUM: male fish reproductive organ

ICHTHYOLOGY: the branch of zoology dealing with fish

INVERTEBRATES: animals without backbones

KILLIFISH: small egg-laying freshwater fish that live only one year; seldom available in pet stores

MARINE FISH: fish for saltwater aquariums

OPERCLE: gill cover

PECTORAL FINS: the first paired fins, one on each side of the body; correspond to the forelegs of land animals or the arms of a human being; also called "breast fins"

**PELVIC FINS:** see Ventral fins

**pH:** the acid or alkaline intensity of water, 7.0 being neutral

**PISCIVOROUS:** fish-eating

**SPINY-RAYED FISH:** fish which have several spines in the dorsal and anal fins

**VENTRAL FINS:** close behind each other on the underside of the fish (often mistakenly called "breast fins"); correspond to the hindlegs of land animals and the legs of humans; also called "pelvic fins"

---

**JACK'S FACTS: Five Top Books for Fish Folks**

*The Manual of Fish Health* by Chris Andrews, Adrian Exell, and Neville Carrington (Tetra Press)

*Baensch Aquarium Atlas* by Hans A. Baensch and Dr. Rudiger Riehl (Tetra Press)

*Exotic Aquarium Fishes* by Dr. William T. Innes (Dutton)

*The Basic Book of Fishkeeping* by Elizabeth Randoph (Fawcett Crest)

*The Fascination of Breeding Aquarium Fish* by H. R. Axelrod and M. Sweeney

Plus: *Aquarium Fish Magazine*, P.O. Box 53351, Boulder, CO 80322–3351. (303) 786–7306. A monthly publication for the novice and seasoned aquarist, with all the latest information on the care and keeping of fish.

# 11

# Creepy Crawly Critters

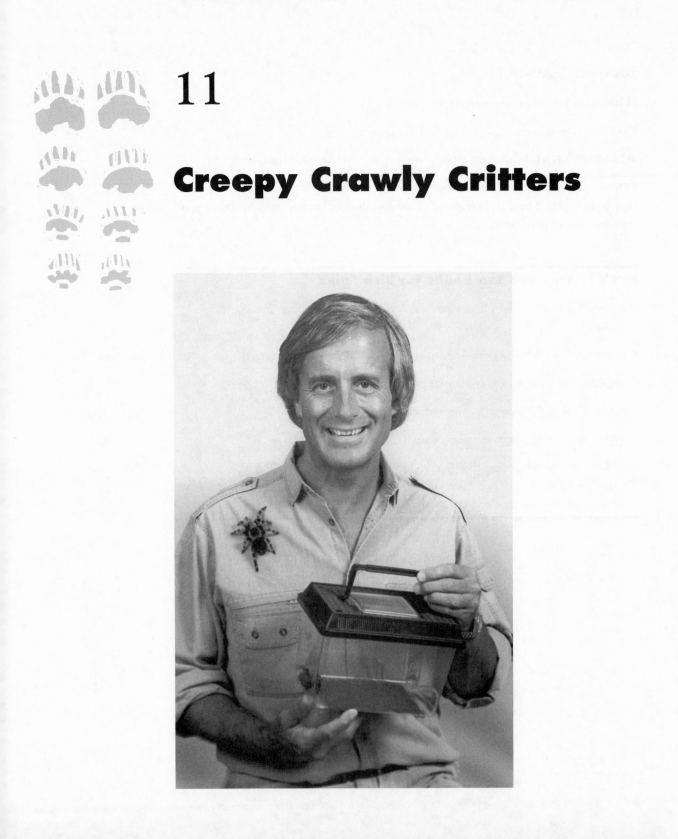

## What You Should Know

There are over 30,000 known species of spiders; over 3,500 species of cockroaches; over 6,500 species of millipedes, and more than 250,000 species of beetles (and that's not counting John, Paul, George, and Ringo)! And though many of these creatures spend more time in more people's homes than dogs, cats, birds, and fish combined—it is rarely as pets. But for those who are interested in them as animal companions, there are some interesting things you should know.

## *Bug Basics*

- Many states prohibit the raising of cockroaches as household pets without a permit from the Department of Agriculture—usually only granted to educators, researchers, and scientists. (Bet you never realized there was so much research going on in your neighborhood.)
- Of the more than 3,500 species of cockroaches in the world, less than 1 percent have any pest status.
- Despite their name, millipedes do not have 1,000 legs. They have two pairs of legs on each body segment. Since most millipedes have thirty to forty body segments, that makes the average number of millipede legs somewhat between 120 to 160 legs. (Can you imagine how long it must take them to wipe their feet on a rainy day?)
- Millipedes are *not* the same as centipedes. Centipedes have just one pair of legs per body segment. On the other hand . . . er, foot, centipedes may have up to 173 body segments, which means 346 legs! (But who's counting?)
- Millipedes grow between molts, when they shed their exoskeleton, emerging with a new soft one. (Because they're vulnerable at this time, they usually lie low before flaunting their new looks.)
- Centipedes are venomous carnivores; millipedes are essentially scavengers that enjoy uneventful meals of decaying plant matter.
- Centipedes sometimes become vegetarians, devouring lettuce, onions, and celery. (Even centipedes go through phases.)
- All species of cockroach are omnivorous; they'll eat virtually anything. (Perfect for people fed up with feeding picky pets.)
- Housing cockroaches as pets requires a cage structure with a tight-fitting lid and a quality mesh to allow for airflow.
- If captive cockroaches don't get enough food, they'll eat the cage they're in—as well as each other.

JACK'S FACTS:
## Why I Love Cockroaches

When I'm traveling to a TV show, I always pack a couple of cockroaches in my left-hand pocket. (Yes, deliberately.) They're my buddies. My calling card even has a cockroach on it. So, what's this thing I have with cockroaches? Well, they're quiet, they don't smell, they eat leftovers and, if I bring them out at the right moment, the little buggers are showstoppers!

---

### JACK'S FACTS: **Missing Hissing Cockroach**

Just because an animal is raised in captivity doesn't mean you can train it to behave when it's on TV. I brought a four-inch Madagascar hissing cockroach with me on the Lifetime cable show *Attitudes,* and before the segment was over—it split. It wasn't the first time an animal had bolted, but we usually have no trouble rounding up a runaway when the segment ends. As I learned, there is always a first time. We searched that studio high and low (sighting a couple of our roach's American cousins along the way), but no luck. Two weeks later, our hungry little fugitive, Poppy (her name was Poppy Cockroach), turned up. That was the good news. The bad news was it was during a cooking segment and the person who was on really, *really* didn't like bugs. Fortunately, the producer knew who *that* bug belonged to, moved faster than the guest's foot, and Poppy was spared, returned, and eager for another stint on TV.

---

- The Madagascar hissing cockroach (unlike her egg-laying American cousins) bears numerous *live* young. Frequently.
- When keeping millipedes in a converted aquarium, feed them pieces of decaying fruits and veggies and you'll be able to raise fruit flies for nothing. (*For turtle and lizard owners, this could be like having in-house food delivery.*)
- There is enough heart stimulant in ten fireflies to kill a human being.
- Ladybugs are actually ladybird beetles—and there are more than 3,000 different kinds of ladybird beetles alone!
- Even if a ladybird beetle is a male, he's still a lady (*not a laddie*).

---

### JACK'S FACTS: **Not Her Favorite Beetle**

When Florence Henderson invited me on her Nashville TV show, I brought along a Goliath beetle. (It is the heaviest known insect in the world and nearly five inches long!) I thought it would be very impressive. Well, it made an impression all right—but not the one I had planned. Before I could stop it, the bug dug its pincers into Florence's shirt, right through her bra, and I could not get it off. I wasn't going to grab her there! I told her not to move, because if she did it would pinch even more. Tears were coming out of her eyes and she was screaming. She told the audience, "I'm sure Jack is just doing this on purpose." I wish I was, but there are very few things you can get a Goliath beetle to do on purpose—and letting go certainly wasn't one of them. I had no way of opening up those powerful pinches. They had to stop taping. All we could do was wait. After eight very long minutes, it happened—the beetle finally got bored and let go. (*It's a good thing it wasn't* The Dolly Parton Show; *it could have taken hours!*)

---

## Spiders You Can Live With

The large, hairy mygalomorph spiders, which most of us know as tarantulas, have in recent years become fairly popular exotic pets. Unfortunately, many of these spiders have been overcollected from the wild and now, along with many other species, have been added to CITES (Convention on International Trade in Endangered Species) as an Appendix II species, meaning that a permit must be issued by the country of origin for each spider it wants to export to the United States or any other CITES-observing country.

Owning a pet is a wonderful thing; endangering a species is an unforgivable thing. By creating a demand for exotic animals, birds, snakes, lizards, and spiders we speed up a terrible timetable for extinction. The only way to turn back that clock is to BUY ONLY CAPTIVE BRED CREATURES. Many exotic spiders are now being bred successfully in captivity. Be sure, before you purchase one, that you've read all about it and will be able to care for it, that the dealer is reputable, and that the spider is homegrown.

### Spiders You Can Handle

**PRO:** Quiet, exotic, happy to act as resident insect exterminators. Need no walks, exercise, shots, or grooming.

**CON:** Not cuddly, can bite, and almost all are cannibalistic. *(They take to roommates the way most of us take to buffets!)* They will never learn to recognize you, most will pay no attention to you at all, and zoos won't want it if things don't work out.

**CREATURE COMFORT:** A five- to ten-gallon terrarium, screen cover or secure commercial aquarium lid. Sterilized substrate, sand, gravel, potting soil. A hiding place (clay flowerpot with hole, mug), rocks, sterilized wood; heater or light to keep temperature between 70–80° Fahrenheit; flat, non-metallic water dish (glass ashtray, saucer).

**DIET NEEDS AND TREATS:** Meals for spiders should be portion-controlled according to size—in other words, live prey should be about one quarter the size of your spider. Store-bought crickets and mealworms are preferable because they're more likely to be disease-free than wild insects. Tarantulas may eat baby mice or fish.

### KEEP IN MIND
- Males have shorter life spans than females.
- Most spiders are nocturnal and will not be very active during the day.

- Exotic spiders, such as tarantulas and scorpions, are now sold in pet shops—but that doesn't mean they're all safe to handle.
- Spiders and scorpions can escape through smaller holes than you think.
- Large spiders can get by in captivity on one or two feedings (or crickets) a week.
- Smaller spiders need smaller food and more frequent feedings than larger relatives.
- Some spiders wrap their prey (*no, not in Saran wrap*) in their silk and save it for later.
- Most spiders require only a little water. (For tropical species that enjoy higher humidity, spraying a mist of water daily is recommended.)
- Spiders and scorpions can sometimes go for months in the wild without eating—but captive ones should be fed regularly.
- Spiders preparing to molt often refuse to eat.

## Captive Bred Choices

DWARF METALLIC TREESPIDER: Medium-sized (about three inches), this is a gentle, semitropical spider that thrives on insects and is said to do well in community vivariums. Owners have claimed it frolics actively on your arm if removed from the cage.

HANNA'S HINT: An actively frolicking spider outside its cage can disappear faster than a fly in a frog pond.

ECUADORIAN PURPLE: Much like the pinktoe, may grow to about three inches in size. Vivid purple hues on head and upper body (carapace). Arboreal, tropical, and docile, this insect-eater is reputed to be a good "pet" tarantula.

MEXICAN REDLEG: Large (about four inches), but expensive, classic hobby tarantula. Captive bred because they are listed on CITES as an Appendix II species (see above), these spiders feed on large insects and small mice. Adults are dark brown with bright orange-red hair on the abdomen and orange and tan bands on all legs, and are said to often have pleasant temperaments (not *always*, but often).

PERUVIAN PINKTOE: Fuzzy, with pink toes on all legs and a yellowish upper body and head (carapace). Medium sized (about three inches), arboreal, tropical, and docile. An insect-eater and gentle.

PINKTOE: Jet-black with pink feet and two to three inches in size. After molting (slipping out of old exoskeleton), the newly hardened head shield (carapace) takes on a bluish hue and red hairs appear on abdomen and back legs. Arboreal, tropical, and docile, the insect-eating Pinktoe is said to coexist well with others of its species in a large vivarium.

## Did You Know . . .

- Spiders feel, hear, and smell with their legs.
- Most spiders lay 100 eggs at a time.
- Spiders actually recycle old webs by swallowing and absorbing the threads.
- Spiders are *not* insects; they're arachnids. (Insect bodies are divided into three parts, spider bodies are divided into only two parts—and no spiders have wings.)
- The name "spider" comes from the old English which means "to spin."
- Though spiders usually live alone, many small ones will often share a web for protection.
- Some scorpions can live their entire life without drinking water, relying only on the moisture in their food.
- Spiders may not be royalty, but they are blue-bloods; instead of red-blood cells, their blood contains a blue pigment called hemocyanin.
- Spiders are cold-blooded and have temperature receptors on their body surface.
- Despite the fact that they have double, triple, and even quadruple the number of eyes that most animals do, the majority of spiders (even those with eight eyes!) do not depend at all on their eyesight for capturing prey, and their sight is extremely poor.
- The strongest types of spider silk have a breaking strain greater than that of steel wire of the same diameter.
- Some spiderwebs, if straightened out, could span more than 300 miles.
- Spiderweb silk is more elastic than rubber or any synthetic material.
- Spiders don't eat their victims—they drink them. They immobilize them with venom, then coat the prey with a fluid that causes it to dissolve so they can suck it up.
- A spider's penis is at the end of one leg.

## Breeding Tips

Unless you're a professional in the field, forget it. Putting the wrong twosome to-gether can be deadly for both. Even if the mating is successful, the couple must be separated immediately afterward. And once the spiderlings hatch, you have to separate each of them—providing individual housing and food. It's expensive, time consuming, and not recommended.

## Cautions for Arachnid Owners

- Handling a spider during or immediately after a molt can endanger the spider's life.
- Keeping poisonous spiders, such as the brown recluse and the black widow, can endanger *your* life!
- A dropped spider can be seriously harmed.
- Keep spider-handling to a minimum to prevent escapes.
- Never forget that even non-poisonous spiders can bite—and do.
- Keep your spider's vivarium out of direct sunlight.
- All insects do not make good spider meals, avoid feeding ants, bees, wasps, or any others that should sting your pet.
- Do not gather insects from areas that have been sprayed with pesticides.
- Never leave live food for any extended period with a spider while it is molting.
- During molting a spider is virtually defenseless and should not be disturbed.

## Compatible—and Incompatible—Household Pets

As long as you keep your spiders in their own spider habitats, all household pets are compatible.

## Children

Spiders are not advised as pets for children—each can be hazardous to the other's health and safety.

### KEEP IN MIND

- Young children do not know their own strength and can inadvertently kill harmless pets.
- Spiders are meant to be observed, rather than played with, and we all know the attention span of young kids is about that of a mosquito.
- Young children have a dangerous tendency to put anything small in their mouths.

JACK'S FACTS: **Beetle Juice Beaters**

The bombardier beetle defends itself by squirting jets of hot irritating liquid formed by chemicals secreted into a reservoir inside its body where this liquid mixture heats up to the boiling point of water. The scalding liquid doesn't harm the beetle (*doesn't even give it heartburn*) but it does repel most attackers—with the exception of one savvy group of spiders. *Argiope* spiders sneak up on the beetle, wrap it in silk, and then leave it until it has used up its liquid defense supply. Once that is depleted, the beetle is defeated and the spiders will eat it.

## Questions and Answers About Creepy Crawly Pets

### Knock-Knock

I've read that some spiders eat other spiders by entering their victim's web and turning the resident predator into prey. How do they do this?

Very cleverly. While the waiting web-spinner waits, the attacking spider shakes the web in the same way a trapped insect would. Wondering what it has snared for dinner, the unlucky resident spider is tricked into becoming dinner itself. The "trapped insect" ploy used by the predatory spider is called aggressive mimicry.

### Dancing in the Dark

How can people keep tarantulas as pets? Aren't tarantulas the spiders whose bite causes victims to dance wildly until they drop from exhaustion or death?

With the possible exception of a spider that's been dropped in your underwear, there are no spiders that cause people to dance wildly at all. This is a myth that apparently began in medieval times near the city of Taranto, Italy, where wild dancing—forbidden by authorities at that time—claimed to be caused by the bite of a local spider (the tarantula), causing a disease known as tarantism, which could only be cured by more dancing, with music and magical antidotes (*known today as cocktails*). But that tarantula was a wolf spider belonging to the genus Lycosa, not the hairy *mygalomorph* that these days we call a tarantula and is sold as a pet. In either case (or genus) neither of these spiders' bites cause any such frenzied Fred and Ginger-vitus dancing. Pain? Yes. Saturday Night Fever? No.

### The Scoop on Poop

If I get a spider as a pet, what sort (or amount) of poop cleaning will I be dealing with?

Speaking as someone who has, at one time or another, cleaned up after virtually every animal under the sun (well, at least the sun that shines on the Columbus, Ohio, Zoo), you're in for minimal-poop patrol. Spider excretion is odorless, typically white liquid and quick drying. (*Sounds like a great house paint, doesn't it?*) Periodic cleanups should do it. Every few months, though, you should change whatever substrate or floor cover is in the habitat and give the whole place a thorough cleaning.

## Web Talk Spider Owners Should Know

APPENDAGES: any attachments to the spider's body—legs, palps, jaws, or spinnerets

BALLOONING: a method by which young and small adult spiders, suspended from lengths of silk, are carried by air currents to a new environment

CARAPACE: the tough shield that covers the upper surface of the head and thorax in spiders; protects internal organs and acts as an anchor for muscles used to suck up the predigested liquid contents of prey

CEPHALOTHORAX: the front part of the spider formed by the fusion of the head and thorax and covered by the carapace

CHELLICERAE: spiders' jaws; each half having a sharp fang for injecting poison

CRIBELLUM: a special structure which produces a multistranded silk

CRYPSIS: a camouflage coloring

CUTICLE: the hard body covering forming the exoskeleton

DRAGLINE: the silk that spiders trail behind them as they move from place to place

EPIGYNE: the structure at the entrance to the female reproductive opening, which varies from species to species of spiders

EXOSKELETON: external skeleton, made of tubes and plates, which protects internal organs and to which the body is attached

**PALPAL ORGAN:** the spider's penis, the terminal segment on one of the legs in front of its walking legs

**PEDICEL:** the spider's waist; between the cephalothorax and the abdomen

**PEDIPALPS:** the two appendages on the segment in front of the spider's walking legs; "palps"

**SPIDERLING:** baby spider

**SPINNERETS:** abdominal appendages from which spider silk is extruded

**STRIDULATION:** producing noise as a means of communication (though they have no ears, they have vibration receptors on their bodies that "hear"—see *trichobothria.*)

**SUCKING STOMACH:** the part of the cephalothorax used to suck up the predigested liquid that was its prey

**TRICHOBOTHRIA:** fine hairs on a spider's outer surface that pick up vibrations (in effect "hear")

---

JACK'S FACTS: **Five Top Books on Creepy Crawly Critters**

*The Book of Spiders and Scorpions* by Rod Preston-Mafham (Crescent Books)

*The Book of the Spider* by Paul Hillyard (Random House)

*The Story of Spiders* by Dorothy E. Shuttlesworth, illustrated by Su Zan Noguchi Swain (Doubleday)

*Insect Pets: Catching and Caring for Them* by Carla Stevens, illustrated by Karl W. Stuecklen (Greenwillow Books)

*Pets in a Jar* by Seymour Simon (Viking)

NOTE: For serious collectors who would like more information about spiders, you can write to: AMERICAN ARACHNOLOGICAL SOCIETY, American Museum of Natural History, Central Park West at 79th Street, New York, NY 10024, *Attention: Dr. Norman I. Platnick.*

---

# Part Three

# Pet Situations and Solutions

# When Visitors Don't Like Your Pet and Vice Versa

**12**

## Behavior Problems That Might Make Your Pet Unlovable

BARKING: Dogs bark for many reasons—hunger, fear, attention, anger, boredom, excitement; you name it, they'll bark at it. But that doesn't make incessant barking any less annoying for those who have to listen to it.

*Solution:* Correct your pet immediately. Some dogs require nothing more than a firm "No"; others need the "No" accompanied by a leash correction or loud noise. (Noisemakers can be a store-bought throw chain, a heavy key ring, a metal shake can containing marbles or pennies, a pot and metal spoon.)

BEGGING: Beggars can be chewers—of your guests' food. It's rude to invite company for dinner and then let your pets badger them for handouts. This behavior is not only unbecoming to pets and annoying to people, it's unhealthy for both.

*Solution:* Never feed your pets from the table. If your dog starts sniffing around (whirling on hindlegs, doing back flips, tap dancing, whatever) tell it to "go to place" (a special spot you've trained it to sit and stay at) or put it in another room. Same goes for cats who think they own the world and birds that would like to.

BITING: It's difficult to get people to like pets that bite them. Whether it's a cat, dog, bird, or snake, biting does not endear animals to visitors, owners, or other animals.

*Solution:* This is a habit that should be nipped in the bud, so to speak. Holding a dog's muzzle closed and issuing a firm "No," and then giving it a chew toy that's a "Yes"—every time—is a good start. Basic obedience training is strongly recommended.

For cats that bite, I'd suggest you warn visitors to keep their paws away from puss. (Cats don't like being "taught" anything; it's a lot easier to train guests.) If your bird is "peckish" for fingers, try a wobble correction (moving finger up and down while bird is standing on it) or simply keep all company on the other side of the cage door. As for snakes, if yours bites, it shouldn't be handled by strangers.

CHEWING: Few things turn visitors against your pet faster than having their things (shoes, sweaters, coats, papers) shredded by your animal companion.

*Solution:* Keep your pet's chew toys within reach when company comes—and keep your company's belongings out of your pet's reach. Also, early correction of inappropriate chewing—by catching your pet in the act, holding its muzzle closed and giving it a firm "No"—can save you a drawer full of single, unmatched socks.

**INAPPROPRIATE PIT STOPS:** If your pet—no matter what it is—relieves itself inappropriately on or about visitors, they might not feel the same affection you do for the poopertraitor.

*Solution:* Feed and walk your dog on a regular schedule and, if not housebroken, keep in a confined area when guests are around. Birds need to relieve themselves frequently (to keep their bodies as light as possible for flying), so warn your guests beforehand if they want to see your feathered friend's out-of-cage antics—or else keep budgie in the cage.

---

**JACK'S FACTS:  On-Air Splash Down**

It's one thing when your animal misbehaves in front of guests, quite another when you're the guest and your animal urinates all over your host's floor—with hundreds of people watching! This happened to me on *Zoo Day,* a weekly feature of a Columbus, Ohio, news show, when my favorite camel, Betty White, made her on-air debut by letting out what sounded like a torrential downpour on the studio floor. (Think of a busted gutter in a thunderstorm.) It was too loud to ignore, so I said to the anchorperson, Angela Pace, "Oh, look, Angela, Betty's going to the bathroom."

While Angela was trying to step out of the camel's way, I was trying to get the camel out of the camera's way. But when I pulled Betty's rope, she slipped and sent Angela and me sprawling.

We got to our feet and I assumed the worst was over, but my assumptions leave a lot to be desired. The next animals out were a few little goats. Happy little goats. Happy, because they had just eaten. And before you could say, "Oh, no!" they all started going to the bathroom, too. By then, I was laughing so hard I was crying; Angela was just trying to hang on to her composure—and her career!

Thinking I could save the day, I said, "Let's have one more look at Betty White."

Angela said, "No, uh . . . I don't think we have time." But no sooner were the words out of her mouth than Betty came storming back in, butting Angela out of her way and onto the floor again.

As Angela picked herself up to sign off, I tried to pull Betty White from the studio. In traditional camel fashion, she wouldn't budge. The last thing viewers saw was me tugging on that camel, the picture jumping up and down as the cameraman laughed us off to commercial rescue.

MOUNTING: It's not cute, it's not funny, and very few guests take it as a compliment when a dog mounts their leg.

*Solution:* Neutering always helps, but it's not guaranteed to be 100% effective for all dogs. In addition, you should issue a firm "NO" whenever the dog attempts to jump on you, discourage rough physical play, and provide your pet with adequate daily exercise.

SPRAYING: Your guests won't be saying, "Here, kitty kitty!" if their noses know your cat is definitely around.

*Solution:* Neutering. Also, frequent litterbox cleaning.

---

JACK'S FACTS: **A Gorilla with a Grate Problem**

Toni, one of the female gorillas at the Columbus Zoo, had a lot of behavioral problems—not the least of which was refusing to go outside into the play yard. For years! We tried everything from tempting foods to good-looking guy gorillas, but Toni was determined to stay indoors. We finally consulted with an animal behaviorist. It turned out that the grated floor of the tunnel leading outside, which rose in the air, terrified her. Once we covered the grating, Toni was back on firm emotional ground and out in the play yard, which I'm delighted to report she frequents to this day.

Most animal difficulties originate with humans. We create the problems, and we must be responsible for creating the solutions.

---

## Training Your Pets to Behave

Pets don't need to learn tricks but they should learn basic manners. And if you don't know how to teach them, you can learn how—or you can hire someone who knows how.

### *How to Go About It*

- Contact your local animal shelter for information about dog-obedience classes.
- Ask for trainer recommendations from local dog clubs and veterinarians.
- Inquire at your pet food store about different trainers.
- Check your library for the books recommended at the end of this chapter (and at the end of Chapter 6) and see which one works best for training you to train your pet.

## Think Your Pet Needs a Shrink?

It's possible. Neurotic behavior is not confined just to humans. Dogs, cats, and birds—as well as some wild animals—may develop it. Whether it's caused by trauma, suppressed rage, or fear, animals often act out their problems through negative behavior.

When an animal develops a behavior problem, such as a fear of noises, cars, heights, confined spaces; tail-chasing, biting, forgetting housetraining, destructive chewing, hiding under furniture, wild scratching at doors or walls, feather-plucking, false pregnancy, fur-biting, feces-eating, digging, pacing, or other negative behavior, the first thing to do is find out if there is a medical reason that's causing it. (Anything from parasites and inner-ear disturbances to toothaches, poor nutrition, viruses, and insect bites can alter normal pet behavior.)

Once medical reasons are eliminated, you might want to seek professional help in uncovering the cause of your pet's negative behavior, and find out how you can best modify it. For simple problems, consulting a reputable pet trainer (or a recommended pet-training guide) may be sufficient. For animals with more complex or ingrained problems, it would be in your pet's best interest to consult an animal behaviorist. Animal behaviorists are trained psychologists who specialize in animal behavior; most have Ph.D.s. These people are certified professionals and should not be confused with self-proclaimed "pet therapists," who frequently have no veterinary accreditation and often claim to communicate with animals telepathically—even over the telephone. (I'm not saying they don't; just that I wouldn't.)

To find an animal behaviorist in your area, you can ask your veterinarian or local animal hospital. Or you can contact the New York Animal Medical Center, 510 East 62nd Street, New York, NY 10021; or phone the Cornell Veterinary Helpline (1–800–548–8937).

---

JACK'S FACTS: **Too Close for Comfort**

You never know what an animal is going to do with a stranger. I brought a flying squirrel on the *Regis & Kathie Lee* show, and it leaped onto Regis's shirt, found an open buttonhole, and crawled inside. Before anyone could stop it, it started wriggling around on Regis's stomach and heading south. I told him to stand still, but with that critter in there it was sort of out-of-the question. He finally unbuttoned his shirt, unbuckled his belt, and reached down into his pants and pulled out the squirrel. It was quite a sight—especially for anyone tuning in just at that moment!

---

## Questions and Answers About When Visitors Don't Like Your Pet

### Pet Public Relations

I travel everywhere with my Doberman, Clancy. He's really very well behaved, but a lot of people are terrified of him just because he's a Doberman, and the breed has gotten a bad rap. Do you have any suggestions on how I can get people to relax around him?

You can try to brief people about your pet before you arrive, but the fact is that people either are comfortable or they aren't with certain animals. If someone has a phobia, as *Good Morning America*'s Joan Lunden does with snakes, I don't force the issue. And you shouldn't, either. It's not necessary for people to love your Doberman or for you to try to get them to love him. A well-behaved pet is its own reward.

Actually, I've found that a bigger problem is people who have no fear of—or respect for—an animal, and who feel that "all animals love them." These are the people who move in where they don't belong, reach out, and that's when accidents can happen. It's my responsibility to keep situations like that under control; the same holds true for pet owners.

---

**JACK'S FACTS: Five Top Books on Pet Behavior Problems**

*When Good Dogs Do Bad Things* by Mordecai Siegal and Matthew Margolis (Little, Brown)

*How to Get Your Dog to Do What You Want* by Warren Eckstein (Fawcett Columbine)

*No Naughty Cat: The First Guide to Intelligent Cat Training* by Debra Pirotin, D.V.M., and Sherry Suib Cohen (Harper & Row)

*Twisted Whiskers: Solving Your Cat's Behavior Problems* by Pam Johnson (The Crossing Press, CA)

*How to Get Your Pet into Show Business* by Arthur J. Haggerty and Carol L. Benjamin (Howell Books)

---

# 13

# Traveling with Your Pet

## What to Do Before You Leave

Ask yourself: "Do I really want to do this?" If the answer is an unequivocal—or un-avoidable—yes, then before you go you should check the checklist below. Remember, being forearmed is better than being caught shorthanded.

### *Prepping for Pet Travel*

- Make sure your pet is in good health and has all its vaccinations.
  HANNA'S HINT: Tell your veterinarian where you're going, and ask if any additional vaccinations are advisable.
- If you are traveling by car, test-drive your pet a few miles before you set out on a long journey.
  HANNA'S HINT: If your pet does get carsick, or is overly agitated, ask your veterinarian about herbs or medicines that can help.
- If your pet will be traveling in a crate, let the animal get used to it before you set out.
  HANNA'S HINT: Put the open crate in your house and let your pet explore it. Planting a treat inside usually speeds up dog and cat curiosity. Personally, I feel that crates are great for transporting animals. Not only does it keep the animal secure, but it can give your pet a sense of denlike security while en route as well as in strange surroundings.
- Make sure your pet has a flat-buckled ID on its collar, with its name and your phone number.
- If you're planning to stay in hotels or motels, make sure they are pet-friendly.
  HANNA'S HINT: Every year, one in three accommodations change management—meaning pet policies can change, too. Call ahead just to make sure you're going to be welcome—otherwise you, your family, and your pet might find yourselves in the doghouse.
- Pack any medications that your pet is taking—as well as the prescriptions (in case of loss).
- Ask your vet about a basic first-aid kit for your pet—with treatments for minor cuts, diarrhea, and motion sickness (along with recommended dosages).
- Don't forget your pet's water and food dishes.
- A favorite toy or blanket comes in handy for pets on any trip.
  HANNA'S HINT: When the surroundings are strange, animals are comforted by familiar things.
- For finicky eaters, a supply of your pet's regular food.

HANNA'S HINT: Many cats and dogs are hooked on one brand of food, and trying to introduce a new food while on the road can be . . . well, trying, for all involved.

## How to Find Pet-Friendly Accommodations

For an annually updated list of more than 10,000 pet-friendly hotels, motels, and campgrounds, as well as "pet-sitters" and kennels, you can contact CLAWS AND PAWS for a copy of *Pets-R-Permitted*. The book costs $11.95 plus shipping and handling and takes two to three weeks for delivery. For three-to-five-day delivery the price is $14.95 (at the time of this writing). You can order *Pets-R-Permitted* by phoning CLAWS AND PAWS at 1–800–274–7297, and charge it to your Visa or MasterCard. Or you can send a check or money order to: CLAWS AND PAWS, 17121 Palmdale Street, Unit A, Huntington Beach, CA 92647.

The AAA (American Automobile Association) has a Tour Guide, free to members, that lists hotels and motels that accommodate pets.

The Chamber of Commerce of most cities can help you find pet-friendly accommodations in the area.

Many major hotel and motel chains have pet-friendly policies. You can check by calling their toll-free numbers or writing for a free brochure.

HANNA'S HINT: Some "pet-friendly" establishments are "friendly" for small pets only. Be sure your pet is not too big for your reservation before you get there.

## Good and Bad Travelers

CATS: Most do not like traveling in general, let alone in trains, planes, or automobiles. They seem to respond well enough to trips in RVs, but buying one seems an expensive way to make your pet feel at home away from home—no matter how much you love the little fluff ball! Keeping your cat in a carrier, with a toy and blanket, is recommended for air and land travel. (See "Planes, Trains, and Automobiles," p. 224, and "Cautions," p. 227, for more feline travel tips.)

DOGS: In general, they enjoy coming along for the ride. Even if they hate traveling, most prefer it to being left behind. But never—and I know I've said this before but it bears repeating—never leave your dog alone in a parked car on a hot day. (See "Planes, Trains, and Automobiles," p. 224, and "Cautions," p. 227, for more canine travel tips.)

**BIRDS:** They don't tolerate temperature extremes, so if you're going somewhere by car be sure it's preheated before you buckle up your feathered friend's cage. If you're flying with your flying buddy, check with your airline to see if you can keep it in an avian kennel under your seat. (Include pieces of fruit—grapes, oranges—to supply liquid.)

**GERBILS, HAMSTERS, MICE:** They're portable but shouldn't be subjected to temperature extremes. They can travel by car in a plastic storage box, lined with shavings, and covered with a lid that has airholes punched in it and is secured by a rubber band. (Ordinary shoeboxes are too easy for them to chew their way out of.) You can add food, small pieces of fruit for liquid, or sipper bottles. If they have to be shipped by plane, check with airline for regulations.

**GUINEA PIGS:** Like other laptop pets, they should not be subjected to temperature extremes. In cars, they can travel in a plastic storage box, outfitted in the same manner as that for gerbils, hamsters, and mice. Because of their need for vitamin C, their on-the-road combination fruit snack 'n' beverage should be orange slices. If traveling by plane, check with airline for regulations.

**LIZARDS:** Not great travelers (*or conversationalists*). They should not be subjected to temperature extremes—especially cool temperatures, which can be dangerous to their health. Because they don't need to eat every day, keep them off food for at least a day before your trip. They can travel by car in a temporary vivarium, with carpet or newspaper on the bottom, and a hot water bottle wrapped in towels for warmth. If traveling by plane, check with airline for regulations.

**SNAKES:** If the kids—or you—absolutely refuse to leave Slinky home, be sure you don't subject it to temperature extremes. Snakes are not goers and doers, but they can travel by car in a cotton pillowcase or laundry bag (**not a plastic bag!**) knotted at the top with plenty of room for air to circulate. A hot-water bottle, well wrapped in towels, will supply warmth. It's wise, too, when transporting the snake from its temperature-controlled environment to the car, to put the pillowcase in a Styrofoam container to prevent exposure to sudden heat or cold. For air travel, be sure to check with your airline for regulations—there are special rules for snakes.

**RABBITS:** Not great travelers because they can suffer heatstroke very easily. Never leave them alone in a car on a hot day! (See "Cautions" section, p. 227.) When traveling by car, they do best in large carriers, with food and water available at all times. Lettuce is a good provider of liquid, but be sure you have a thermos of water to refill your pet's sipper bottle if it's empty. For air travel, check with your airline for regulations.

**FISH:** Land travel is not something they enjoy. But if you must, for one reason or another, travel with your underwater companions on terra firma, remember that they do need air to survive. (*You can't just plop them into closed, water-filled Mason jars and pack them in the trunk!*) If you are carrying them in a plastic bag with water from the tank, make sure there is sufficient air in the bag for the trip, approximately three-quarters water to one-quarter air. (On long trips, open the bag every few hours to provide fresh air.) If you are transporting them in a fishbowl or aquarium, fill it only halfway. Also, it's best not to feed fish before traveling—for reasons that might quickly become obvious. And, again, be careful about exposing them to temperature extremes.

**SPIDERS:** Bad travelers (and great escape artists). But if for some reason you can't leave home without yours, make sure its container has enough air and a secure lid. Most can do without food for long periods of time, at least until you arrive at your destination. If you're traveling by air, be sure you check airline regulations or you and your pet may part company—like it or not.

**TURTLES:** If yours can't be left at home, a semi-aquatic type may be transported by car in a plastic plant propagator with a shallow water tray and adjustable ventilation slots in the top; a terrestrial can travel in a ventilated shoebox with shredded newspaper (non-toxic ink) flooring. Lettuce should be offered to supply water en route. A rock, shallow water dish, and, if necessary, a light bulb positioned for heat can be set up when you arrive at your destination. (*One assumes you are not going camping with your turtle.*) If traveling by air, check with your carrier on rules and regulations.

**FROGS AND TOADS:** Unless you are on your way to the Calavaras County Fair, these pets are better left at home. Though they are used to traveling by leaps and bounds, traveling by car is another story. But if you must, a plastic plant propagator with a shallow tray and adjustable ventilation slots or a ventilated shoebox with peat moss on the bottom can serve as a temporary carrier. Worms, fresh bugs, and other frog favorites can be gathered en route. Avoid temperature extremes. If traveling by plane, check with your airline on rules and regulations.

## Rules for Planes, Trains, and Automobiles

### Planes

- Book direct flights whenever possible.
- If a non-stop flight is unavailable, a one-stop or connecting flight is the best alternative.
- In hot weather, try to book a night—or very early morning—flight. (Do the same if you're traveling to a hot climate.)
- Whenever possible, travel in the morning, before airline traffic builds up and delays begin.
- Airline regulations may vary from carrier to carrier, from one month to another, so double-check on what you need before packing your pet for departure.
- Take any animal small enough to fit under the seat in an airline-approved carrier on the plane with you. (Reservations must be made in advance, prices range from $25 to $60, depending on the airline, and not all airlines allow pets in the passenger area.)
- Find out how much in advance of check-in time you should arrive when traveling with your pet. (When animals travel as cargo, you usually have to get there two to six hours before.)
- For foreign travel, check with the consulate of the country you're visiting to find out what paperwork your pet requires for admittance.
  HANNA'S HINT: Also, be sure you know what sort of extended quarantine you might be subjecting your pet to when you *return!*
- Make sure your pet's crate or kennel is USDA approved. (They are available from pet stores and airlines, but you have a larger selection at pet stores.)
- If you are buying a crate from the airline, make sure you reserve it. (Reconfirming that the crate you reserved will be there is a wise idea, as is arriving early in case there's a problem.)
- Write "LIVE ANIMAL" on top and sides of crate with arrows pointing to show upright position.
- All carriers for pets should be clearly marked with your name, pet's name, address, phone number, and destination.
- Provide food, food dish, water dish, extra food, and feeding instructions for a lengthy trip, and attach to crate.
- Crate should be securely closed but unlocked so that in the event of an emergency it can be opened quickly.
- Unless the weather is very hot, do not give your pet water within two hours of traveling.

- Do not feed your pet any later than four hours before flight time.
- Line bottom of carrier with shredded newspaper or towels.
- Include a favorite toy in crate, but avoid anything with bells, squeakers, or shreddable material that your pet might swallow (see other "Cautions" section, p. 227.)
- Air travel usually requires that your pet have a certificate of health signed by a veterinarian.
- Keep your pet's necessary documents with your own most important papers.
- Exercise your pet before the trip.
- Dr. Richard Crawford, Assistant Deputy Administration for Animal Care of the United States Department of Agriculture (USDA), suggests that when boarding the plane, you give one of the cabin crew a note for the pilot with a picture of your pet that is in the cargo compartment. Thank the pilot for remembering that your animal is on board.

## Trains

- Trains in the United States do not allow any pets on board, except for guide dogs, even as cargo.
- When traveling with your pet in other countries, especially where language and landscape are unfamiliar, you can lessen stress on your pet—and yourself— by going to the train station alone before your date of departure to make reservations and find out exactly where you'll have to go, what you'll have to do, and when you'll have to do it.

## Buses

- Major bus lines in the United States do not allow any pets on board, except for guide dogs, even as cargo.

## Automobiles

- Do not feed your pet for several hours before departure.
- Unless the weather is hot, do not give your pet water for two hours before travel.
  HANNA'S HINT: If you're traveling with a dog, you might want to take along ice cubes to dole out during the ride. Ice cubes are also good for pets that tend to drink too quickly.
- Be sure to bring along your pet's food and water dishes, as well as food and water to put in them.

HANNA'S HINT: Fast food might be fun for you on the road, but it can wreak havoc with a dog or cat's digestive system. Traveling with a sick pet is not an experience you'll want to remember; unfortunately, it's also not an experience easy to forget!

- Bring towels. Paper ones for emergency cleanups and a regular one to dry off a wet pet. (*The smell of a soggy dog in your car can put a real damper on the trip.*)
- Plan on frequent rest stops so your pet can stretch its legs and relieve itself—but don't open the car door without putting your pet on a leash.

  HANNA'S HINT: If your cat won't "go" while on a leash, taking a litterbox along for kitty's comfort is a good idea.)
- Change any bedding your pet has soiled as soon as possible—for everyone's comfort.
- Never leave your pet alone in a parked car (*and <u>definitely not</u> in a moving one*).

  HANNA'S HINT: If you must leave your pet in the car, be sure to carry an extra set of keys. Active dogs have been known to jump around and lock their owners out. Also, in the event that you absolutely must leave your pet in the vehicle for a short while, an extra set of keys will allow you to lock it and leave the heat or air-conditioning on for your pet's comfort.
- Use window ventilation grills to provide fresh air, protect your pets from injury, and prevent escapes.
- Pets should be crated, harnessed in specially made animal car restraints, or kept safely in the back of the vehicle and away from the driver with a steel mesh or net barrier.
- Always reconfirm hotel or motel reservations to make sure they are expecting you *and* your pets.

---

### JACK'S FACTS: **Travel Alert**

Pets can travel easily to all the United States, with one exception—Hawaii. Because it is an island with no incidences of rabies, any animal brought in must be quarantined for at least four months to be certain that the animal is not infected. Many island nations around the world have the same policy, for the same reason. Before you pack your pet's bags for travel abroad, contact the local consulate at your destination to be sure you comply with their requirements.

Also, if you're planning to go hiking with your pet, be aware that many state and national parks do not allow them—even if they're on a leash!

---

## Cautions

- Never leave your pet unattended in a car, especially in hot weather! A car interior can heat up enough to kill an animal even if the temperature outside is only 70° Fahrenheit.
- Leaving your pet alone in a parked car is illegal in many places.
- An unrestrained pet in a car can endanger everyone.
- Don't leave your pet on a leash in the car; the leash can get caught around its neck and cause strangulation.
- Be sure to ask your veterinarian if your pet's vaccinations have had time to become effective; some take as long as two weeks.
- A window that's open wide enough for your pet to hang its head out of is one that its whole body can squeeze through, too.
- Cats tend to wander off and get lost in unfamiliar territory and should be confined to a house, a pen, or walks on a leash.
  HANNA'S HINT: Get your cat used to walking on a lead *before* you go on vacation—or it won't be a vacation for either of you.
- Be sure your cat's carrier is well-ventilated and securely fastened.
- A cardboard box with airholes is okay to take kitty on a quick trip to the vet, but on long journeys a bored cat may scratch its way out and get lost.
- Taking your pet on a boating trip can be hazardous to all on board.
- Always keep your dog on lead when you let it out to exercise or relieve itself near a busy road.
- Just because your dog roams free in the local park doesn't mean it's safe to allow it off lead in the country. If it picks up the scent of an animal and chases it, your pet could get lost; if it confronts an animal that's dangerous, it could be injured; if it harms a farm or game animal, it could be shot!

## JACK'S FACTS: **You Think You Have Problems?**

If you've ever traveled with a dog or cat, you know it's not always easy to find hotels and motels that allow them. Well, imagine having to find friendly accommodations for the likes of lions, tigers, alligators, goats, orangutans, and aardvarks—to say nothing of hippos, elephants, and camels! I've traveled thousands of miles with hundreds of animals, but I'll tell you right now that I could never have done it without my dauntless keeper staff and quick-thinking zoo assistants. Many animals we take on the road are nocturnal; an owl will hoot, an alligator might thrash and splash in the bathtub all night. (I can't begin to tell you how many wild tales we've had to come up with to cover up the really wild tails that were in our rooms!) Fortunately, there are animal-friendly places, such as New York's Mayflower Hotel on Central Park West, where we're welcome—warthogs and all. But even when it is okay to bring an animal, when you've been requested to do so, you have to be sure that the accommodations can accommodate the size of the animal you're bringing. I learned this, as usual, the hard way—going on *The David Letterman Show*.

I'd brought a couple of full-grown camels with me. I'd weighed and measured them, as I do with all the animals before we go on a show, but I forgot to measure their humps. They had plenty of room in the elevator, but the ceiling where they got off was too low. (A fact we discovered too late.) You have to understand, once a camel's walking straight in a narrow hallway, you can't turn it around. And as those two traipsed down to the studio, their unmeasured humps took out just about every ceiling panel—lights and all. To call it a mess would be an understatement; the damage was in the thousands.

The camels were unscathed and couldn't have cared less. I, on the other hand, was a wreck about the wreck and apologized, but Dave's producer told me not to worry. In fact, they brought in a camera to shoot the whole fiasco and used it in the opening of the show. It was a big hit and I felt relieved—until I discovered that while we were on the air, the maintenance people had fixed most of the panels and lights, unaware that the camels had to get back downstairs the same way they came up. And so they did, exactly the same carefree way—humps punching out lights and panels all the way. It was an exit worthy of Lawrence of Arabia—and about as costly as a trip there.

## Questions and Answers About Traveling with Your Pet

### *Flying Cats and Dogs*

Due to illness, I can no longer care for my six-year-old cat and my four-year-old Irish setter. I do not want them separated, but the only person I know who'll care for both of them is my son in California, which means I'll have to fly them out. They will have to travel as cargo. Is this dangerous for them?

We've all heard stories about lost luggage, but the truth is that pets travel by air every day. Safely. In fact, according to the ASPCA (American Society for the Prevention of Cruelty to Animals) more than 275,000 animals fly each year without a hitch—except, of course, they never get to watch the movie. If your cat and dog are in good health, they should be perfectly fine.

### *Tranqs? No, Thanks!*

What's your feeling about pet tranquilizers for travel?

Personally, I prefer a good book and a refreshing beverage. But for animals, my feeling—and the feeling of most vets these days—is that if any pet is so stressed by traveling that it needs a tranquilizer, it should be left home. If being left home or at a kennel is not an option, be sure to ask your vet about the kinds of tranquilizers available, the risks involved, so that you can make the best—and safest—choice for your pet.

---

### JACK'S FACTS: **Five Top Books on Traveling with Your Pet**

*Take Your Pet: A Guide of Accommodations for Pets and Their Owners* by Arthur Frank (Artco)

*Pet Lovers' Guide to Touring America* by J. Hampton (Summit)

*Travel with Your Pet* by Paula Weideger and Geraldine Thorsten (Simon & Schuster)

*The Portable Pet: How to Travel Anywhere with Your Dog or Cat* by Barbara Nichols (Harvard Common Press)

*On the Road Again with Man's Best Friend* by Dawn and Robert Habgood (Dawbert Press)

---

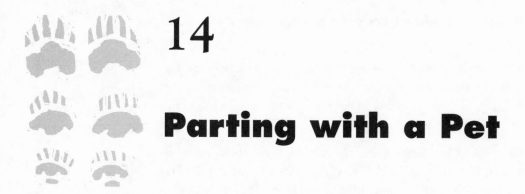

# 14

# Parting with a Pet

## Dealing with Separations

As much as you love your pet, it's unlikely that you can be with it twenty-four hours a day. And whether the separation is a couple of hours, a couple of days, or even a couple of weeks, both of you are going to have to deal with it. And the earlier in your relationship that you deal with it, the easier it's going to be.

### Dogs

- A good way to get your puppy used to being home alone without you, and without making a fuss or a mess, is to get it used to being in a crate. Far from being a negative thing, domestic canines, much like their ancestors in the wild, appreciate and enjoy the security of an indoor denlike enclosure.
  HANNA'S HINT: Put a few safe, non-shreddable toys inside the crate. Keep your first trips away short to get your pup used to being alone, lengthen the time gradually.
- Older dogs allowed to roam the house should not be left alone for much longer than eight hours. It's asking a lot of your pet to behave (and be comfortable) for that period of time. And if you punish it for having an "accident," chances are you'll worsen the problem. (Also, check the "Cautions" section on p. 98 to be sure your home is pet-proofed in your absence.)
- Frequently, a dog that has just had an operation or returned from a kennel will be upset about your leaving and revert to destructive behavior. Be patient. Try short forays out so that you can return and praise your pet for being good, encouraging it to do so. If that doesn't work, consult with your vet, a reputable trainer, or an animal behaviorist for the best way to handle the situation—before it worsens.

### Cats

- They rarely object to being left alone. (In fact, you're lucky if yours acknowledges that you're around.)
- Leaving a scratching post and toys for the cat while you're gone can keep your pets paws off the furniture, out of the garbage, and happily occupied. (See the "Cautions" section on p. 73 to make sure your house is pet-proofed in your absence.)
- Providing they don't have a health problem, most cats can be left alone safely for a weekend with sufficient dry food and water.

### Birds

- Pet birds without in-cage feathered friends do NOT like being left alone, but supplying them with cage toys to keep their beaks busy makes your stays away easier on them.
- Some birds can be left alone for a weekend with sufficient food and water, but you should check with your vet about your particular pet before doing so.
- If you're going away for an extended period of time, be sure to have someone come in to feed *and* play with (or talk to) your pet. (Birds used to full-time human companionship have been known to die of loneliness.)

### Mice, Gerbils, Hamsters, Guinea Pigs, and Rabbits

- They don't seem to mind being alone for a day or two, provided they have sufficient food, water, and toys in their cages to keep them busy.

### Fish

- They won't mope while you're out and about. In fact, most common aquarium fish can get by for a day or two quite nicely without you, provided the tank temperature remains intact.

## Finding a Pet-Sitter

If you can't take your pet with you, and you don't want to leave it at a kennel or cattery, don't trust your neighbor's kids to be responsible; there are alternatives—pet-sitters. Usually hired by the hour, these are capable, bonded individuals who will come to your home—once, twice, three times a day (or more)—and feed, exercise, and play with your pet. To find one in your area, ask your vet or phone the National Association of Professional Pet Sitters at 1–800–296–7387. Be sure to leave feeding instructions, your veterinarian's name and phone number, as well as a phone number where you can be reached in case of emergency.

## When Boarding a Pet

Shop around for a kennel before you need one. Ask for recommendations from your veterinarian and local animal clubs, then visit the places they suggest. You want to be sure they're clean, that the animals there look healthy, that they have runs for your pet to exercise in. Also, speak to the owners. You don't want to leave your happy-go-lucky pet with down-in-the-mouth caretakers.

- If your dog hates cats, or vice versa, be sure that the kennel where you leave your pet has well-separated boarding areas for both.
- Ask about exercise; don't just assume your pet will get enough.
- Find out about feeding schedules and the establishment's willingness to use your pet's favorite food.
- Make sure they have a veterinarian on twenty-four-hour call for emergencies.
- Don't leave your pet without leaving the name of your pet's vet and a number where you can be reached.
- Make sure your pet has all necessary inoculations before going to a kennel.
- Ask your vet about giving your pet an inoculation against kennel cough (*tracheobronchitis*).

## Finding a New Home for Your Pet

### *Temporarily*

Finding a good home for your pet while you're away on a long trip, or hospitalized, is not easy—even when you have friends and family members willing to do it. They might have pets who are unwilling to accept a newcomer. Your pet might not behave with them the way it does with you. Cats that are used to being let outside may run away. Dogs, if unfamiliar with their temporary caretakers, may become confused, disobedient, and also try to escape.

- Before leaving your pet at someone else's home for an extended period, let the animal get acquainted with its foster parents on short visits and become familiar with its future surroundings.
- Be sure to leave your pet with as many of its familiar items—bedding, food dishes, toys—as the host family can handle.
- Provide food (or payment for food), feeding schedule, your veterinarian's name, and assurance that you will pay for any necessary medical care.
- Tell your pet where you are going and why. I'm not saying that the animal will understand or that it will make him or her feel better about being left behind, but it will help you because you'll know that you tried.

### *Permanently*

There are, unfortunately, times and circumstances when people have to give up their pets—permanently. But as difficult as it is for a loving owner to part with an animal, it's more important that the animal be given the chance to enjoy the rest of its life in a good home.

- Ask your veterinarian, local animal clubs, and pet stores for suggestions for potential new owners for your pet.
- If you advertise "free to a good home," make inquiries about the people who answer your ad before turning over your pet to them. (Unscrupulous petnappers often collect animals for unsavory purposes by answering these ads.)
- For a purebred (or purebred look-alike), call the breed rescue service to help in placement.
- Call the local animal shelter to see if there have been any inquiries for a pet like yours.
- When turning your animal over to a new owner, do your absolute best to make the experience as positive as possible for your pet's sake. (I know, I know—this is easier said than done. But you want your pet to be happy—so try.)

## Providing for Your Pets

If you love your pet, you'll want to provide for it in case you won't be around to do so. Three situations that should be planned for are:

1. In the event of your death, provisions to provide for the comfort and care of the animal should be in your will.
2. Advance arrangements should be made to protect the pet during the period between your death and the admission of the will to probate—which could be several weeks or even months!
3. Advance arrangements to care for the pet in the event of your emergency hospitalization or incapacity.

### Planning Should Include
- Designating caretakers.
- Providing funds for your pet's care.
- Designating a humane society or shelter to care for pets, with a cash bequest.
- Establishing an honorary trust for your chosen caretaker to use solely for the upkeep of your animal's health and well-being.
- Providing for euthanasia if caretakers are not found.

- Emergency instructions, to carry in your wallet, in the event you are unable to return home due to an accident, hospitalization, or death.

For sample wills and free instructions on how to best provide for your pet, you can write for a copy of *Providing for Your Pets*, prepared by the Association of the Bar of the City of New York, Committee on Legal Issues Pertaining to Animals. The address is Association of the Bar of the City of New York, Office of Communications, 42 West 44th Street, New York, NY 10036–6690. Or, you can phone (212) 382–6695.

## What to Do If Your Pet Is Lost

LOOK FOR IT IMMEDIATELY: Search the neighborhood; drive around; have a picture of your pet, plus a card with your phone number, and ask runners, garbage collectors, store owners, mailpersons, pedestrians, to let you know if they see your animal.

USE YOUR VOICE: I don't care if your pet's name is "Stinky," it knows it. And if it can hear your voice, it will recognize that, too.

CONTACT LOCAL SHELTERS: Dogs are easier to describe over the phone than cats; bring a color photo of your cat to the shelter as soon as possible.

CALL LOCAL VETERINARIANS: Injured animals are usually brought to a vet before being sent to a shelter.

LEAVE YOUR PET A MARKER: Put a piece of clothing you've worn recently or your pet's favorite pillow outside. For indoor cats that have gone out and gotten lost, sometimes the familiar scent of their litterbox can bring them home. If it's your bird that has flown the coop, put its cage outside and leave the door open. That's the bird's home, and once your pet sees it, he or she might realize that there's no place like it.

ADVERTISE AND OFFER A REWARD: Run an ad in local papers; put flyers with your pet's photo up in any public place or store that you can.

DON'T GIVE UP: Frightened or injured animals may travel a long way from home. If your child, sibling, parent, or spouse was missing for a week you wouldn't give up. Well, your pet's a family member, too!

---

JACK'S FACTS: **Cockroach Missing in New York**

I'm always extremely careful about the safety of the animals I travel with, but accidents can happen. While staying at a hotel in New York a few years ago, one of my favorite cockroaches—a four-inch hissing Madagascar specimen—escaped from its usually secure travel compartment in my left pocket. Now, in New York City (which is a wonderful place, don't get me wrong), looking for a missing cockroach can be a little like searching for a needle in a haystack. Also, you can't go around putting up flyers asking people, "Have you seen this cockroach?" Especially in a classy hotel! After two days, I had just about given up hope when the hotel manager knocked on my door. "Mr. Hanna," he said, "I believe this belongs to you." And very carefully, as if he were turning over the keys to Fort Knox, he handed me a sock. Inside, well fed and no worse for his travels, was my cockroach. "We found it in the lobby and knew instantly it wasn't one of ours. Fortunately, one of the porters had seen you with it on television." Fortunately, indeed—for me and especially for the cockroach!

---

## Prevention Tactics

The following measures can increase your chances of having a missing pet returned, and decrease the chances of having your pet stolen.

- Identification tag with your phone number. (Be sure that tag is affixed securely to collar; "S" hook attachments are easily lost.)
- Register your pet with a service that guarantees to pick up your pet, provide any necessary veterinary attention, and hold it until they can contact you. (Ask your local shelter, animal club, or vet for recommendations.) These services will give you a tag with an identification number and a toll-free number for the finder of your pet to call. (Some services will even guarantee a reward.) Most important, someone is there to answer the call around the clock!
- Have your pet tattooed (most shelters will not destroy a tattooed animal) and be sure to register the number. The National Dog Registry charges a one-time fee, but then you can register other pets with the same number. (Use a number that won't change—birth date, anniversary, social security number.)
- Ask your vet about an injected microchip. Several companies manufacture them and have their own database that you register with. By paying annual dues, your microchip tag registry will keep extra numbers and important information on file, including your pet's medical condition, necessary treatments, even behavioral quirks that might need to be addressed in stress situations.

## When It's Time to Say Goodbye

One of the inescapable facts of life is death. And one of the saddest passages for pet owners is having to decide if it's the right time—or the right way—to let our companion depart.

If your pet is seriously ill, a heart-to-heart talk with your veterinarian and your conscience is in order. Before subjecting your animal to surgery or hospitalization, you should consider its chances for recovery—not only of health but of a comfortable quality of life. Prolonging a pet's life because you can't bear to part with it is understandable, but not necessarily the best decision for the animal you love.

Financial considerations aside (and I say this because for most of us pets are family members, and if there is a way—even an expensive way—to restore them to health, we'll usually find the means somehow to do so, despite having to listen to friends' and relatives' cries of, "You spent all that money on a *cat!*") deciding on whether or not to pursue heroic but futile efforts, allowing your pet to die naturally, or having the animal humanely euthanized are painful choices that often come with the joys of pet owning.

When recovery is not an option, and the animal is not in physical distress, letting nature take its course can be a compassionate farewell—if you and your family are emotionally reconciled to dealing with it. There is also extra time and work involved in keeping a dying pet comfortable (helping it eat or relieve itself outside); but knowing how much happier your animal is being at home, in familiar surroundings, can more than compensate for the effort. Ask your vet's advice on foods or liquids that might make your pet more comfortable, but trust yourself and your human-animal bond and you'll make all the right choices.

### *Euthanasia*

Making the decision that it is best for your beloved animal to be euthanatized— "put to sleep," "put down"—may be the right one, but that does not make it any less emotionally wrenching. It's advisable to discuss any fears or reservations you have with your veterinarian, and then weigh your options. Remember, there is nothing wrong with getting a second opinion on your pet's health any more than there is in seeking it for a loved one.

Most veterinarians will allow you, if you wish, to be with your pet in the final moments of its life. You can hold it, stroke it, talk to it as goes into a deep sleep. The intravenous drug used for euthansia does not cause any pain. But whether you choose to be present for the procedure, prefer to bid goodbye afterward, or would rather say farewell to your friend in other surroundings, if you follow your heart your pet will know that you were there.

## Final Resting Places

When your pet dies, the one last decision you must make is where its final resting place should be. This is an important part of dealing with the loss of an animal companion—particularly for a child for whom this may be a first encounter with death.

Veterinarians can help you in deciding what to do by explaining the various options; they can also facilitate arrangements. Pet cemeteries exist in virtually all major cities in the United States, with costs varying from around $200 for a simple interment to thousands of dollars for an elaborate service. Much less costly are communal burials, which are also offered by most of these cemeteries—all of which should adhere to established standards. For a free list of these established standards you can write to the International Association of Pet Cemeteries, Box 1346, South Bend, Indiana 46624. Or call (219) 277–1115.

If you live in the country or the suburbs, burying your pet on the property can offer comfort as well as closure. For children, especially. I was just a little kid when my pet parakeet Petey died, but I remember the sadness and the day like it was yesterday. I placed the little guy in a Rice Krispies box and buried him on the top of the hill at our farm in Tennessee. Many, many years have gone by, but I'll tell you when I close my eyes I can still see the exact spot where Petey is. Some municipalities have laws prohibiting animal burials on private property for local health reasons, but dispensations for household pets can usually be obtained.

A cremated pet can be buried anywhere. Many owners plant memorial shrubs or flowers with their pet's ashes, or scatter them in areas that their pet used to frequent. A veterinarian can arrange for your pet to have an individual cremation, which costs between $75 to $250. Or you can ask your vet or local humane society about communal cremation which is relatively inexpensive.

Pet memorial markers are available through catalogues and pet cemeteries. But you might also keep in mind that a donation to an animal shelter, pet hospital or research cause in your pet's name is a memorial that not only keeps your pet's memory alive, but other animals alive as well.

JACK'S FACTS: **Funeral for a Friend**

When Mac (Macombo), the beloved patriarch of the Columbus Zoo gorilla community—and the first to sire a gorilla born in captivity—died at the age of thirty-eight, it was a great loss for the keepers and the public, who loved him more than any other animal in the zoo. I loved Mac, too, because to me he represented both the old and the new zoo. He had been caught in Africa and lived in a cage most of his life. And being that he was the first gorilla to breed successfully in captivity, his contribution to the survival of the species would live on long after we were all gone.

Because of the keepers' affection for Mac, they asked if he could be buried at the zoo. This is something that is never done, but Mac was special and I'm pushy. The trustees gave their okay. I decided the best thing to do was have an intimate "immediate family" type of affair. Well, the next thing I knew, there were phone calls from everyone who'd worked with Mac over the years wanting to attend. And, of course, there was Mac's public.

The day of the ceremony, there were about three hundred people gathered outside the gates. The maintenance people had built a beautiful casket with "Mac" inscribed in rope on the top. It took eight powerful pallbearers to lift it to the grave site, which was next to the gorilla habitat that Mac had grown to love.

What followed was a funeral I'll never forget. There were flowers everywhere and speeches by people who knew him, loved him, and respected him (even when, as was said, he could be a colossal pain in the butt). But we had learned a great deal from Mac, which was why he was buried on zoo grounds. I closed with, "Ashes to ashes, dust to dust; Mac did a great job for all of us," Mac's two grandgorillas, Oscar and Toni, were outdoors looking on. It was real quiet, and people said later those apes knew what was going on. I don't know if they knew *what* was going on, but they knew something was. And it was. There is a plaque there today to commemorate it.

## Coping with Your Pet's Death

The loss of a pet can be devastating, particularly because far too often friends and relatives do not think of it as a cause for serious grieving. People unaware of the powerful human-animal bond that exists between owner and pet seem to believe that one pet is replaceable by another. (Sort of like, "Oh, the light bulb burned out, here's a new one.") And not getting emotional support and understanding from friends and relatives makes dealing with the death of a pet even more difficult.

Sharing tears and memories with family members and friends who knew and loved your pet, too, is enormously helpful. Grief and sadness are not signs of weakness, they are human emotions appropriate to loss and they should not be squelched.

Sometimes a pet means more to one member of the family than another; some people are better than others at coping with loss, whatever the reasons for different expressions of grief or length of mourning, they are all valid!

It helps the healing process to find others who understand your need to talk about your pet, your feelings, your sense of aloneness. Fortunately, this need is now being taken seriously by veterinary colleges and hospitals around the country and support groups and pet bereavement counseling is available—and encouraged—for people whose beloved pets have died or who are dealing with those that are terminally ill.

If you feel in need of counseling, or just understanding, contacting any of the following institutions, individuals and agencies can help a lot:

- Susan Phillips Cohen, Director of Counseling, The Animal Medical Center, New York, NY (212) 838–8100, Ext. 269. (For further information on human-animal bond services, you can write to: The Animal Medical Center, Human-Animal Bond Programs, 510 East 62nd Street, New York, NY 10021–8383.)
- M. Patricia Gallagher, Darien, CT (203) 656–2669.
- Dorothea Iannuzzi, Tufts University School of Veterinary Medicine, North Grafton, MA (508) 839–5302, Ext 4750.
- The MSPCA, Boston, MA (617) 522–7400.
- The University of California at Davis Pet Loss Support Hotline (916) 752–4200 between 6:30 PM and 9:30 PM Pacific Time. (For information on pet loss support groups in your area, you can write to: Human-Animal Program, School of Veterinary Medicine, University of California, Davis, CA 95616.)
- Victoria Voith, The University of Pennsylvania School of Veterinary Medicine, Philadelphia, PA (215) 898–4525.

---

JACK'S FACTS: **Five Top Books on Parting with a Pet**

*Pet Love* by Betty White (William Morrow & Company)

*Euthanasia of the Companion Animal: The Impact on Pet Owners, Veterinarians & Society,* edited by William J. Kay, DVM; Susan P. Cohen, CSW, ACSW; Carole E. Fudin, Ph.D., CSW, ACSW; Austin H. Kutscher, DDS; Herbert A. Nieburg, Ph.D.; Ross E. Grey, DVM; Mohamed M. Osman, DVM, Ph.D. (The Charles Press, Philadelphia.)

*Coping with the Loss of a Pet: A Gentle Guide for All Who Love a Pet* by Christina M. Lemieux (W. R. Clark Co.)

*The Loss of a Pet* by Wallace Sife (Howell Books)

*Pet Loss: A Thoughtful Guide for Adults and Children* by Herbert A. Nieberg, Ph.D., and Arlene Fischer (Harper Perennial)

---

## Questions and Answers About Parting with a Pet

### When Pets Are Parted

We had to have our 13-year-old cat, Sherlock, put to sleep last month. Our other cat, Watson, who's only six years old, didn't seem to notice his absence at first, but now he keeps going over to where Sherlock's bed used to be, looking behind the couch where Sherlock took to hiding toward the end, and he's hardly eating at all. Watson looks healthy, but he certainly isn't happy. Is it possible that he knows Sherlock is gone forever and that he's grieving?

I'd say that Watson is definitely mourning the loss of his buddy. He might not understand what has happened to him, but he knows he's gone. (Especially if you've removed Sherlock's bed or food dish.) Pets miss their pals the way people do, usually for several weeks. Give him a lot of extra TLC and attention. This should help him see that there can be an upside to being an only cat. But if Watson's appetite and personality don't pick up, I'd have him checked out for medical problems. If there are none, well, maybe he's just not happy being solo. Bringing in a new playmate, if *you're* ready for one, too, may be just the thing to perk him up.

When Pete, a hippopotamus and our oldest resident at the Columbus Zoo died at the age of forty-four, his longtime companion Cleo knew something was wrong and lost her hippo-sized appetite for months! She was so sad that we decided to get her another companion. He was a younger guy, a ten-month-old hippo, but he was a full 650 pounds and quite mature for his age. When he got to the zoo he relaxed right into his new home next to Cleo. In fact, he got so comfortable that he and Cleo were expecting much earlier than anyone had expected they would. And it turned out to be a big bundle of joy for everyone!

# **Afterword**

I have never doubted the power of the human-animal bond—to comfort, to heal, to motivate and, especially, to enrich lives. I hope that this book has provided an understanding of the wide variety of pets available, their needs and their natures, so that more will be done in years to come to acknowledge and strengthen that bond.

Ten years ago, I visited a severely ill twelve-year-old girl suffering from encephalitis in a Houston hospital. I brought a tiny hedgehog and a few other small animals to her bedside, and something special happened between the two of us and those animals that day. She wrote to me soon afterward a moving letter of appreciation and renewed faith in herself that I have always treasured—just as I will always treasure this recent letter from her which arrived a few weeks ago:

*Dear Jack,*

*I don't know if you really know how much of an effect you had on me. I truly believe I would probably be bedridden if it weren't for you coming to visit the hospital. After touching those animals and seeing you and how much you cared, it really made me want to get well. I even had a dog at home that would not eat because I was in the hospital. When I was well, I fed her every day and played with her. Well, when she realized I was gone, she wouldn't eat for anybody. So I knew I had to get better for her, so she would eat.*

*I've always loved animals . . . I bought a camera so I could take pictures of them. For the longest time I was taking pictures from the wheelchair. I never had the best view from the wheelchair, but I still wanted to take them. Just going outdoors and seeing all the animals inspired me so much. I believe animals love you unconditionally. They don't care how you look at all. It doesn't matter if you are too thin, too fat, too ugly, if your hair is brushed or if you are wearing makeup or not. My dog especially showed me that. She never cared what I looked like just as long as I would pet her on the head was good enough for her.*

*Anyway . . . I don't know if you realize, but it was ten years ago when I first met you. I will never forget until the day I die. You will always have a place in my heart, always! I think of you as my hero. You and those animals saved my life . . . I hope you will never forget me . . . Trust me, I could never forget you.*

*Thinking of you often,*
*Kristen Dixon McClure*

Today Kristen is healthy, married, and working happily as a veterinary technician. She and her husband are also the proud pet-parents of three parakeets, two cats, two German shepherds, a sheltie, a rabbit, and a pigeon. They believe, as I do, that the time for loving all live things is always now.

I hope that with this book I've ignited at least a spark of that belief in all of you.

# Bibliography

The following list is given to fully acknowledge my sincere appreciation to the many authors, trainers, breeders, veterinarians, psychologists, zoologists, biologists, and animal lovers whose wonderfully written, often painstakingly researched books, articles, and published works have enriched my understanding of the animal world and made this pet guide possible.

Ackerman, Diane. *Vanishing Animals, Timeless Worlds*. New York: Random House, 1996.

Allude, Gretchen P. "Winter Coats." *Dog Fancy*, November 1994.

Angier, Natalie. "Guinea Pigs Not Rodents? DNA Weighing In." *The New York Times*, June 13, 1996.

Asbell, Bernard, and Karen Wynn. *What They Know About You*. New York: Random House, 1991.

Barger, Sherie, and Linda Johnson. *Boa Constrictors*. Mahwah, NJ: Watermill Press, 1986.

Bennett, Bob. *Rabbits as a Hobby*. Neptune City, NJ: T.F.H. Publications, 1991.

Bicks, Jane R., D.V.M. *The Revolution in Cat Nutrition*. New York: Rawson Associates, 1986.

Brasch, R. *How Did It Begin?* New York: David McKay Company Inc., 1965.

Brewster Tietjen, Sari. "From Italy with Love." *Dog Fancy*, April 1996.

Climo, Shirley. *Someone Saw a Spider*. New York: Thomas Y. Crowell, 1985.

Comfort, David. *The First Pet History of the World*. New York: Simon & Schuster, 1994.

Cooper, Paulette. "Did You Know . . . ?" *Dog Fancy*, March 1996.

Cooper, Paulette, and Paul Noble. *277 Secrets Your Dog Wants You to Know*. Berkeley, CA: Ten Speed Press, 1995.

Cruickshank, Allen D., and Helen G. Cruickshank. *1001 Questions Answered About Birds*. New York: Grosset & Dunlap, 1958.

Dannen, Kent, and Donna Dannen. "Weathering Winter." *Dog Fancy*, November 1994.

Davenport, Robert. *Pets' Names of the Rich and Famous*. Santa Monica, CA: General Publishing Group, 1995.

DePrisco, Andrew, and James B. Johnson. *The Mini-Atlas of Cats*. Neptune City, NJ: 1991.

Dibra, Bashkim, with Elizabeth Randolph. *Dog Training by Bash*. New York: Dutton, 1991.

Dolensek, Nancy, and Barbara Burn. *Mutt*. New York: Clarkson N. Potter, Inc., 1978.

Dossey, Donald E., Ph.D. *Holiday Folklore, Phobias and Fun*. Los Angeles, CA: Outcomes Unlimited Press, 1992.

Emrich, Duncan. *The Hodgepodge Book*. New York: Four Winds Press, 1972.

Feldman, David. *When Do Fish Sleep?* New York: Harper & Row, 1986.

———. *Who Put the Butter in Butterfly?* New York: Harper & Row, 1989.

———. *Why Do Dogs Have Wet Noses?* New York: HarperCollins Publishers, 1990.

*Ferrets*. Fancy Publications Inc., Irvine, CA, 1995.

Fogelson, Gail. "Making A Difference." *Dog Fancy*, May 1993.

*4-H Rabbit Production*. The Cooperative Extension Services of the Northeast States.

Gaddis, Vincent, and Margaret Gaddis. *The Strange World of Animals and Pets*. New York: Cowles Book Company, Inc., 1970.

Gannon, Robert. *Starting Right with Goldfish*. Neptune City, NJ: T.F.H. Publications, 1973.

———. *Starting with Tropical Fish*. Neptune City, NJ: T.F.H. Publications, 1974.

Garrison, Webb. *Why You Say It*. Nashville, Tennessee: Rutledge Hill Press, 1992.

Gerstenfeld, Sheldon, L., V.M.D. "Have Pet Will Travel." *Parents*, August 1993.

Gordon, Myron, and Herbert R. Axelrod. *Siamese Fighting Fish*. Neptune City, NJ: T.F.H. Publications, 1968.

Haggerty, Arthur J. and Carol Lea Benjamin. *Dog Tricks*. Garden City, NY: Doubleday, 1978.

Hanna, Jack. *Monkeys on the Interstate*. New York: Doubleday, 1989.

Healey, Neale. *Birds for Pets and Pleasure*. New York: Delacorte Press, 1981.

Hedgepeth, William. *The Hog Book*. Garden City, NY: Doubleday & Company, Inc., 1978.

Horwitz, Debra, D.V.M. "Recognizing Aggression." *Dog Fancy*, April 1996.

Hunt, John. *A World Full of Animals*. New York: David McKay Company, Inc., 1969.

Johnes, Carolyn Boyce. *Please Don't Call Me Fido*. New York: Berkeley Publishing Corporation, 1977.

Knott, Thomas A., and Dolores Oden Cooper. *The Complete Handbook of Dog Training*. New York: Howell Book House, 1994.

Koppel, Kale. *Amazing But True Cat Facts*. Boca Raton, FL: Globe Communications Corp., 1995.

Lawson, Deborah. "Purebred Trends." *Dog Fancy*, March 1996.

Leinwoll, Stanley. *The Book of Pets*. New York: Julien Messner, 1980.

Lemonick, Michael D. "A Terrible Beauty." *Time*, December 12, 1994.

Lewinsohn, Richard. *Animals, Men and Myths*. New York: Harper and Brothers, 1954.

Marrs, Texe, and Wanda Marrs. *A Perfect Name for Your Pet*. San Francisco, CA: Heian International Inc., 1983.

Masson, Jeffrey Moussaieff, and Susan McCarthy. *When Elephants Weep*. New York: Delacorte Press, 1995.

Mattison, Christopher. *The Care of Reptiles and Amphibians in Captivity*. New York: Blandford Books, Ltd., 1982.

McLennan, Bardi. "Ask Dog Fancy." *Dog Fancy*, March 1996.

Mehrtens, John M. *Living Snakes of the World*. New York: Sterling Publishing Co., Inc. 1987.

*Merck Veterinary Manual*, Fourth Edition. Rahway, NJ: Merck & Co., 1973.

Mery, Fernand. *The Life, History and Magic of the Cat.* New York: Grosset & Dunlap Inc., 1971.

Meyer, Stephen M. "Disease Treatment." *Aquarium Fish*, October 1994.

Michael, Scott W. "Fishes for the Marine Aquarium." *Aquarium Fish*, October 1994.

The Monks of New Skete. *The Art of Raising a Puppy.* New York: Little, Brown and Company, 1991.

————. *How to Be Your Dog's Best Friend.* Boston-Toronto: Little, Brown and Company, 1978.

Morris, Scott. *The Emperor Who Ate the Bible.* New York: Doubleday, 1991.

Mullally, Linda. "Traveling with Dogs." *Dog Fancy*, February 1995.

Neville, Peter. *Do Cats Need Shrinks?* Chicago, IL: Contemporary Books, 1990.

Newman, L. Hugh. *How's Your Pet?* London: Max Parris and Company, 1967.

Opie, Iona, and Peter Opie. *The Lore and Language of Schoolchildren.* London: Oxford University Press, 1959.

Palika, Liz. "Alphabet Soup." *Dog Fancy*, February 1995.

————. "Living with Dogs." *Dog Fancy*, May 1993.

Panati, Charles. *Panati's Browser's Book of Beginnings.* Boston: Houghton Mifflin Company, 1984.

Parker Guidry, Virginia. "Lovable Rascals." *Dog Fancy*, March 1996.

————. "Poodles Rule!" *Dog Fancy*, February, 1995.

Pavia, Audrey. "A Little White Spark." *Dog Fancy*, April 1996.

————. "25 Vacation Fun Spots." *Dog Fancy*, March 1996.

Preston-Mafham, Rod. *The Book of Spiders and Scorpions.* New York: Crescent Books, 1991.

*Rabbits: Guide to Buying and Caring for Pet Rabbits.* Fancy Publications Inc., Irvine, CA, 1996.

Radford, Edwin, and A. Mona. *Encyclopedia of Superstition.* New York: The Philosophical Library, 1949.

Randolph, Vance. *Ozark Superstitions.* New York: Dover Publications, Inc. 1947.

Rataj, K., and R. Zukal. *Aquarium Fishes and Plants.* New York: The Hamlyn Publishing Group Limited, 1971.

Raver, Ann. "With Nary a Seed in Sight, Birds Need Help Now." *The New York Times*, January 14, 1996.

*Reptiles: Guide to Keeping Reptiles and Amphibians.* Irvine, CA: Fancy Publications, Inc., February 1995.

*Reptiles: Guide to Keeping Reptiles and Amphibians.* Irvine, CA: Fancy Publications, Inc., March 1996.

Rindels, Forrest. "Keeping Teeth Clean." *Dog Fancy*, March 1995.

Rosen, Barbara. "Is Your Dog Lonely?" *Dog World*, February 1995.

Rothwell, John H., and Rudd B. Weatherwax. *The Story of Lassie.* New York: Duell, Sloan and Pearce, 1950.

Schuler, Elizabeth Meriwether. *The Dog Lover's Answer Book.* New York: Simon & Schuster, 1975.

Seuling, Barbara. *Elephants Can't Jump.* New York: E. P. Dutton, 1985.

————. *The Loudest Screen Kiss.* Garden City, NY: Doubleday & Company, 1976.

Shannon, Michelle. "The Chinese Crested." *Dog Fancy*, May 1993.

Shuttlesworth, Dorothy. *The Story of Spiders*. Garden City, NY: Doubleday & Company, 1959.

Siegel, Micki. "Taking Pets on the Road." *Good Housekeeping,* June 1994.

Siegel, Mordecai, and Matthew Margolis. *When Good Dogs Do Bad Things*. New York; Little, Brown and Company, 1986.

Siegel, Scott, and Barbara Siegel. *The Encyclopedia of Hollywood*. New York: Avon Books, 1990.

Sikora Siino, Betsy. "Dollars for Dogs." *Dog Fancy,* November 1994.

Simon, Seymour. *Pets in a Jar*. New York: Viking Press, 1975.

Socolof, Loise. *Gerbils as Pets*. Neptune City, NJ: T.F.H. Publications, Inc., 1966.

Stevens, Carla. *Insect Pets: Catching and Caring for Them*. New York: Greenwillow Books, 1978.

Swift, W. Bradford, D.V.M. "Shampoo Therapy." *Dog Fancy,* May 1993.

Trayford, Arthur, D.V.M., and Gladys Hall. *McCall's Complete Family Guide to Puppy & Dog Care*. New York: The McCall Publishing Company, 1970.

Truman, Margaret. *White House Pets*. New York: David McKay Company, Inc., 1969.

Uridel, Faith A. "Gentle Majesty." *Dog Fancy,* March 1996.

Vine, Louis L. *Common Sense Book of Complete Cat Care*. New York: Warner Books Inc., 1978.

Wallace, Robert, A. *How They Do It*. New York: William Marrow and Company, Inc., 1980.

Wallechinsky, David, and Irving Wallace. *The People's Almanac*. New York: Doubleday & Company, 1975.

Warzecha, Mary. "Happy Camping." *Dog Fancy,* May 1993.

Weatherwax, Rudd. *The Lassie Method*. Western Publishing Co., Inc, 1971.

Weideger, Paula, and Geraldine Thornsten. *Travel with Your Pet*. New York: Simon & Schuster, 1973.

Weis, Peter. "Blue Tongued Skinks." *Reptiles,* February 1995.

Zim, Herbert S., and Hobart M. Smith, Ph.D. *Reptiles and Amphibians*. New York: Western Publishing Co., 1956.

# Index